SPURGEON
ON PRAYER

CHARLES H.
SPURGEON

BRIDGE
LOGOS
FOUNDATION

Alachua, Florida 32615

Bridge-Logos
Alachua, FL 32615 USA

Spurgeon on Prayer
by Charles H. Spurgeon

Compiled and edited by Harold J. Chadwick

Printed in the United States of America.

Library of Congress Catalog Card Number: 2009936344
International Standard Book Number: 978-0-88270-639-9

Scripture quotations are from the *King James Version* of the Bible.

CONTENTS

SPURGEON'S SUNDAY MORNING PRAYERS

SPURGEON'S PULPIT PRAYERS

FOREWORD

C. H. SPURGEON was known as "the prince of preachers," a title he well deserved. But he could also have been called "the prince of prayers (pray-ers)," which would have been a title he also equally deserved.

In the preface to a collection of the Sunday morning prayers that he gave as preludes to his sermons, this was written:

> Mr. D. L. Moody in commencing his first address in the [Metropolitan] Tabernacle, October 9th, 1892, pathetically recalled the time when he first entered the building, twenty-five years ago. He had come four thousand miles to hear Mr. Spurgeon. What impressed him most was not the praise, though he thought he had never heard such grand congregational singing; it was not Mr. Spurgeon's exposition, fine though it was, nor even his sermon; it was his prayer. He seemed to have such access to God that he could bring down the power from heaven; that was the great secret of his influence and his success.

In his introduction to *Spurgeon's Pulpit Prayers*, Dinsdale T. Young wrote, "Lovers of C. H. Spurgeon will delight in this treasury of devotion. They will not open the book without keen anticipation, and assuredly they will not close it with disappointment. I am glad that the publishers have associated with these prayers one of C. H. Spurgeon's delightful and pungent sermons on prayer—an art, of all arts the greatest, in which he was a master indeed. Few could use "The Golden Key of Prayer" as he so deftly could. May many be enabled, through grace, by the study of these prayers, to pray more abundantly and more effectually!"

The same can be said for this Pure Gold Classic, *Spurgeon on Prayer*. In this book, we have gathered forty-five of Spurgeon's short devotionals on prayer, nine of his best sermons on prayer—including his famous, "The Golden Key of Prayer," six of his Sunday morning prayers, and six of his pulpit prayers that he gave at other times. So in this book you will not only be able to study what Spurgeon said about prayer, but also how he himself prayed.

We believe that this combination of Spurgeon's writings on prayer and his vocal prayers, will instruct and inspire you, and deepen your personal prayer life. It certainly did so for us as we compiled and edited this selection of Spurgeon's works for your spiritual enjoyment and edification. We pray it will do the same for you.

Harold J. Chadwick

BIOGRAPHY

CHARLES HADDON SPURGEON

1834–1926

Charles Haddon Spurgeon, often called "the prince of preachers," was born at Kelvedon (40 miles northeast of London), Essex, England, on June 19, 1834. From early in his life it was obvious he was destined to be a preacher, like his father and grandfather, who were both independent ministers. W. Y. Fullerton, his biographer, relates this story about him.

When he was but six years of age, he gave evidence of his vocation. His Aunt Ann tells the story. During his first visit to Stambourne he heard his grandfather lamenting time and again over the inconsistent life of one of his flock, and one day he suddenly declared his intention to kill old Roads, the man in question. In spite of the warning his grandfather gave him about the awful fate of murderers, he persisted in his resolve. "I'll not do anything bad," he declared, "but I'll kill him." Shortly afterwards he astonished them by asserting that he had done the deed. In answer to all questions he declared he had done no wrong but that he had been about the Lord's work, that he had killed old Roads, who would never trouble his grandfather any more.

The mystery was solved by the appearance of old Roads himself, who shortly afterwards called at the manse, and told how he had been sitting in the public house, with his paper and mug of beer, when the boy entered and, pointing to him, said, "What doest thou here, Elijah, sitting with the ungodly, and you a member of the church, and breaking your pastor's heart? I'm ashamed of you. I wouldn't break my pastor's heart, I'm sure." The sermon in its brevity and simplicity and directness might also be put alongside that other which ten years afterward led the young preacher himself to surrender his life to Christ, as this one led old Roads. During the four years that followed, the old man lived an exemplary life. He could not read, but he knew that the words of life were in the Bible, and with pathetic love for the Book, he counted the very leaves of it.

Spurgeon's own conversion took place on January 6, 1850, ten years after his encounter with old Roads. He was fifteen years old. Here in his own words is how it happened.

I sometimes think I might have been in darkness and despair now, had it not been for the goodness of God in sending a snowstorm one Sunday morning, when I was going to a place of worship. When I could go no further, I turned down a court and came to a little Primitive Methodist Chapel. In that chapel there might be a dozen or fifteen people. The minister did not come that morning: snowed up, I suppose. A poor man, a shoemaker, a tailor, or something of that sort, went up into the pulpit to preach. He was obliged to stick to his text, for the simple reason that he had nothing else to say. The text was, "Look unto me, and be ye saved, all the ends of the earth" (Isaiah 45:22).

He did not even pronounce the words rightly, but that did not matter.

There was, I thought, a glimpse of hope for me in the text. He began thus: "My dear friends, this is a very simple text indeed. It says, 'Look.' Now that does not take a deal of effort. It ain't lifting your foot or your finger; it is just 'look.' Well, a man need not go to college to learn to look. You may be the biggest fool, and yet you can look. A man need not be worth a thousand a year to look. Anyone can look; a child can look. But this is what the text says. Then it says, 'Look unto me.' Ay," said he, in broad Essex, "many of ye are looking to yourselves. No use looking there. You'll never find comfort in yourselves." Then the good man followed up his text in this way: "Look unto me: I am sweating great drops of blood. Look unto me; I am hanging on the Cross. Look: I am dead and buried. Look unto me; I rise again. Look unto me; I ascend; I am sitting at the Father's right hand. O look to me! Look to me!" When he had got about that length, and managed to spin out ten minutes, he was at the length of his tether.

Then he looked at me under the gallery, and I daresay, with so few present, he knew me to be a stranger. He then said, "Young man, you look very miserable." Well, I did; but I had not been accustomed to have remarks made on my personal appearance from the pulpit before. However, it was a good blow struck. He continued: "And you will always be miserable—miserable in life and miserable in death—if you do not obey my text. But if you obey now, this moment, you will be saved."

Then he shouted, as only a Primitive Methodist can, "Young man, look to Jesus Christ." There and then the cloud was gone, the darkness had rolled away, and that moment I saw the sun. I had been waiting to do fifty things, but when I heard the word look, I could have almost looked my eyes away. I could have risen that instant and have sung with the most enthusiastic of them of the precious blood of Christ, and the simple faith that looks alone to Him.

I thought I could dance all the way home. I could understand what John Bunyan meant when he declared he wanted to tell the crows on the plowed land all about his conversion. He was too full to hold. He must tell somebody.

There was no doubt about his conversion, it went through every part of his being. "As Richard Knill [a missionary] said, 'At such a time of the day, clang went every harp in Heaven, for Richard Knill was born again'; it was even so with me." Spurgeon later said that if there had been a pile of blazing faggots [bundles of sticks] next to the church door, he could have stood in the midst of them without chains, happy to give his flesh and blood and bones to be burned, if only such action might have testified of the love he felt for Jesus. "Between half past ten, when I entered that chapel, and half past twelve, when I returned home, what a change had taken place in me!"

On April 4, 1850, Spurgeon, who was soon to become known as "the boy preacher," was admitted to the church at

Newmarket. At that time he had not yet received the Lord's Supper, because though he had never heard of Baptists until he was fourteen, he had become convinced, by the Church of England catechism and by study of the New Testament, that believers in Christ should be baptized in His name after they received Him, and so he naturally desired baptism before his first communion.

He could not find a Baptist minister anywhere nearer than Isleham, where a Rev. W. W. Cantlow, who was a former missionary in Jamaica, ministered. Having decided to go there to be baptized, he first wrote to his parents to ask permission. They readily consented, although his father warned him that he must not trust in his baptism, and his mother reminded him that though she often prayed that her son would be a Christian, she had never asked that he would be a Baptist. Spurgeon playfully responded that the Lord had dealt with her in His usual bounty, and had given her exceedingly abundantly above all that she had asked.

It was on his mother's birthday, May 3, 1850, that Spurgeon "put on Christ," just short of his sixteenth birthday. He rose early on that Friday morning, spent two hours in prayer and dedication, and walked eight miles to Isleham Ferry, on the river Lark, which is a beautiful stream that divides Suffolk from Cambridgeshire. Though there were not as many people at this Friday baptism as there normally were on a Sunday baptism, there were a sufficient number watching to make Spurgeon, who had never seen a baptism before, a bit nervous. Here is his description of the scene.

> The wind blew down the river with a cutting blast
> as my turn came to wade into the flood; but after I

had walked a few steps, and noted the people on the ferryboat, and in boats, and on either shore, I felt as if Heaven and Earth and hell might all gaze upon me, for I was not ashamed, then and there, to own myself a follower of the Lamb. My timidity was washed away; it floated down the river into the sea, and must have been devoured by the fishes, for I have never felt anything of the kind since. Baptism also loosed my tongue, and from that day it has never been quiet.

That evening a prayer meeting was held in the Isleham vestry, at which the newly baptized Spurgeon prayed openly— "And people wondered and wept for joy as they listened to the lad." In the morning he went back to Newmarket, and the next Sunday he had communion for the first time, and was appointed a Sunday school teacher.

Some years later he wrote:

I did not fulfill the outward ordinance to join a party and to become a Baptist, but to be a Christian after the apostolic fashion; for they, when they believed, were baptized. It is now questioned whether John Bunyan was baptized, but the same question can never be raised concerning me. I, who scarcely belong to any sect, am nevertheless by no means willing to have it doubted in time to come whether or not I followed the conviction of my heart.

Later that year he moved to Cambridge. In the winter of 1850/1851, when he was just sixteen, he preached his first sermon in a cottage at Teversham, Cambridge. He hadn't planned on preaching there; in fact, hadn't know he was going to, but he was tricked into it by a Mr. James Vinter in

Cambridge, who was president of the Preachers' Association. Bishop Vinter, as he was generally known, called on Spurgeon one morning just as school was dismissed, and told him "to go over to Teversham the next evening, for a young man was to preach there who was not much used to services, and very likely would be glad of company."

Bishop Vinter apparently knew Spurgeon well, for a direct request for him to preach probably would have been refused. But Vinter knew that the young man had in him those qualities that make great preachers, and he only had to get started. Considering Vinter's reason for the ruse, it was excusable— it was also successful.

Spurgeon and the other young man Vinter had mentioned, started off in the early evening along the Newmarket Road to Teversham. After walking some distance in silence, Spurgeon expressed the hope that his companion, who was a bit older, would sense the presence of God when he preached. Horrified, the older man said that he had never preached, could not preach, and would not preach. Unless Spurgeon preached, he said, there would be no sermon at all. Spurgeon hesitated at first, saying he did not know what he could preach. The older man replied that if Spurgeon would just give one of his Sunday school teachings it should do quite well. Spurgeon then agreed to preach, and reproached himself for his hesitation: "Surely I can tell a few poor cottagers of the sweetness and love of Jesus, since I feel them in my own soul." Now having settled the matter, it was as if the Lord himself walked with them as He did with the two men on the road to Emmaus.

Spurgeon's text that memorable evening was, "Unto you therefore which believe he is precious" (1 Peter 2:7).

Then he expounded the praises of his Lord for nearly an hour, while those gathered in that thatched cottage listened attentively, enthralled with the eloquence of the young lad. When he finished, happy with the fact that he had been able to complete his sermon, which showed how little he thought of his preaching ability, he picked up a hymnbook to close out the service with praise and worship songs. Before they could start singing, however, an aged woman called out, "Bless your dear heart, how old are you?" Perhaps a bit prideful, or embarrassed to tell how young he was, Spurgeon replied, "You must wait until the service is over before making any such inquiries. Let us now sing."

During the friendly conversation that followed the singing, the old woman asked Spurgeon again, "How old are you?"

To this Spurgeon replied, "I am under sixty."

"Yes," said the old woman, "and under sixteen."

"Never mind," Spurgeon said, "think of the Lord Jesus Christ and His preciousness." Then upon the urging of several of the church members, he promised he would come back—if Bishop Vinter thought he was fit to preach again.

From that small but notable beginning, Spurgeon's fame as a preacher spread around the countryside, and he was invited to preach in Teversham both on Sundays and weekdays. Over the years in his writings and sermons, Spurgeon described his daily routine in those days. He would rise early in the morning for prayer and reading the Bible, then he would attend to school duties until about five in the evening. Almost every evening he would visit the villages near Cambridge to tell the people what he had learned during the day. He found that those things took solid hold of him when he proclaimed them to others. He also said that he made many blunders in those days, but he usually had a friendly audience and there were no reporters at that time writing down his every word.

In October 1851, he promised to preach at the small Baptist church in Waterbeach, six miles from Cambridge. This is the village where Rowland Hill (1744-1833) was said to have preached his first open air sermon. He had not, however, been licensed to preach, and so for preaching in the open air in and around Cambridge without a license, Hill was often opposed by the secular and church authorities and frequently assaulted by mobs. Finally, in 1773, after he had been refused ordination into the Church of England by six bishops, he was ordained by the Bishop of Bath and Wells and offered the curacy of Kingston in Somerset, but was subsequently denied priest's orders and continued his ministry as an independent or nonconformist. Later, having inherited considerable wealth from his father, Sir Rowland Hill, he built his own free chapel, Surrey Chapel, on Blackfriars Road in London. It opened in 1783. Hill was also one of the founders, and chairman, of the Religious Tract Society, and an active promoter of the interests of the British and Foreign Bible Society and the London Missionary Society.

The chapel at Waterbeach was a primitive building with a thatched roof, which was common in those days. Spurgeon promised to preach for a few Sundays, but continued for more than two years. It was here that he published his first literary work: a gospel tract written in 1853.

When Spurgeon took up the pulpit at Waterbeach, the village was notorious for its ungodliness and public drunkenness and profanity, like many of the towns where Charles Finney preached during the Great American Awakening. And like those towns, Waterbeach was soon to come under the power of the gospel, for God had sent His chosen messenger there. Here is Spurgeon's account of the changes that took place.

In a short time the little thatched chapel was crammed, the biggest vagabonds of the village were weeping floods of tears, and those who had been the curse of the parish became its blessing. I can say with joy and happiness that almost from one end of the village to the other, at the hour of eventide, one might have heard the voice of song coming from every roof-tree and echoing from almost every heart.

Spurgeon's first convert in Waterbeach was a laborer's wife, and he said he prized that soul more than the thousands that came afterward. She received Christ at the Sunday service, and early the next morning the seventeen-year-old Spurgeon hurried down to see his first spiritual child. "If anybody had said to me, 'Somebody has left you twenty thousand pounds,' I should not have given a snap of my fingers for it compared with the joy which I felt when I was told that God had saved a soul through my ministry. I felt like a boy who had earned his first guinea, or like a diver who had been down to the depth of the sea and brought up a rare pearl."

From the beginning of his ministry Spurgeon's style and ability were considered to be far above average. Of these early days, his brother James wrote:

> When I drove my brother about the country to preach, I thought then, as I have thought ever since, what an extraordinary preacher he was. What

wonderful unction and power I remember in some of those early speeches! The effect upon the people listening to him I have never known exceeded in after years. He seemed to have leaped full-grown into the pulpit. The breadth and brilliance of those early sermons, and the power that God's Holy Spirit evidently gave to him, made them perfectly marvelous. When he went to Waterbeach his letters came home, and were read as family documents, discussed, prayed over and wondered at. We were not surprised, however, for we all believed that it was in him.

It's a measure of how much Spurgeon ministered in the country where God had placed him that by the time he was called to London he had preached 670 sermons.

While the young Spurgeon was busy in Waterbeach and content to stay there, the New Park Street Baptist Church in London was looking for a pastor who could revive its fallen condition. It was an influential church because of having probably the largest chapel of any Baptist church building—it could seat nearly 1200 people, and was one of only six churches that had a listed membership of over three hundred. For a number of years, however, the church had been unable to find pastors of any distinction and the active membership had dwindled to less than two hundred. At this time the pastorate had been vacant for three months, and then they discovered nineteen-year-old Charles Spurgeon.

It happened unexpectedly. George Gould, a deacon of the church at Loughton, Essex, was in Cambridge and attended the anniversary meeting of the Cambridge Sunday School Union. Spurgeon was one of the speakers. During their speeches, the two older speakers scorned Spurgeon's youth. Spurgeon asked if he could reply. Both his speech and his reply so impressed Gould that when he returned to London and Thomas Olney, a New Park Street deacon, complained to him that they had been unable to find a suitable pastor, he suggested young Spurgeon. The suggestion was ignored the first time it was made, but when it was made again at a later date, Olney spoke to another New Park Street deacon and they agreed "to try the experiment" and wrote to Waterbeach, which was the only address they had, and invited Spurgeon to preach one Sunday.

When the invitation reached Spurgeon on the last Sunday of November of 1853, he was certain it was a mistake and passed the letter to Robert Coe, one of his church deacons. Coe said he was certain it *wasn't* a mistake, that what he had long dreaded had happened. But he was surprised at the invitation coming so soon and coming from London, which was "a great step from this little place."

Spurgeon still wasn't convinced, but on November 28 he wrote a cautious answer to the invitation, and said that he was willing to go to London for a Sunday, but suggested that the invitation was probably a mistake since he was only nineteen, and was quite unknown outside of the Waterbeach area. A second letter from London, however, eased his mind and he arranged to preach at New Park Street on December 18, 1853.

When the reluctant Spurgeon reached London he was greeted with a total lack of hospitality. Rather than house him in the home of one of the affluent members, as was often the custom with visiting clergy, they sent him to a boarding house in Queen's Square, Bloomsbury, where he was given a bedroom barely large enough to hold a bed. The clothing he wore clearly showed his country breeding, and upon hearing he was going to preach at New Park Street, the other young boarders told him tall tales of London's wonderful preachers. By the time Spurgeon went to his small bedroom to sleep, he was thoroughly discouraged, which, added to the unaccustomed street noise, kept him awake most of the night.

When he went to New Park Street the next morning and saw the imposing building, he was amazed at his own recklessness at thinking he could preach there. If he hadn't been certain of his calling, he probably would have returned immediately to Waterbeach.

But once in front of the sparse congregation that attended that morning—only about eighty people, he regained his normal confidence and delivered his sermon from the James 1:17: "Every good gift and every perfect gift is from above, and cometh down from the Father of lights, with whom is no variableness, neither shadow of turning." His message so affected the congregation that after the meeting one of the deacons said that if Spurgeon was only with them for three months the church would be filled. News of the splendid young preacher from Waterbeach spread by word-of-mouth all Sunday afternoon, and that evening the congregation had more than tripled what it was in the morning. Among them was the young lady who was later to become Spurgeon's wife. His text that evening was from Revelation 14:5: "They are without fault before the throne of God."

The people were so excited at the end the service that they would not leave until the deacons had convinced Spurgeon to come again, and before he left the building he agreed to return. Here is his account of that service.

> The Lord helped me very graciously. I had a happy Sabbath in the pulpit, and spent the interval with warm-hearted friends; and when at night I trudged back to the Queen's Square narrow lodging, I was not alone, and I no longer looked on Londoners as flinty-hearted barbarians. My tone was altered, I wanted no pity of anyone; I did not care a penny for the young gentlemen lodgers and their miraculous ministers, nor for the grind of the cabs, nor for anything else under the sun. The lion had been looked at all round, and his majesty did not appear to be a tenth as majestic as when I had heard his roar miles away.

No other preacher who had spoken at New Park Street during the three months when the pastorate was vacant had been invited a second time, but Spurgeon was invited back on the first, third, and fifth Sundays of January, 1854. His ministry was so successful that on January 25th, the Wednesday before the last Sunday, he was invited to occupy the pulpit for six months, with a view to becoming their new pastor.

Spurgeon was in Cambridge when the invitation from the church reached him, and he immediately wrote back stating that he dared not accept an unqualified invitation for such a long time. "My objection is not to the length of the time of probation, but it ill becomes a youth to promise to preach to a London congregation so long until he knows them and they know him. I would engage to supply for three months of that time, and then, should the congregation fail or the church disagree, I would reserve to myself the liberty, without breach of engagement, to retire, and you on your part would have the right to dismiss me without seeming to treat me ill. Enthusiasm and popularity are often like the crackling of thorns, and soon expire. I do not wish to be a hindrance if I cannot be a help."

The suggested probation was cut short, however, when fifty of the men members signed a request to the deacons that a special meeting be called. The meeting was held on April 19, 1854, and a resolution was passed in which they expressed with thankfulness the esteem in which their new preacher was held, and the extraordinary increase in attendance at all the church meetings. Thus they "consider it prudent to secure as early as possible his permanent settlement among us."

On April 28, just over four months after he arrived in London, the nineteen-year-old Spurgeon replied, "There is but one answer to so loving and candid an invitation. I accept it." Then he asked for their prayers, "Remember my youth and inexperience, and I pray that these may not hinder my usefulness. I trust also the remembrance of these will lead you to forgive mistakes I may make, or unguarded words that I may utter."

Spurgeon was a man of great courage, especially when it came to spiritual matters and defense of the Bible. He once said, "I have hardly ever known what the fear of man means." Along with this, God increasingly added courage to his faith, until there was literally nothing that could stop him from doing the work to which God had called him. In his exposition of the ninety-first Psalm in *The Treasury of David*, perhaps one of his greatest works, he wrote this:

> In the year 1854, when I had scarcely been in London twelve months, the neighborhood in which I lived was visited by Asiatic cholera, and my congregation suffered from its inroads. Family after family summoned me to the bedside of the smitten, and almost every day I was called to visit the grave. I gave myself up with youthful ardor to the visitation of the sick, and was sent for from all quarters of the district by persons of all ranks and religions. I became weary in body and sick at heart. My friends seemed falling one by one, and I felt or fancied that I was sickening like those around me. A little more work and weeping would have laid me low among the rest; I felt that my burden was heavier than I could bear, and I was ready to sink under it. As God would have it, I was returning mournfully from a funeral, when my curiosity led me to read a paper which was wafered [taped] up in a shoemaker's shop in the Dover Road. It did not look like a trade announcement, nor was it, for it bore in a good bold handwriting these words: "Because thou hast made the LORD, which is my refuge, even the most High, thy habitation; there shall no evil befall thee, neither shall any plague come nigh thy dwelling" (Psalm 91:9-10). The effect on my heart was immediate. Faith appropriated the passage as her own. I felt secure, refreshed, girt with immortality. I went on with my visitation of the dying in a calm and peaceful spirit; I felt no fear of evil and I suffered no harm. The providence which moved the tradesman to place those verses on the window I gratefully

acknowledge, and in the remembrance of its marvelous power I adore the Lord my God.

Though only about eighty people attended Spurgeon's first service at New Park Street, it soon became impossible to crowd into the building all the people who wanted to hear and see "the boy preacher," and the services moved to increasingly larger buildings. Soon the decision was made to enlarge the New Park Street Chapel, and the services were moved to a public building, Exeter Hall. Although using a public place for church services is common practice today, it was virtually unheard of in Spurgeon's day. But while Exeter Hall held several thousands more than the Park Street Chapel, it also wasn't large enough to contain the increasing crowds flocking to his meetings.

The work on the chapel took place from February 11 to May 27, 1855, and during this time Spurgeon became increasingly busy. Besides all his other ministerial duties and his writing, he was preaching as much as thirteen times a week. Soon his voice was overtaxed and the services in Exeter Hall were too much for him (keep in mind that there were no sound systems in those days and the preacher had to speak loudly enough for all in even the largest hall to hear him). About his voice, his wife later wrote:

> Sometimes his voice would almost break and fail as he pleaded with sinners to come to Christ, or magnified the Lord in His sovereignty and righteousness. A glass of chili vinegar always stood on a shelf under the desk before him, and I knew what to expect when he had recourse to that remedy. I remember with strange vividness the Sunday evening when he preached from

the text, "His name shall endure forever." It was a subject in which he reveled, it was his chief delight to exalt his glorious Savior, and he seemed in that discourse to be pouring out his very soul and life in homage and adoration before his gracious King. But I really thought he would have died there, in face of all those people. At the end he made a mighty effort to recover his voice; but utterance well nigh failed, and only in broken accents could the pathetic peroration be heard—"Let my name perish, but let Christ's name last for ever! Jesus! Jesus! JESUS! Crown Him Lord of all! You will not hear me say anything else. These are my last words in Exeter Hall for this time. Jesus! Jesus! JESUS! Crown Him Lord of all!" and then he fell back, almost fainting in the chair behind him.

When they returned to the enlarged New Park Street Chapel on May 31, it was discovered that the money spent on it was almost wasted, for while several hundred more could get into the chapel, the crowds were larger than before and thousands were disappointed. Services were held in the chapel for only about a year before it became necessary to rent Exeter Hall again.

Meanwhile, like George Whitefield, Spurgeon preached in the open air whenever the opportunity was offered, once in a field to a crowd of almost twenty thousand. Writing on June 3 of the same year to the soon-to-be Mrs. Spurgeon, Spurgeon said:

> Yesterday I climbed to the summit of a minister's glory. My congregation was enormous, I think ten thousand, but certainly twice as many as at Exeter

Hall. The Lord was with me, and the profoundest silence was observed; but oh, the close—never did mortal man receive a more enthusiastic oration! I wonder I am alive! After the service five or six gentlemen endeavored to clear a passage, but I was borne along, amid cheers, and prayers, and shouts, for about a quarter of an hour—it really seemed more like a week! I was hurried round and round the field without hope of escape until, suddenly seeing a nice open carriage, with two occupants, standing near, I sprang in, and begged them to drive away. This they most kindly did, and I stood up, waving my hat, and crying, "The blessing of God be with you!" while from thousands of heads the hats were lifted and cheer after cheer was given. Surely amid these plaudits I can hear the low rumbling of an advancing storm of reproaches; but even this I can bear for the Master's sake.

And come the storms did. Spurgeon soon had almost as many detractors as he did admirers. On one occasion when his carriage was driven through a crowd in London, he was heartily hooted and booed. And throughout his ministry a portion of the press was scornfully critical of him. Spurgeon once said, "A true Christian is one who fears God, and is hated by the *Saturday Review*." But no matter how highly and often he was criticized, he never changed one dot of what he believed to be the truth of God. His Pauline Calvinism, his sturdy Puritanism, his old-fashioned apostolic gospel, remained unchanged to the end.

One criticism that followed him all his life was that he was conceited. About this his biographer W. Y. Fullerton wrote:

As to the question of conceit,... in later years he gave a sufficient answer. "A friend of mine was calling upon him some time ago," wrote one after his death, "and happened to say, 'Do you know, Mr. Spurgeon, some people think you're conceited?' The great preacher smiled indulgently, and after a pause said, 'Do you see those bookshelves? They contain hundreds, nay, thousands of my sermons translated into every language under Heaven. Well, now, add to this that ever since I was twenty years old there never has been built a place large enough to hold the numbers of people who wished to hear me preach, and, upon my honor, when I think of it, I wonder I am not more conceited than I am.'" Upon which the writer remarks, "That is the kind of bonhomie [geniality] that disarms criticism."

Spurgeon had become known through much of London, but not all its inhabitants had heard of him. Strangely, what quickly made him known in every nook and cranny of the city was an accident. The owners of Exeter Hall said they could no longer rent the hall to one congregation, so plans were immediately formulated to build a structure larger than the Hall that would hold the thousands the Hall could not accommodate. But some temporary building was needed. Fortunately, the Surrey Music Hall, which could hold ten to twelve thousand people, became available. The news that Spurgeon was to preach in the Music Hall spread like wildfire, and on Sunday evening, October 19, 1856, the hall was jammed with ten thousand people and another ten thousand in the gardens surrounding the hall.

The building was so crowded that the service began before its appointed time. A prayer was offered, then a hymn with the customary running commentary, then another hymn. Prayer before the sermon was being offered when suddenly a loud cry of "Fire!" rang throughout the hall. There was instant panic and bedlam. In the ensuing rush for the door, a stairway gave way and toppled people to the floor, others were knocked down and trampled underfoot. Seven were killed and twenty-eight were taken to the hospital seriously injured. There was, however, no fire; it was a false alarm, given perhaps out of malice against Spurgeon.

In the midst of it all, Spurgeon was unaware of the extent of the disaster, and did not know there had been any fatal injuries. He attempted to quiet the people, and at the urging of repeated cries endeavored to preach. He told the crowd that the text he had intended to use was the thirty-third verse of the third chapter of Proverbs, "The curse of the LORD is upon the house of the wicked: but he blesseth the habitation of the just," and asked the people to remain quiet or retire gradually if they felt they must leave. But there was more disturbance, and the service had to be discontinued. Spurgeon was so distressed by it all, he had to be carried from the pulpit.

The next day every newspaper in London carried vivid descriptions of the disaster and the deaths and injuries and vilified Spurgeon for holding services in a public Music Hall. Said one leading newspaper, "This hiring of places of amusement for Sunday preaching is a novelty, and a powerful one. It looks as if religion were at its last shift. It is a confession of weakness, rather than a sign of strength. It is not wrestling with Satan in his strongholds—to use the old earnest Puritan language—but entering into a very coward truce and alliance with the world." Within days every part of London was talking about the young preacher, and when he resumed preaching, after spending several days deeply depressed and discouraged, the crowds were larger than ever. Hoping to turn people against Spurgeon, the newspapers had done just the opposite, and made him the best known preacher in all of London. What the enemy had intended for evil, God had turned to good.

Over the years after that, Spurgeon's popularity increased until he was known all over the civilized world. His sermons were reproduced by the millions in virtually every language. Even today they are read more than any other sermons ever printed.

On March 25, 1861, Spurgeon preached his first sermon in his newest and largest building, the Metropolitan Tabernacle at Elephant and Castle, Southwark. The building would seat 4,600 people, but often another thousand—and often more—found some place to sit or stand. A deacon once claimed that on a special occasion they had crammed eight thousand people into it. "We counted eight thousand out of her" he said. "I don't know where she put 'em, but we did."

D. L. Moody had not yet arrived on the London scene, but Spurgeon invited him to preach at the tabernacle, to which Moody replied, "In regard to coming to your tabernacle, I consider it a great honor to be invited; and, in fact, I should consider it an honor to black your boots, but to preach to your people would be out of the question. If they will not turn to God under your preaching, neither will they be persuaded though one rose from the dead." Moody did later preach for Spurgeon, and in writing to thank him and invite him to his church to preach, Moody said, "I wish you could give us every night you can for the next sixty days. There are so few men who can draw on a weeknight."

That was the wonder of it, Spurgeon built a tabernacle seating between five and six thousand persons, able to contain over seven thousand, and for thirty-eight years he maintained that congregation there and elsewhere in London. Other great preachers, like Wesley and Whitefield, gathered as great crowds, but they traveled to various places to do so. Spurgeon remained rooted to London.

At a prayer meeting on May 26, 1890, Spurgeon looked around the Metropolitan Tabernacle and exclaimed, "How many thousands have been converted here! There has not been a single day but what I have heard of two, three, or four having been converted; and that not for one, two, or three years, but for the last ten years!" It is an interesting note that additions to the church year by year were double the additions to New Park Street in the same periods of time, which shows that the number of new converts bears a relationship to the size of the congregation. With few exceptions, that great building was crowded every Sunday morning and evening for thirty years, and the attendance at the Thursday night meeting was usually even larger.

Spurgeon once said:

> Somebody asked me how I got my congregation. I never got it at all. I did not think it was my duty to do so. I only had to preach the gospel. Why, my congregation got my congregation. I had eighty, or scarcely a hundred, when I preached first. The next time I had two hundred. Everyone who heard me was

saying to his neighbor, "You must go and hear this young man!" Next meeting we had four hundred, and in six weeks, eight hundred. That was the way in which my people got my congregation. Now the people are admitted by tickets. That does very well; a member can give his ticket to another person and say, "I will stand in the aisle," or "I will get in with the crowd." Some persons, you know, will not go if they can get in easily, but they will go if you tell them they cannot get in without a ticket. That is the way congregations ought to bring a congregation about a minister. A minister preaches all the better if he has a large congregation. It was once said by a gentleman that the forming of a congregation was like the beating-up of game, the minister being the sportsman. But there are some of our ministers that can't shoot! I really think, however, that I could shoot a partridge if I fired into the midst of a covey, though I might not do so if there were only one or two.

On October 26, 1891, Spurgeon, who was feeling increasingly ill and weak from a combination of rheumatism, gout, and Bright's disease (kidney disease) which he had suffered from for many years, started out on a journey to Menton, France, where he often went to rest and recuperate. They reached the Hotel Beau-Rivage, where they were staying, without difficulty, and despite his weakness enjoyed three months of "earthly paradise." By the middle of January, however, he began to weaken rapidly, though he conducted brief services in his room on January 10 and 17. They were the last of his earthly work for his Lord. He died on January 31, 1892. His wife and two sons outlived him, as did his father, who died at the age of almost ninety-two.

The news of his home-going flashed around the world. One London newspaper had the terse headline, "Death of Spurgeon." That day it was difficult to obtain a newspaper anywhere in England, the demand was so great. Spurgeon's coffin was brought back from Menton, France, and arrived at Victoria Station, London, on Monday, February 9, 1892. It was met by a small group of friends and taken to the Pastor's College, where it remained for the rest of the day. That night it was carried into the Metropolitan Tabernacle, and over sixty thousand people passed by it to pay their homage. Four funeral services were held on Wednesday to accommodate the crowds. Ira D. Sankey, Moody's associate, was there and sang twice. Herber Evans, a Welsh Nonconformist minister, spoke briefly and concluding said, "But there is one Charles Haddon Spurgeon whom we cannot bury; there is not earth enough in Norwood to bury him—the Spurgeon of history. The good works that he has done will live. You cannot bury them."

The funeral was on Thursday, and one newspaper said you could search all of London and not find three women who were not wearing black. At the graveside, Archibald G. Brown, a close friend and one of Spurgeon's most distinguished associates, gave a eulogy that some have said will be remembered forever.

Beloved President, faithful Pastor, Prince of Preachers, brother beloved, dear Spurgeon—we bid you not "Farewell," but only for a little while "good night." Thou shalt rise soon at the first dawn of the resurrection day of the redeemed. Yet is the good night not ours to bid, but thine; it is we who linger in the darkness; thou art in God's holy light. Our night shall soon be passed, and with it all our weeping. Then, with thine, our songs shall greet the morning of a day that knows no cloud nor close; for there is no night there.

Hard worker in the field, thy toil is ended. Straight has been the furrow thou hast ploughed. No looking back has marred thy course. Harvests have followed thy patient sowing, and Heaven is already rich with thine ingathered sheaves, and shall still be enriched through the years yet lying in eternity.

Champion of God, thy battle, long and nobly fought, is over; thy sword, which clave to thy hand, has dropped at last; a palm branch takes it place. No longer does the helmet press thy brow, oft weary with its surging thoughts of battle; a victor's wreath from the great Commander's hand has already proved thy full reward.

Here, for a little while, shall rest thy precious dust. Then shall thy Well-beloved come; and at His voice thou shalt spring from thy couch of Earth, fashioned like unto His body, into glory. Then spirit, soul, and body shall magnify the Lord's redemption. Until then, beloved, sleep. We praise God for you, and by the blood of the everlasting covenant, hope and expect to praise God with you. Amen.

Spurgeon's coffin was then lowered into the ground. On it was a Bible open to the text that led Spurgeon to the Lord and Savior that he had served faithfully for more than forty years, "Look unto me, and be ye saved, all the ends of the earth: for I am God, and there is none else" (Isaiah 45:22).

A Brief Chronology of Spurgeon's Life

- June 19, 1834, born at Kelvedon, Essex, England

- January 6, 1850, born-again at Colchester

- May 3, 1850, baptized in the River Lark at Isleham, becomes a Baptist

- Winter of 1850/1851, preaches his first public sermon at a cottage in Teversham

- October 12, 1851, preaches his first sermon at Waterbeach Baptist Chapel

- December 18, 1853, preaches his first sermon at New Park Street Chapel, London—about 80 people attend the service

- April 28, 1854, accepts pastorate at New Park Street Chapel, which has 232 members

- January 10, 1855, publishes his first sermon in the "New Park Street Pulpit"

- January 8, 1856, marries Miss Susannah Thompson (born 1/15/1832)

- Spring 1856, takes a 10-day wedding trip to Paris, France

- September 20, 1856, fraternal (non-identical) twin sons, Thomas and Charles, born

- June 1856, Metropolitan Tabernacle Building Committee formed

- 1856, establishes the Pastor's College, expands it in 1857

- March 18, 1861, Metropolitan Tabernacle opens with a great prayer meeting

- March 25, 1861, preaches first sermon in Metropolitan Tabernacle

- 1866, Metropolitan Tabernacle Colportage Association Founded (to peddle literature)

- 1867, Stockwell Orphanage (boy's side) founded, foundation stone laid September 9, 1869

- May 6, 1867, foundation stone laid by Senior Deacon Thomas Olney for the Pastor's College building

- March, 1868, construction of Pastor's College building completed

- December 1871, begins annual vacations to Menton in southern France for rest and relaxation

- February 1873, congregation now numbers 4,417 members

- October 14, 1873, foundation stone laid for a newer Pastor's College Building

- 1879, Stockwell Orphanage (girl's side) founded

- June 22, 1880, foundation stone for orphanage laid

- 1888, his mother Eliza dies at age 75

- June 7, 1891, delivers last sermon at Metropolitan Tabernacle—during his pastorate, 14,692 were baptized and joined the tabernacle—at end of 1891 it had 5,311 members

- June and July, 1891, suffers much pain and sickness from his long-endured combination of rheumatism, gout, and Bright's disease

- October 26, 1891, starts trip to Menton, France, for the last time

- January 20, 1892, illness overcomes him and he takes to his bed

- January 31, 1892, his spirit leaves his body

- February 9, 1892, coffin arrives back in London

- February 11, 1892, buried at Norwood Cemetery

- March 22, 1899, brother, James, Assistant Tabernacle Pastor, dies

- June 14, 1902, his father, John, dies, just short of 92, having been born on July 15, 1910

- October 22, 1903, his wife, Susannah, dies at age 71

- October 17, 1917, son Thomas, a pastor, dies at age 61

- December 13, 1926, son Charles, a pastor, dies at age 70

ILLUSTRATION PORTFOLIO

The Birthplace of Charles H. Spurgeon
June 19, 1834 in Kelvedon, Essex, England

Rev. John Spurgeon
father of C.H. Spurgeon

Eliza Spurgeon
mother of C.H. Spurgeon

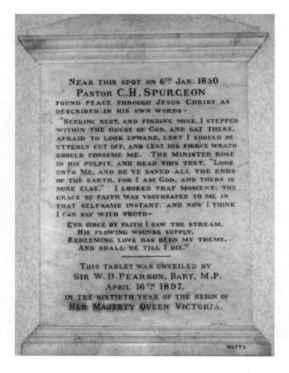

Near this spot on 6th Jan. 1850

Pastor C.H. Spurgeon

FOUND PEACE THROUGH JESUS CHRIST AS DESCRIBED IN HIS OWN WORDS –
"SEEKING REST, AND FINDING NONE, I STEPPED WITHIN THE HOUSE OF GOD,
AND SAT THERE, AFRAID TO LOOK UPWARD, LEST I SHOULD BE UTTERLY CUT OFF, AND
LEST HIS FIERCE WRATH SHOULD CONSUME ME. THE MINISTER ROSE IN HIS PULPIT,
AND READ THIS TEXT, "LOOK UNTO ME, AND BE YE SAVED ALL THE ENDS OF THE
EARTH, FOR I AM GOD, AND THERE IS NONE ELSE."
I LOOKED THAT MOMENT: THE GRACE OF FAITH WAS VOUCHSAFED TO ME IN THAT
SELFSAME INSTATNT; AND NOW I THINK I CAN SAY WITH TRUTH –
E'ER SINCE BY FAITH I SAW THE STREAM,
HIS FLOWING WOUNDS SUPPLY,
REDEEMING LOVE HAS BEEN MY THEME,
AND SHALL BE TILL I DIE."

THIS TABLET WAS UNVEILED BY
SIR W.D. PEARSON, BART, M.P.
APRIL 16TH 1897.
IN THE SIXTIETH YEAR OF THE REIGN OF
HER MAJESTY QUEEN VICTORIA

Above: The cottage where Mr. Spurgeon preached his first sermon at age 16. Left: Susannah Tompson became Mrs. Charles Spurgeon on January 8, 1856. Despite fragile health, she was a strong partner to her husband and his ministry. Below: The Spurgeons lived a comfortable but modest life at Westwood, and used the majority of their income to help ministers, the poor, and people in need.

WESTWOOD

33

THE NEW PARK STREET CHAPEL
Spurgeon accepted his first pastorate in December 1853,
at the age of 19.

MUSIC HALL IN THE ROYAL SURREY GARDENS
In spite of a disastrous beginning, the congregation used this
building as a meeting place for five years.

THE METROPOLITAN TABERNACLE
Above: Completed in 1861, the new
home of the Park Street congregation
was built in the Greek style. It was
the largest church in the world at the
time and held nearly 6,000 people.
Left: Spurgeon sometimes needed to
be helped into the pulpit because of
the pain he suffered from gout.

STOCKWELL ORPHANAGE
Spurgeon oversaw and raised funds to support the Boy's
School and Girl's School at Stockwell Orphanage (*above*), as
well as the Pastor's College he founded (*bottom*).

THE PASTOR'S COLLEGE

THE SWORD AND
THE TROWEL
Spurgeon published
this monthly
magazine beginning
in 1865, in which he
essentially continued
preaching Christ,
but also touched on
issues of doctrine
within the church.

Spurgeon in
his study at
Westwood, his
family home.

Spurgeon's study at Westwood (*above*) contained more than 12,000 volumes. Mr. Spurgeon's work was enormous. Besides editing and furnishing most of the matter for his monthly magazine, *The Sword and the Trowel*, since January 1, 1865, he wrote *The Saint and His Saviour*, *The Treasury of David, an Exposition of the Psalms* in seven octavo volumes; *The New Park Street Pulpit* and the *Metropolitan Tabernacle Pulpit*, which contains about two thousand of his weekly sermons from 1855 to 1889, making thirty large volumes. Also *Lectures to My Students, Commenting and Commentaries, John Ploughman*, the *Cheque Book of the Bank of Faith*, and various other

Mark XVI. 14.

This shows us the way in w[hich] we must deal with
unbelief in ourselves, & in others. It is a sin
& should be treated as such. Jesus w[oul]d not have
upbraided had not this been the case.

In the case before us they had repeated
testimonies, from their own brethren, & backed by
his own word — but we have even more
guilt for we know him to be risen & y[e]t doubt

I. _Let us consider its evil in itself_

Suppose some one doubted us.
Think of who he is & what he has done. —
Consider his near & dear relation to us.
The many times in w[hich] we have doubted
And upon the same matter.
Where his promises forbade unbelief
Despite our own declarations.
What have we believed in preference?

II. _Let us observe the evils w[hich] it causes_

It grieves the Spirit of God.
It causes distress in our own hearts
It weakens us for action or suffering
It depresses others.
It leaves an ill impress on sinners
It cannot but gender to bondage

III. _Let us reflect upon its sinfulness where
it reigns_

It gives God the lie.
It argues hatred in the heart
It is the sign of utter moral death.
It is the essence of hell.

SERMON NOTES

This one page of handwritten notes is all Spurgeon took with
him into the pulpit when he preached the sermon titled
"Unbelievers Upbraided."

PART 1

SPURGEON'S
DEVOTIONALS
ON PRAYER

AFTER THIS MANNER PRAY

"After this manner therefore pray ye:
Our Father which art in heaven." (Matthew 6:9)

This prayer begins where all true prayer must commence, with the spirit of adoption, "Our Father." There is no acceptable prayer until we can say, "I will arise, and go unto my Father." This childlike spirit soon perceives the grandeur of the Father "in Heaven," and ascends to devout adoration, "Hallowed be thy name." The child lisping, "Abba, Father," grows into the cherub crying, "Holy, Holy, Holy."

There is but a step from rapturous worship to the glowing missionary spirit, which is a sure outgrowth of filial love and reverent adoration: "Thy kingdom come, thy will be done on earth as it is in heaven." Next follows the heartfelt expression of dependence upon God: "Give us this day our daily bread." Being further illuminated by the Spirit, he discovers that he is not only dependent, but sinful, hence he entreats for mercy, "Forgive us our debts as we forgive our debtors," and being pardoned, having the righteousness of Christ imputed, and knowing his acceptance with God, he humbly supplicates for holy perseverance, "Lead us not into temptation."

The man who is really forgiven, is eager not to offend again; the possession of justification leads to an eager desire for sanctification. "Forgive us our debts," that is justification; "Lead us not into temptation, but deliver us from evil," that is sanctification in its negative and positive forms. As the result of all this, there follows a triumphant ascription of praise, "Thine is the kingdom, the power, and the glory, for ever and ever, Amen."

We rejoice that our King reigns in providence and shall reign in grace, from the river even to the ends of the Earth, and of His dominion there shall be no end. Thus from a sense of adoption, up to fellowship with our reigning Lord, this short model of prayer conducts the soul. Lord, teach us thus to pray.

CALL ON THE LORD

"He was sore athirst, and called on the LORD, and said, Thou hast given this great deliverance into the hand of thy servant: and now shall I die for thirst?" (Judges 15:18)

Samson was thirsty and ready to die. The difficulty was totally different from any that the hero had met before. Merely to get thirst satisfied is nothing like so great a matter as to be delivered from a thousand Philistines! But when the thirst was upon him, Samson felt that little present difficulty more weighty than the great past difficulty out of which he had so specially been delivered. It is very usual for God's people, when they have enjoyed a great deliverance, to find a little trouble too much for them. Samson slays a thousand Philistines, and piles them up in heaps, and then faints for a little water! Jacob wrestles with God at Peniel, and overcomes Omnipotence itself, and then goes "halting on his thigh!" (Genesis 32:31). Strange that there must be a shrinking of the sinew whenever we win the day. As if the Lord must teach us our littleness, our nothingness, in order to keep us within bounds.

Samson boasted right loudly when he said, "I have slain a thousand men" (Judges 15:16). His boastful throat soon grew hoarse with thirst, and he betook himself to prayer. God has many ways of humbling His people. Dear child of God, if after great mercy you are laid very low, your case is not an unusual one.

When David had mounted the throne of Israel, he said, "I am this day weak, though anointed king" (2 Samuel 3:39). You must expect to feel weakest when you are enjoying your greatest triumph. If God has wrought for you great deliverances in the past, your present difficulty is only like Samson's thirst, and the Lord will not let you faint, nor suffer the daughter of the uncircumcised to triumph over you. The road of sorrow is the road to Heaven, but there are wells of refreshing water all along the route.

So, tired brother, tired sister, cheer your heart with Samson's words, and rest assured that God will deliver you before long.

CONTINUE IN PRAYER

"Continue in prayer." (Colossians 4:2)

It is interesting to remark how large a portion of sacred writ is occupied with the subject of prayer, either in furnishing examples, enforcing precepts, or pronouncing promises. We scarcely open the Bible before we read, "Then began men to call upon the name of the Lord" (Genesis 4:26); and just as we are about to close the volume, the "Amen" of an earnest supplication meets our ear. (See Revelation 22:20-21.) Instances are plentiful.

Here we find a wrestling Jacob—there a Daniel who prayed three times a day—and a David who with all his heart called upon his God. On the mountain we see Elijah; in the dungeon Paul and Silas. We have multitudes of commands and myriads of promises.

What does this teach us, but the sacred importance and necessity of prayer? We may be certain that whatever God has made prominent in His Word, He intended to be conspicuous in our lives. If He has said much about prayer, it is because He knows we have much need of it. So deep are our necessities, that until we are in Heaven we must not cease to pray. Do you want nothing? Then, I fear you do not know your poverty. Have you no mercy to ask of God? Then, may the Lord's mercy show you your misery!

A prayerless soul is a Christless soul. Prayer is the lisping of the believing infant, the shout of the fighting believer, the requiem of the dying saint falling asleep in Jesus. It is the breath, the watchword, the comfort, the strength, the honor of a Christian. If you are a child of God, you will seek your Father's face, and live in your Father's love. Pray that this year you may be holy, humble, zealous, and patient; have closer communion with Christ, and enter oftener into the banqueting house of His love. Pray that you may be an example and a blessing unto others, and that you may live more to the glory of your Master.

The motto for this year must be, "Continue in prayer."

CRY UNTO THE LORD

"Unto thee will I cry, O LORD my rock; be not silent to me: lest, if thou be silent to me, I become like them that go down into the pit." (Psalm 28:1)

A cry is the natural expression of sorrow, and a suitable utterance when all other modes of appeal fail us; but the cry must be directed to the Lord alone, for to cry to man is to waste our entreaties upon the air. When we consider the readiness of the Lord to hear, and His ability to aid, we shall see good reason for directing all our appeals at once to the

God of our salvation. It will be in vain to call to the rocks in the Day of Judgment, but our Rock attends to our cries.

"Be not silent to me." Mere formalists may be content without answers to their prayers, but genuine suppliants cannot; they are not satisfied with the results of prayer itself in calming the mind and subduing the will—they must go further, and obtain actual replies from Heaven, or they cannot rest; and those replies they long to receive at once, they dread even a little of God's silence. God's voice is often so terrible that it shakes the wilderness; but His silence is equally full of awe to an eager suppliant.

When God seems to close His ear, we must not therefore close our mouths, but rather cry with more earnestness; for when our note grows shrill with eagerness and grief, He will not long deny us a hearing. What a dreadful case should we be in if the Lord should become forever silent to our prayers? "Lest, if you be silent to me, I become like them that go down into the pit." Deprived of the God who answers prayer, we should be in a more pitiable plight than the dead in the grave, and should soon sink to the same level as the lost in hell. We must have answers to prayer: ours is an urgent case of dire necessity; surely the Lord will speak peace to our agitated minds, for He never can find it in His heart to permit His own elect to perish.

DAVID ENQUIRED OF THE LORD

"And David enquired of the LORD." (2 Samuel 5:23)

When David made this enquiry he had just fought the Philistines, and gained a signal victory. The Philistines came up in great hosts, but, by the help of God, David had easily put them to flight. Note, however, that when they came a second time, David did not go up to fight them without enquiring of the Lord. Once he had been victorious, and he might have said, as many have in other cases, "I shall be victorious again; I may rest quite sure that if I have conquered once I shall triumph yet again. Wherefore should I tarry to seek at the Lord's hands?" Not so, David. He had gained one battle by the strength of the Lord; he would not venture upon another until he had ensured the same. He enquired, "Shall I go up against them?" He waited until God's sign was given.

Learn from David to take no step without God. Christian, if you would know the path of duty, take God for your compass; if you would steer your ship through the dark billows, put the tiller into the hand of the Almighty. Many a rock might be escaped, if we would let our Father take the helm; many a shoal or quicksand we might well avoid, if we would leave to His sovereign will to choose and to command.

The Puritan said, "As sure as ever a Christian carves for himself, he'll cut his own fingers;" this is a great truth. Said another old divine, "He that goes before the cloud of God's providence goes on a fool's errand;" and so he does. We must mark God's providence leading us; and if providence tarries, tarry till providence comes. He who goes before providence will be very glad to run back again. "I will instruct thee and teach thee in the way which thou shalt go" (Psalm 32:8), is God's promise to His people. Let us, then, take all our perplexities to Him, and say, "Lord, what wilt thou have me to do?" (Acts 9:6).

Leave not your chamber this morning without enquiring of the Lord.

DELIVER US FROM EVIL

"Lead us not into temptation;
but deliver us from evil." (Luke 11:4)

What we are taught to seek or shun in prayer, we should equally pursue or avoid in action. Very earnestly, therefore, should we avoid temptation, seeking to walk so guardedly in the path of obedience, that we may never tempt the devil to tempt us. We are not to enter the thicket in search of the lion. Dearly might we pay for such presumption. This lion may cross our path or leap upon us from the thicket, but we have nothing to do with hunting him. He that meets with him, even though he wins the day, will find it a stern struggle. Let the Christian pray that he may be spared the encounter. Our Savior, who had experience of what temptation meant, thus earnestly admonished His disciples: "Pray that ye enter not into temptation."

But let us do as we will, we shall be tempted; hence the prayer "deliver us from evil." God had one Son without sin; but He has no son without temptation. The natural man is born to trouble as the sparks fly upwards, and the Christian man is born to temptation just as certainly. We must be always on our watch against Satan, because, like a thief, he gives no intimation of his approach. Believers who have had experience of the ways of Satan, know that there are certain seasons when he will most probably make an attack, just as at certain seasons bleak winds may be expected; thus the Christian is put on a double guard by fear of danger, and the danger is averted by preparing to meet it.

Prevention is better than cure: it is better to be so well armed that the Devil will not attack you than to endure the perils of the fight, even though you come off as a conqueror. Pray this evening first that you may not be tempted, and next that if temptation be permitted, you may be delivered from the evil one.

DO AS THOU HAST SAID

"Do as thou hast said." (2 Samuel 7:25)

God's promises were never meant to be thrown aside as waste paper; He intended that they should be used. God's gold is not miser's money, but is minted to be traded with. Nothing pleases our Lord better than to see His promises put in circulation; He loves to see His children bring them up to Him, and say, "Lord, do as thou hast said." We glorify God when we plead His promises.

Do you think God will be any the poorer for giving you the riches He has promised? Do you dream that He will be any the less holy for giving holiness to you? Do you imagine He will be any the less pure for washing you from your sins? He has said, "Come now, and let us reason together, saith the LORD: though your sins be as scarlet, they shall be as white as snow; though they be red like crimson, they shall be as wool" (Isaiah 1:18).

Faith lays hold upon the promise of pardon, and it does not delay, saying, "This is a precious promise, I wonder if it is true?" but it goes straight to the throne with it, and pleads, "Lord, here is the promise, 'Do as thou hast said.'" Our Lord replies, "Be it unto thee even as thou wilt" (Matthew 15:28).

When a Christian grasps a promise, if he does not take it to God, he dishonors Him; but when he hastens to the throne of grace, and cries, "Lord, I have nothing to recommend me but this, 'Thou hast said it;'" then his desire shall be granted.

Our heavenly banker delights to cash His own notes. Never let the promise rust. Draw the sword of promise out of its scabbard, and use it with holy violence. Think not that God will be troubled by your importunately reminding Him of His promises. He loves to hear the loud outcries of needy souls. It is His delight to bestow favors. He is more ready to hear than you are to ask. The sun is not weary of shining, nor the fountain of flowing. It is God's nature to keep His promises; therefore, go at once to the throne with "Do as thou hast said."

FOR THIS CHILD I PRAYED

"For this child I prayed." (1 Samuel 1:27)

Devout souls delight to look upon those mercies that they have obtained in answer to supplication, for they can see God's special love in them. When we can name our blessings *Samuel*, that is, "asked of God," they will be as dear to us as her child was to Hannah. Peninnah had many children, but they came as common blessings unsought in prayer: Hannah's one Heaven-given child was dearer far, because he was the fruit of earnest pleadings. How sweet was that water to Samson which he found at "the well of him that prayed!"

Quassia cups turn all waters bitter, but the cup of prayer puts a sweetness into the draughts it brings.

Did we pray for the conversion of our children? How doubly sweet, when they are saved, to see in them our own petitions fulfilled! Better to rejoice over them as the fruit of our pleadings than as the fruit of our bodies. Have we sought of the Lord some choice spiritual gift? When it comes to us it will be wrapped up in the gold cloth of God's faithfulness and truth, and so be doubly precious. Have we petitioned for success in the Lord's work? How joyful is the prosperity that comes flying upon the wings of prayer! It is always best to get blessings into our house in the legitimate way, by the door of prayer; then they are blessings indeed, and not temptations. Even when prayer speeds not, the blessings grow all the richer for the delay; the child Jesus was all the more lovely in the eyes of Mary when she found Him after having sought Him sorrowing.

That which we win by prayer we should dedicate to God, as Hannah dedicated Samuel. The gift came from Heaven, let it go to heaven. Prayer brought it, gratitude sang over it, let devotion consecrate it. Here will be a special occasion for saying, "Of your own have I given unto you." Reader, is prayer your element or your weariness? Which?

FORSAKE ME NOT

"Forsake me not, O LORD." (Psalm 38:21)

Frequently we pray that God would not forsake us in the hour of trial and temptation, but we too much forget that we have need to use this prayer at all times. There is no moment of our life, however holy, in which we can do without His constant upholding. Whether in light or in darkness, in communion or in temptation, we alike need the prayer, "Forsake me not, O LORD." "Hold thou me up, and I shall be safe" (Psalm 119:117). A little child, while learning to walk, always needs the nurse's aid. The ship left by the pilot drifts at once from her course.

We cannot do without continued aid from above; let it then be your prayer today: "Forsake me not, Father; forsake not your child, lest he fall by the hand of the enemy. Shepherd, forsake not your lamb, lest he wander from the safety of the fold. Great Husbandman, forsake not your plant, lest it wither and die. 'Forsake me not, O LORD' now; and forsake me not at any moment of my life. Forsake me not in my joys, lest they absorb my heart. Forsake me not in my sorrows, lest I murmur against thee. Forsake me not in the day of my repentance, lest I lose the hope of pardon and fall into despair; and forsake me not in the day of my strongest faith, lest faith degenerate into presumption. Forsake me not, for without you I am weak, but with you I am strong. Forsake me not, for my path is dangerous, and full of snares, and I cannot do without your guidance. The hen forsakes not her brood; do, Lord, evermore cover me with your feathers, and permit me under your wings to find my refuge. 'Be not far from me; for trouble is near; for there is none to help' (Psalm 22:11). 'Leave me not, neither forsake me, O God of my salvation!' (Psalm 27:9)."

> O ever in our cleansed breast,
> Bid thine eternal Spirit rest;
> And make our secret soul to be
> A temple pure and worthy of thee.

GIVE YOURSELF UNTO PRAYER

"But I give myself unto prayer." (Psalm 109:4)

Lying tongues were busy against the reputation of David, but he did not defend himself; he moved the case into a higher court, and pleaded before the great King himself. Prayer is the safest method of replying to words of hatred.

The Psalmist prayed in no cold-hearted manner; he gave himself to the exercise—threw his whole soul and heart into it—straining every sinew and muscle, as Jacob did when wrestling with the angel. Thus, and thus only, shall any of us speed at the throne of grace. As a shadow has no power because there is no substance in it, even so that supplication, in which a man's proper self is not thoroughly present in agonizing earnestness and vehement desire, is utterly ineffectual, for it lacks that which would give it force. "Fervent prayer," says an old divine, "like a cannon planted at the gates of Heaven, makes them fly open."

The common fault with most of us is our readiness to yield to distractions. Our thoughts go roving hither and thither, and we make little progress towards our desired end. Like quicksilver our mind will not hold together, but rolls off this way and that. How great an evil this is! It injures us, and what is worse, it insults our God. What should we think of a petitioner, if, while having an audience with a prince, he should be playing with a feather or catching a fly?

Continuance and perseverance are intended in the expression of our text. David did not cry once, and then relapse into silence; his holy clamor was continued till it brought down the blessing. Prayer must not be our chance work, but our daily business, our habit and vocation. As artists give themselves to their models, and poets to their classical pursuits, so must we addict ourselves to prayer. We must be immersed in prayer as in our element, and so pray without ceasing. Lord, teach us so to pray that we may be more and more prevalent in supplication.

GO FORTH TO MEET HIM

"Isaac went out to meditate in the field at the eventide."
(Genesis 24:63)

Very admirable was his occupation. If those who spend so many hours in idle company, light reading, and useless pastimes, could learn wisdom, they would find more profitable society and more interesting engagements in meditation than in the vanities that now have such charms for them. We should all know more, live nearer to God, and grow in grace, if we were more alone. Meditation chews the cud and extracts the real nutriment from the mental food gathered elsewhere. When Jesus is the theme, meditation is sweet indeed. Isaac found Rebecca while engaged in private musings; many others have found their best beloved there.

Very admirable was the choice of place. In the field we have a study hung round with texts for thought. From the cedar to the hyssop, from the soaring eagle down to the chirping grasshopper, from the blue expanse of Heaven to a drop of dew, all things are full of teaching, and when the eye is divinely opened, that teaching flashes upon the mind far more vividly than from written books. Our little rooms are neither so healthy, so suggestive, so agreeable, or so inspiring as the fields. Let us count nothing common or unclean, but feel that all created things point to their Maker, and the field will at once be hallowed.

Very admirable was the season. The season of sunset as it draws a veil over the day, befits that repose of the soul when

Earth-born cares yield to the joys of heavenly communion. The glory of the setting sun excites our wonder, and the solemnity of approaching night awakens our awe. If the business of this day will permit it, it will be well, dear reader, if you can spare an hour to walk in the field at eventide, but if not, the Lord is in the town, too, and will meet with you in your chamber or in the crowded street. Let your heart go forth to meet Him.

GOD OFTEN DELAYS HIS ANSWER

"Therefore will the LORD wait, that he may be gracious unto you." (Isaiah 30:18)

God often *delays in answering prayer*. We have several instances of this in sacred Scripture. Jacob did not get the blessing from the angel until near the dawn of day—he had to wrestle all night for it. The poor woman of Syrophoenicia was answered not a word for a long while. Paul prayed to the Lord three times that "the thorn in the flesh" (2 Corinthians 12:7) might be taken from him, and he received no assurance that it should be taken away, but instead thereof a promise that God's grace should be sufficient for him.

If you have been knocking at the gate of mercy and have received no answer, shall I tell you why the mighty Maker has not opened the door and let you in? Our Father has reasons peculiar to himself for keeping us waiting. Sometimes it is to show His power and His sovereignty, that men may know that Jehovah has a right to give or to withhold. More frequently the delay is for our profit.

You are perhaps kept waiting in order that your desires may be more fervent. God knows that delay will quicken and increase desire, and that if He keeps you waiting, you will see your necessity more clearly, and will seek more earnestly; and that you will prize the mercy all the more for its long tarrying. There may also be something wrong in you that has need to be removed, before the joy of the Lord is given. Perhaps your views of the gospel plan are confused, or you may be placing some little reliance on yourself, instead of trusting simply and entirely in the Lord Jesus. Or, God makes you tarry awhile that He may the more fully display the riches of His grace to you at last.

Your prayers are all filed in Heaven, and if not immediately answered; they are certainly not forgotten, but in a little while shall be fulfilled to your delight and satisfaction. Let not despair make you silent, but continue instant in earnest supplication.

GOD WILL ANSWER

"I will answer thee, and shew thee great and mighty things which thou knowest not." (Jeremiah 33:3)

There are different translations of these words. One version renders it, "I will shew thee great and fortified things." Another, "Great and reserved things." Now, there are reserved and special things in Christian experience: all the developments of spiritual life are not alike easy of attainment. There are the common frames and feelings of repentance, faith, joy, and hope, that are enjoyed by the entire family; but there is an upper realm of rapture, communion, and conscious union with Christ, which is far from being the common dwelling place of believers. We have not all the high privilege of John, to lean upon Jesus' bosom; nor of Paul, to be caught up into the third heaven.

There are heights in experimental knowledge of the things of God that the eagle's eye of acumen and philosophic thought has never seen: God alone can bear us there; but the chariot in which He takes us up, and the fiery steeds with which that chariot is pulled, are prevailing prayers. Prevailing prayer is victorious over the God of mercy, "By his strength he had power with God: yea, he had power over the angel, and prevailed: he wept, and made supplication unto Him: he found Him in Bethel, and there He spake with us" (Hosea 12:3-4).

Prevailing prayer takes the Christian to Carmel, and enables him to cover Heaven with clouds of blessing and Earth

61

with floods of mercy. Prevailing prayer bears the Christian aloft to Pisgah, and shows him the inheritance reserved; it elevates us to Tabor and transfigures us, till in the likeness of his Lord, as He is, so are we also in this world. If you would reach to something higher than ordinary groveling experience, look to the rock that is higher than you (see Psalm 61:2), and gaze with the eye of faith through the window of importunate prayer. When you open the window on your side, it will not be bolted on the other.

HE PRAYED ALL NIGHT

"And it came to pass in those days, that He went out into a mountain to pray, and continued all night in prayer to God." (Luke 6:12)

If ever one of woman born might have lived without prayer, it was our spotless, perfect Lord, and yet none was ever so much in supplication as He! Such was His love to His Father, that He loved much to be in communion with Him; such was His love for His people, that He desired to be much in intercession for them. The fact of this eminent prayerfulness of Jesus is a lesson for us—He has given us an example that we may follow in His steps.

The time He chose was admirable, it was the hour of silence, when the crowd would not disturb Him; the time of inaction, when all but himself had ceased to labor; and the season when slumber made men forget their woes, and cease their applications to Him for relief. While others found rest in sleep, He refreshed himself with prayer. The place was also well selected. He was alone where none would intrude, where none could observe: thus was He free from Pharisaic ostentation and vulgar interruption. Those dark and silent hills were a fit oratory for the Son of God. Heaven and Earth in midnight stillness heard the groans and sighs of the mysterious Being in whom both worlds were blended.

The continuance of His pleadings is remarkable; the long watches were not too long; the cold wind did not chill His devotions; the grim darkness did not darken His faith, or loneliness check His importunity. We cannot watch with Him one hour, but He watched for us whole nights. The occasion for this prayer is notable; it was after His enemies had been enraged—prayer was His refuge and solace; it was before He sent forth the twelve apostles—prayer was the gate of His enterprise, the herald of His new work. Should we not learn from Jesus to resort to special prayer when we are under peculiar trial, or contemplate fresh endeavors for the Master's glory? Lord Jesus, teach us to pray.

I AM THY SALVATION

"Say unto my soul, I am thy salvation." (Psalm 35:3)

What does this sweet prayer teach me? It shall be my evening's petition, but first let it yield me an instructive meditation. The text informs me first of all that David had his doubts, for why should he pray, "Say unto my soul, I am thy salvation," if he was not sometimes exercised with doubts and fears? Let me, then, be of good cheer, for I am not the only saint who has to complain of weakness of faith.

If David doubted, I need not conclude that I am no Christian because I have doubts. The text reminds me that David was not content while he had doubts and fears, but he repaired at once to the mercy seat to pray for assurance, for he valued it as much fine gold. I too must labor after an abiding sense of my acceptance in the Beloved, and must have no joy when His love is not shed abroad in my soul. When my Bridegroom is gone from me, my soul must and will fast. I learn also that David knew where to obtain full assurance. He went to his God in prayer, crying, "Say unto my soul I am thy salvation." I must be much alone with God if I would have a clear sense of Jesus' love.

Let my prayers cease, and my eye of faith will grow dim. Much in prayer, much in Heaven; slow in prayer, slow in progress. I notice that David would not be satisfied unless his assurance had a divine source. "Say unto my soul." Lord, do say it! Nothing short of a divine testimony in the soul will ever content the true Christian. Moreover, David could not rest unless his assurance had a vivid personality about it. "Say unto my soul, I am your salvation." Lord, if you should say this to all the saints, it would be nothing, unless you should say it to me. Lord, I have sinned; I deserve not your smile; I scarcely dare to ask it; but oh! say to my soul, even to my soul, "I am your salvation." Let me have a present, personal, infallible, indisputable sense that I am yours, and that you are mine.

⟋∞⟍

JESUS' HIGH PRIESTLY PRAYER

"I pray not that thou shouldst take them out of the world."
(John 17:15)

It is a sweet and blessed event that will occur to all believers in God's own time—the going home to be with Jesus. In a few more years the Lord's soldiers, who are now fighting "the good fight of faith" (1 Timothy 6:12), will have done with conflict, and will have entered into the joy of their Lord. But although Christ prays that His people may eventually be with Him where He is, He does not ask that they may be taken at once away from this world to Heaven. He wishes them to stay here.

Yet how frequently does the wearied pilgrim put up the prayer, "O that I had wings like a dove! for then would I fly away and be at rest" (Psalm 55:6); but Christ does not pray like that, He leaves us in His Father's hands, until, like shocks of corn fully ripe, we shall each be gathered into our Master's garner. Jesus does not plead for our instant removal by death, for to abide in the flesh is needful for others if not profitable for ourselves. He asks that we may be kept from evil, but He never asks for us to be admitted to the inheritance in glory till we are of full age.

Christians often want to die when they have any trouble. Ask them why, and they tell you, "Because I want to be with the Lord." We fear it is not so much because they are longing to be with the Lord, as because they desire to get rid of their troubles; else they would feel the same wish to die at other times when not under the pressure of trial. They want to go home, not so much for the Savior's company, as to be at rest. Now it is quite right to desire to depart if we can do it in the same spirit that Paul did, because to be with Christ is far better, but the wish to escape from trouble is a selfish one. Rather, let your care and wish be to glorify God by your life here as long as He pleases, even though it be in the midst of toil, conflict, and suffering, and leave Him to say when "it is enough."

KEEP ME FROM PRESUMPTUOUS SINS

"Keep back thy servant also from presumptuous sins."
(Psalm 19:13)

Such was the prayer of the "man after God's own heart." Did holy David need to pray thus? How needful, then, must such a prayer be for us babes in grace! It is as if he said, "Keep me back, or I shall rush headlong over the precipice of sin." Our evil nature, like an ill-tempered horse, is apt to run away. May the grace of God put the bridle upon it, and hold it in, that it rush not into mischief.

What might not the best of us do if it were not for the holds which the Lord sets upon us both in providence and in grace! The Psalmist's prayer is directed against the worst form of sin—that which is done with deliberation and willfulness. Even the holiest need to be "kept back" from the vilest transgressions. It is a solemn thing to find the Apostle Paul warning saints against the most loathsome sins. "Mortify therefore your members which are upon the earth; fornication, uncleanness, inordinate affection, evil concupiscence, and covetousness, which is idolatry" (Colossians 3:5). What? Do saints want warning against such sins as these? Yes, they do. The whitest robes, unless their purity is preserved by divine grace, will be defiled by the blackest spots.

Experienced Christian, boast not in your experience; you will trip yet if you look away from Him who is able to keep you from falling. You whose love is fervent, whose faith is constant, whose hopes are bright, say not, "We shall never sin," but rather cry, "Lead us not into temptation." There is enough tinder in the heart of the best of men to light a fire that shall burn to the lowest hell, unless God shall quench the sparks as they fall. Who would have dreamed that righteous Lot could be found drunken, and committing uncleanness? Hazael said, "Is thy servant a dog, that he should do this great thing?" (2 Kings 8:13), and we are very apt to use the same self-righteous question. May infinite wisdom cure us of the madness of self-confidence.

∾∾∾

KEEP THE ALTAR BURNING

*"The fire shall ever be burning upon the altar;
it shall never go out." (Leviticus 6:13)*

Keep the altar of private prayer burning. This is the very life of all piety. The sanctuary and family altars borrow their fires here; therefore, let this burn well. Secret devotion is the very essence, evidence, and barometer of vital and experimental religion.

Burn here the fat of your sacrifices. Let your private prayer seasons be, if possible, regular, frequent, and undisturbed. Effectual prayer avails much. Have you nothing to pray for? Let us suggest the Church, the ministry, your own soul, your children, your relations, your neighbors, your country, and the cause of God and truth throughout the world. Let us examine ourselves on this important matter.

Do we engage in lukewarmness in our private devotion? Is the fire of devotion burning dimly in our hearts? Do the chariot wheels drag heavily? If so, let us be alarmed at this sign of decay. Let us go with weeping and ask for the Spirit of grace and of supplications. Let us set apart special seasons for extraordinary prayer. For if this fire should be smothered beneath the ashes of a worldly conformity, it will dim the fire on the family altar, and lessen our influence both in the Church and in the world.

The text will also apply to the altar of the heart. This is a golden altar indeed. God loves to see the hearts of His people glowing towards himself. Let us give to God our hearts, all blazing with love, and seek His grace, that the fire may never be quenched, for it will not burn if the Lord does not keep it burning. Many foes will attempt to extinguish it, but if the unseen hand behind the wall pours thereon the sacred oil, it will blaze higher and higher. Let us use texts of Scripture as fuel for our hearts' fire—they are live coals. Let us attend sermons, but above all, let us be much alone with Jesus.

LET THE EARTH BE FILLED WITH HIS GLORY

"Let the whole earth be filled with his glory;
Amen, and Amen." (Psalm 72:19)

This is a large petition. To intercede for a whole city needs a stretch of faith, and there are times when a prayer for one man is enough to stagger us. But how far reaching was the Psalmist's dying intercession! How comprehensive! How sublime! "Let the whole earth be filled with his glory." It does not exempt a single country, however crushed by the foot of superstition it maay be; it does not exclude a single nation, however barbarous. For the cannibal as well as for the civilized, for all climes and races, this prayer is uttered—the whole circle of the Earth it encompasses, and it omits no son of Adam.

We must be up and doing for our Master, or we cannot honestly offer such a prayer. The petition is not asked with a sincere heart unless we endeavor, as God shall help us, to extend the Kingdom of our Master. Are there not some who neglect both to plead and to labor? Reader, is it your prayer? Turn your eyes to Calvary. Behold the Lord of life nailed to a Cross, with the thorn crown on His brow, with bleeding head, hands, and feet. What! can you look upon this miracle of miracles, the death of the Son of God, without feeling within your bosom a marvelous adoration that language never can express?

And when you feel the blood applied to your conscience, and know that He has blotted out your sins, you are not a man unless you start from your knees and cry, "Let the whole earth be filled with his glory; Amen, and Amen." Can you bow before the Crucified in loving homage, and not wish to see your Monarch Master of the world? Away with you if you can pretend to love your Prince, and desire not to see Him as the universal ruler. Your piety is worthless unless it leads you to wish that the same mercy which has been extended to you may bless the whole world. Lord, it is harvest time, put in your sickle and reap.

⚬⚬⚬

MOSES' MIGHTY PRAYER

"And his hands were steady until the going down of the sun." (Exodus 17:12)

So mighty was the prayer of Moses, that all depended upon it. The petitions of Moses discomfited the enemy more than the fighting of Joshua. Yet both were needed. No, in the soul's conflict, force and fervor, decision and devotion, valor and vehemence, must join their forces, and all will be well. You must wrestle with your sin, but the major part of the wrestling must be done alone in private with God. Prayer holds up the token of the covenant before the Lord. The rod was the emblem of God's working with Moses, the symbol of God's government in Israel. Learn, O pleading saint, to hold up the promise and the oath of God before Him. The Lord cannot deny His own declarations. Hold up the rod of promise, and have what you will.

Moses grew weary, and then his friends assisted him. When at any time your prayer flags, let faith support one hand, and let holy hope uplift the other, and prayer seating itself upon the stone of Israel, the rock of our salvation, will persevere and prevail. Beware of faintness in devotion; if Moses felt it, who can escape? It is far easier to fight with sin in public, than to pray against it in private.

It is remarked that Joshua never grew weary in the fighting, but Moses did grow weary in the praying; the more spiritual an exercise, the more difficult it is for flesh and blood to maintain it. Let us cry, then, for special strength, and may the Spirit of God, who helps our infirmities, as He helped Moses, enable us like him to continue with our hands steady "until the going down of the sun"—till the evening of life is over, and till we shall come to the rising of a better sun in the land where prayer is swallowed up in praise.

OUR SAVIOR PRAYED

*"And he went a little farther, and fell on his face,
and prayed." (Matthew 26:39)*

There are several instructive features in our Savior's prayer in His hour of trial. It was lonely prayer. He withdrew even from His three favored disciples.

Believer, be much in solitary prayer, especially in times of trial. Family prayer, social prayer, prayer in the Church, will not suffice. Those are very precious, but the best beaten spice will smoke in your censer in your private devotions, where no ear hears but God's.

It was humble prayer. Luke says He knelt, but Matthew says He "fell on His face." Where, then, must be *your* place, you humble servant of the great Master? What dust and ashes should cover *your* head! Humility gives us a good foothold in prayer. There is no hope of prevalence with God unless we abase ourselves, that He may exalt us in due time.

It was filial prayer. "Abba, Father" (Mark 14:36). You will find it a stronghold in the day of trial to plead your adoption. You have no rights as a subject, you have forfeited them by your treason; but nothing can forfeit a child's right to a father's protection. Be not afraid to say, "My Father, hear my cry."

Observe that it was persevering prayer. He prayed three times. Cease not until you prevail. Be as the importunate widow, whose continual coming earned what her first supplication could not win. Continue in prayer, and watch in the same with thanksgiving.

Lastly, it was the prayer of resignation. "Nevertheless, not as I will, but as thou wilt." Yield, and God yields. Let it be as God wills, and God will determine for the best. Be content to leave your prayer in His hands, who knows when to give, and how to give, and what to give, and what to withhold. So pleading earnestly, importunately, yet with humility and resignation, you shall surely prevail.

PLEAD FOR THIS PROMISE

"He shall see his seed; he shall prolong his days,
and the pleasure of the LORD shall prosper in his hand."
(Isaiah 53:10)

Plead for the speedy fulfillment of this promise, all you who love the Lord. It is easy work to pray when we are grounded and bottomed, as to our desires, upon God's own promise. How can He that gave the Word refuse to keep it? Immutable veracity cannot demean itself by a lie, and eternal faithfulness cannot degrade itself by neglect. God must bless His Son, for His covenant binds Him to it. That which the Spirit prompts us to ask from Jesus is that which God decrees to give Him.

Whenever you are praying for the Kingdom of Christ, let your eyes behold the dawning of the blessed day that draws near, when the Crucified shall receive His coronation in the place where men rejected Him. Courage, you that prayerfully work and toil for Christ with success of the very smallest kind, it shall not be so always; better times are before you. Your eyes cannot see the blissful future; borrow the telescope of faith; wipe the misty breath of your doubts from the glass; look through it and behold the coming glory.

Reader, let us ask, do you make this your constant prayer? Remember that the same Christ who tells us to say, "Give us this day our daily bread," had first given us this petition, "Hallowed be thy name; thy kingdom come; thy will be done in earth as it is in heaven." Let not all your prayers be concerning your own sins, your own wants, your own imperfections, your own trials, but let them climb the starry ladder, and get up to Christ himself, and then, as you draw nigh to the blood-sprinkled mercy seat, offer this prayer continually, "Lord, extend the Kingdom of your dear Son." Such a petition, fervently presented, will elevate the spirit of all your devotions. Mind that you prove the sincerity of your prayer by laboring to promote the Lord's glory.

PRAISE SHOULD FOLLOW ANSWERED PRAYER

"I will praise thee, O LORD." (Psalm 9:1)

Praise should always follow answered prayer, as the mist of Earth's gratitude rises when the sun of Heaven's love warms the ground. Has the Lord been gracious to you and inclined His ear to the voice of your supplication? Then praise Him as long as you live. Let the ripe fruit drop upon the fertile soil from which it drew its life. Deny not a song to Him who has answered your prayer and given you the desire of your heart.

To be silent over God's mercies is to incur the guilt of ingratitude; it is to act as basely as the nine lepers, who after they had been cured of their leprosy, returned not to give thanks unto the healing Lord. To forget to praise God is to refuse to benefit ourselves; for praise, like prayer, is one great means of promoting the growth of the spiritual life. It helps to remove our burdens, to excite our hope, to increase our faith. It is a healthful and invigorating exercise that quickens the pulse of the believer, and nerves him for fresh enterprises in his Master's service. To bless God for mercies received is also the way to benefit our fellowmen; "the humble shall hear thereof and be glad" (Psalm 34:2).

Others who have been in like circumstances shall take comfort if we can say, "Oh! magnify the LORD with me, and let us exalt his name together.... This poor man cried, and the LORD heard him" (Psalm 34:3,6). Weak hearts will be strengthened, and drooping saints will be revived, as they listen to our "songs of deliverance." Their doubts and fears will be rebuked, as we teach and admonish one another in psalms and hymns and spiritual songs. They too shall "sing in the ways of the LORD" (Psalm 138:5) when they hear us magnify His holy name.

Praise is the most heavenly of Christian duties. The angels pray not, but they cease not to praise both day and night; and the redeemed, clothed in white robes, with palm branches in their hands, are never weary of singing the new song, "Worthy is the Lamb" (Revelation 5:12).

PRAY AGAIN

"Go again seven times." (1 Kings 18:43)

Success is certain when the Lord has promised it. Although you may have pleaded month after month without evidence of answer, it is not possible that the Lord should be deaf when His people are earnest in a matter that concerns His glory. The prophet on the top of Carmel continued to wrestle with God, and never for a moment gave way to a fear that he should be not suited for Jehovah's courts. Six times the servant returned, but on each occasion no word was spoken but, "Go again." We must not dream of unbelief, but hold to our faith even to seventy times seven.

Faith sends expectant hope to look from Carmel's brow, and if nothing is beheld, she sends again and again. So far from being crushed by repeated disappointment, faith is animated to plead more fervently with her God. She is humbled, but not abashed: her groans are deeper, and her sighing more vehement, but she never relaxes her hold or stays her hand.

It would be more agreeable to flesh and blood to have a speedy answer, but believing souls have learned to be submissive and to find it good to wait upon the Lord. Delayed answers often set the heart searching itself, and so lead to contrition and spiritual reformation; deadly blows are struck at our corruption, and the chambers of imagery are cleansed. The great danger is that men might faint, and miss the blessing.

Reader, do not fall into that sin, but continue in prayer and watching. At last the little cloud was seen, the sure forerunner of torrents of rain, and even so with you, the token for good shall surely be given, and you shall rise as a prevailing prince to enjoy the mercy you have sought. Elijah was a man of like passions as ours; his power with God did not lie in his own merits. If his believing prayer availed so much, why not yours? Plead the precious blood with unceasing importunity, and it shall be with you according to your desire.

PRAY FOR GOD'S MINISTERS

"Brethren, pray for us." (1 Thessalonians 5:25)

This one morning in the year we reserved to refresh the reader's memory upon the subject of prayer for ministers, and we do most earnestly implore every Christian household to grant the fervent request of the text first uttered by an apostle and now repeated by us. Brethren, our work is solemnly momentous, involving welt or woe to thousands; we work with souls for God on eternal business, and our word is either a savor of life unto life, or of death unto death. A very heavy responsibility rests upon us, and it will be no small mercy if at the last we be found clear of the blood of all men.

As officers in Christ's army, we are the special mark of the enmity of men and devils; they watch for our stumbling and labor to take us by the heels. Our sacred calling involves us in temptations from which you are exempt, above all it too often draws us away from our personal enjoyment of truth into a ministerial and official consideration of it. We meet with many complicated cases, and our wits are at a nonplus; we observe very sad backslidings, and our hearts are wounded; we see millions perishing, and our spirits sink. We wish for you to profit by our preaching; we desire to be blessed to your children; we long to be useful both to saints and sinners; therefore, dear friends, intercede for us with our God.

Miserable men are we if we miss the aid of your prayers, but happy are we if we live in your supplications. You do not look to us but to our Master for spiritual blessings, and yet how many times has He given those blessings through His ministers; ask then, again and again, that we may be the earthen vessels into which the Lord may put the treasure of the gospel. We, the whole company of missionaries, ministers, city missionaries, and students, do in the name of Jesus beseech you: "BRETHREN, PRAY FOR US."

PRAY FOR ONE ANOTHER

"Pray one for another." (James 5:16)

As an encouragement cheerfully to offer intercessory prayer, remember that such prayer is the sweetest God ever hears, for the prayer of Christ is of this character. In all the incense that our great High Priest now puts into the golden censer, there is not a single grain for himself. His intercession must be the most acceptable of all supplications—and the more like our prayer is to Christ's, the sweeter it will be; thus while petitions for ourselves will be accepted, our pleadings for others, having in them more of the fruits of the Spirit, more love, more faith, more brotherly kindness, will be, through the precious merits of Jesus, the sweetest oblation that we can offer to God, the very fat of our sacrifice.

Remember again that intercessory prayer is exceedingly prevalent. What wonders it has wrought! The Word of God teems with its marvelous deeds. Believer, you have a mighty power in your hand; use it well, use it constantly, use it with faith, and you shall surely be a benefactor to your brethren. When you have the King's ear, speak to Him for the suffering members of His body. When you are favored to draw very near to His throne, and the King says to you, "Ask, and I will give you what you ask," let your petitions be not for yourself alone, but for the many who need His aid.

If you have grace at all, and are not an intercessor, that grace must be small as a grain of mustard seed. You have just enough grace to float your soul clear from the quicksand, but you have no deep floods of grace, or else you would carry in your joyous bark a weighty cargo of the wants of others, and you would bring back from your Lord, for them, rich blessings which but for you they might not have obtained:

Oh, let my hands forget their skill,
My tongue be silent, cold, and still,
This bounding heart forget to beat,
If I forget the mercy seat!

PRAY THAT THEY BE WITH CHRIST

"Father, I will that they also, whom thou hast given me,
be with me where I am." (John 17:24)

O death! Why do you touch the tree beneath whose spreading branches weariness has rest? Why do you snatch away the excellent of the Earth, in whom is all our delight? If you must use your axe, use it upon the trees that yield no fruit; you might then be thanked. But why do you fell the goodly cedars of Lebanon? O stay your axe, and spare the righteous. But no, it must not be; death smites the goodliest of our friends; the most generous, the most prayerful, the most holy, the most devoted must die. And why? It is through Jesus' prevailing prayer: "Father, I will that they also, whom thou hast given me, be with me where I am." It is that which bears them on eagle's wings to Heaven.

Every time a believer mounts from this Earth to paradise, it is an answer to Christ's prayer. A good old divine remarks, "Many times Jesus and His people pull against one another in prayer. You bend your knee in prayer and say, 'Father, I ask that your saints be with me where I am.' Christ says, 'Father, I will that they also, whom thou hast given me, be with me where I am.'" Thus the disciple is at cross-purposes with his Lord. The soul cannot be in both places; the beloved one cannot be with Christ and with you, too. Now, which pleader shall win the day?

If you had your choice, if the King should step from His throne, and say, "Here are two supplicants praying in opposition to one another, which shall be answered?" Oh! I am sure, though it were agony, you would start from your feet, and say, "Jesus, not my will, but yours be done." You would give up your prayer for your loved one's life, if you could realize the thoughts that Christ is praying in the opposite direction: "Father, I will that they also, whom thou hast given me, be with me where I am." Lord, you shall have them. By faith we let them go.

PRAYER IS A NEVER-FAILING RESORT

"Their prayer came up to his holy dwelling place, even unto heaven." (2 Chronicles 30:27)

Prayer is the never-failing resort of the Christian in any case, in every plight. When you cannot use your sword you may take to the weapon of *all- prayer*. Your powder may be damp, your bow string may be relaxed, but the weapon of *all-prayer* need never be out of order. Leviathan laughs at the javelin, but he trembles at prayer. Sword and spear need furbishing, but prayer never rusts, and when we think it most blunt it cuts the best. Prayer is an open door that none can shut.

Devils may surround you on all sides, but the way upward is always open, and as long as that road is unobstructed, you will not fall into the enemy's hand. We can never be taken by blockade, escalade, mine, or storm, so long as heavenly succors can come down to us by Jacob's ladder to relieve us in the time of our necessities. Prayer is never out of season; in summer and in winter its merchandize is precious. Prayer gains audience with Heaven in the dead of night, in the midst of business, in the heat of noonday, and in the shades of evening. In every condition, whether poverty, sickness, obscurity, slander, or doubt, your covenant God will welcome your prayer and answer it from His holy place. Nor is prayer ever futile. True prayer is evermore true power.

You may not always get what you ask, but you shall always have your real needs supplied. When God does not answer His children according to the letter, He does so according to the spirit. If you ask for coarse meal, will you be angered because He gives you the finest flour? If you seek bodily health, should you complain if instead thereof He makes your sickness turn to the healing of spiritual maladies? Is it not better to have the cross sanctified than removed? This evening, my soul, forget not to offer your petition and request, for the Lord is ready to grant your desires.

PRAYER IS THE FORERUNNER OF MERCY

"Thus saith the Lord GOD; I will yet for this be enquired of by the house of Israel, to do it for them." (Ezekiel 36:37)

Prayer is the forerunner of mercy. Turn to sacred history, and you will find that scarcely ever did a great mercy come to this world unheralded by supplication. You have found this true in your own personal experience. God has given you many an unsolicited favor, but still great prayer has always been the prelude of great mercy with you. When you first found peace through the blood of the Cross, you may have been praying much, and earnestly interceding with God, that He would remove your doubts and deliver you from your distresses. Your assurance was the result of prayer.

When at any time you have had high and rapturous joys, you have been obliged to look upon them as answers to your prayers. When you have had great deliverances out of sore troubles and mighty helps in great dangers, you have been able to say, "I sought the LORD, and he heard me, and delivered me from all my fears" (Psalm 34:4). Prayer is always the preface to blessing. It goes before the blessing as the blessing's shadow. When the sunlight of God's mercies rises upon our necessities, it casts the shadow of prayer far down upon the plain. Or, to use another illustration, when God piles up a hill of mercies, He himself shines behind them, and He casts on our spirits the shadow of prayer, so that we may rest certain; if we are much in prayer, our pleadings are the shadows of mercy.

Prayer is thus connected with the blessing to show us the value of it. If we had the blessings without asking for them, we should think them common things; but prayer makes our mercies more precious than diamonds. The things we ask for are precious, but we do not realize their preciousness until we have sought for them earnestly.

Prayer makes the darkened cloud withdraw;

Prayer climbs the ladder Jacob saw;

Gives exercise to faith and love;

Brings every blessing from above.

PRAYER SOMETIMES TARRIES

"I called him, but he gave me no answer."
(Song of Solomon 5:6)

Prayer sometimes tarries like a petitioner at the gate, until the King comes forth to fill her bosom with the blessings that she seeks. The Lord, when He has given great faith, has been known to try it by long delaying. He has suffered His servants' voices to echo in their ears, as from a brazen sky. They have knocked at the golden gate, but it has remained immovable, as though it were rusted upon its hinges. Like Jeremiah, they have cried, "Thou hast covered thyself with a cloud, that our prayer should not pass through." Thus have true saints continued long in patient waiting without reply, not because their prayers were not vehement, nor because they were unaccepted, but because it so pleased Him who is a Sovereign, and who gives according to His own pleasure.

If it pleases Him to bid our patience to exercise itself, shall He not do as He wills with His own! Beggars must not be choosers either as to time, place, or form. But we must be careful not to take delays in prayer for denials; God's long-dated bills will be punctually honored; we must not suffer Satan to shake our confidence in the God of truth by pointing to our unanswered prayers.

Unanswered petitions are not unheard. God keeps a file for our prayers—they are not blown away by the wind; they are treasured in the King's archives. This is a registry in the court of Heaven where every prayer is recorded. Tried believer, your Lord has a tear bottle in which the costly drops of sacred grief are put away, and a book in which your holy groanings are numbered. By and by your suit shall prevail. Can you not be content to wait a little? Will not your Lord's time be better than your time? By and by He will comfortably appear, to your soul's joy, and make you put away the sackcloth and ashes of long waiting, and put on the scarlet and fine linen of full fruition.

PRAYER TEACHES US OUR UNWORTHINESS

"Let us lift up our heart with our hands unto God in the heavens." (Lamentations 3:41)

The act of prayer teaches us our unworthiness, which is a very salutary lesson for such proud beings as we are. If God gave us favors without constraining us to pray for them, we should never know how poor we are, but a true prayer is an inventory of wants, a catalogue of necessities, a revelation of hidden poverty. While it is an application to divine wealth, it is a confession of human emptiness.

The most healthy state of a Christian is to be always empty in self and constantly depending upon the Lord for supplies; to be always poor in self and rich in Jesus; to be weak as water personally, but mighty through God to do great exploits; and hence the use of prayer, because, while it adores God, it lays the creature where it should be, in the very dust. Prayer is in itself, apart from the answer which it brings, a great benefit to the Christian. As the runner gains strength for the race by daily exercise, so for the great race of life we acquire energy by the hallowed labor of prayer.

Prayer plumes the wings of God's young eaglets, that they may learn to mount above the clouds. Prayer girds the loins of God's warriors and sends them forth to combat with their sinews braced and their muscles firm. An earnest pleader comes out of his prayer closet, even as the sun arises from the chambers of the east, rejoicing like a strong man to run his race. Prayer is that uplifted hand of Moses which routs the Amalekites more than the sword of Joshua; it is the arrow shot from the chamber of the prophet foreboding defeat to the Syrians. Prayer girds human weakness with divine strength, turns human folly into heavenly wisdom, and gives to troubled mortals the peace of God.

We know not what prayer cannot do! We thank you, great God, for the mercy seat, a choice proof of your marvelous, loving, kindness. Help us to use it aright throughout this day!

PRAYING ALWAYS

"Praying always." (Ephesians 6:18)

What multitudes of prayers we have put up from the first moment when we learned to pray. Our first prayer was a prayer for ourselves; we asked that God would have mercy upon us and blot out our sin. He heard us. But when He had blotted out our sins like a cloud, then we had more prayers for ourselves. We have had to pray for sanctifying grace, for constraining and restraining grace; we have been led to crave for a fresh assurance of faith, for the comfortable application of the promise, for deliverance in the hour of temptation, for help in the time of duty, and for succor in the day of trial. We have been compelled to go to God for our souls, as constant beggars asking for everything.

Bear witness, children of God; you have never been able to get anything for your souls elsewhere. All the bread your soul has eaten has come from Heaven, and all the water of which it has drank has flowed from the living rock—Christ Jesus the Lord. Your soul has never grown rich in itself; it has always been a pensioner upon the daily bounty of God; and hence your prayers have ascended to Heaven for a range of spiritual mercies all but infinite. Your wants were innumerable, and, therefore, the supplies have been infinitely great, and your prayers have been as varied as the mercies have been countless. Then have you not cause to say, "I love the LORD, because he hath heard my voice and my supplications" (Psalm 116:1)?

For as your prayers have been many, so also have been God's answers to them. He has heard you in the day of trouble, has strengthened you, and helped you, even when you dishonored Him by trembling and doubting at the mercy seat. Remember this, and let it fill your heart with gratitude to God, who has thus graciously heard your poor, weak prayers. "Bless the LORD, O my soul, and forget not all his benefits" (Psalm 103:2).

PRAYING IN THE HOLY GHOST

"Praying in the Holy Ghost." (Jude 20)

Mark the grand characteristic of true prayer: "In the Holy Ghost." The seed of acceptable devotion must come from Heaven's storehouse. Only the prayer that comes from God can go to God. We must shoot the Lord's arrows back to Him. That desire that He writes upon our heart will move His heart and bring down a blessing, but the desires of the flesh have no power with Him.

Praying in the Holy Ghost is praying in fervency. Cold prayers ask the Lord not to hear them. Those who do not plead with fervency, plead not at all. One may as well speak of lukewarm fire as of lukewarm prayer—it is essential that it be red hot. It is praying perseveringly. The true suppliant gathers force as he proceeds, and grows more fervent when God delays to answer. The longer the gate is closed, the more vehemently does he use the knocker, and the longer the angel lingers, the more resolved is he that he will never let him go without the blessing.

Beautiful in God's sight is tearful, agonizing, unconquerable importunity. It means praying humbly, for the Holy Spirit never puffs us up with pride. It is His office to convince of sin, and so to bow us down in contrition and brokenness of spirit. We shall never sing *Gloria in excelsis* except we pray to God *De profundis*; out of the depths must we cry, or we shall never behold glory in the highest. It is loving prayer. Prayer

91

should be perfumed with love, saturated with love—love to our fellow saints, and love to Christ.

Moreover, it must be a prayer full of faith. A man prevails only as he believes. The Holy Spirit is the author of faith, and strengthens it, so that we pray, believing God's promise. O that this blessed combination of excellent graces, priceless and sweet as the spices of the merchant, might be fragrant within us because the Holy Ghost is in our hearts!

Most blessed Comforter, exert your mighty power within us, helping our infirmities in prayer.

PRAYING IN THE SPIRIT

"Blessed be God, which hath not turned away my prayer."
(Psalm 66:20)

In looking back upon the character of our prayers, if we do it honestly, we shall be filled with wonder that God has ever answered them. There may be some who think their "I" prayers worthy of acceptance, as the Pharisee did; but the true Christian, in a more enlightened retrospect, weeps over his prayers, and if he could retrace his steps, he would desire to pray more earnestly. Remember, Christian, how cold your prayers have been. When in your closet you should have wrestled as Jacob did; instead thereof, your petitions have been faint and few—far removed from that humble, believing, persevering faith that cries, "I will not let thee go except thou bless me" (Genesis 32:26). Yet, wonderful to say, God has heard these cold prayers of yours, and not only heard, but answered them.

Reflect, also, how infrequent have been your prayers, unless you have been in trouble, and then you have gone often to the mercy seat: but when deliverance has come, where has been your constant supplication? Yet, notwithstanding, you have ceased to pray as you once did, God has not ceased to bless. When you have neglected the mercy seat, God has not deserted it, but the bright light of the Shekinah has always been visible between the wings of the cherubim.

Oh, it is marvelous that the Lord should regard those intermittent spasms of importunity that come and go with our necessities. What a God is He to hear the prayers of those who come to Him when they have pressing wants, but neglect Him when they have received a mercy; who approach Him when they are forced to come, but who almost forget to address Him when mercies are plentiful and sorrows are few. Let His gracious kindness in hearing such prayers touch our hearts, so that we may henceforth be found, "Praying always with all prayer and supplication in the Spirit" (Ephesians 6:18).

PRIVATE PRAYER

*"Tell me ... where thou feedest, where thou makest thy
flock to rest at noon." (Song of Solomon 1:7)*

These words express the desire of the believer after Christ,
and his longing for present communion with Him. Where
doest thou feed thy flock? In thy house? I will go, if I may
find thee there. In private prayer? Then I will pray without
ceasing. In the Word? Then I will read it diligently. In thine
ordinances? Then I will walk in them with all my heart. Tell
me where you feed, for wherever you stand as the Shepherd,
there will I lie down as a sheep; for none but you can supply
my need. I cannot be satisfied to be apart from you. My soul
hungers and thirsts for the refreshing of your presence.

"Where dost thou make thy flock to rest at noon?" for
whether at dawn or at noon, my only rest must be where
you and your beloved flock are. My soul's rest must be a
grace given rest, and can only be found in you. Where is the
shadow of that rock? Why should I not repose beneath it?
"Why should I be as one that turneth aside by the flocks of thy
companions?" (Song of Solomon 1:7). You hast companions—
why should I not be one? Satan tells me I am unworthy; but I
always was unworthy, and yet you have long loved me; and,
therefore, my unworthiness cannot be a barrier to my having
fellowship with you now.

It is true I am weak in faith, and prone to fall, but my very
feebleness is the reason why I should always be where you feed

your flock, that I may be strengthened, and preserved in safety beside the still waters. Why should I turn aside? There is no reason why I should, but there are a thousand reasons why I should not, for Jesus beckons me to come. If He withdrew himself a little, it is but to make me prize His presence more. Now that I am grieved and distressed at being away from Him, He will lead me yet again to that sheltered nook where the lambs of His fold are sheltered from the burning sun.

PULL ME OUT OF THE NET

"Pull me out of the net that they have laid privily for me: for thou art my strength." (Psalm 31:4)

Our spiritual foes are of the serpent's brood, and seek to ensnare us by subtlety. The prayer before us supposes the possibility of the believer being caught like a bird. So deftly does the fowler do his work, that simple ones are soon surrounded by the net. The text asks that even out of Satan's meshes the captive one may be delivered; this is a proper petition, and one which can be granted: from between the jaws of the lion and out of the belly of hell can eternal love rescue the saint.

It may need a sharp pull to save a soul from the net of temptations, and a mighty pull to extricate a man from the snares of malicious cunning, but the Lord is equal to every emergency, and the most skillfully placed nets of the hunter shall never be able to hold His chosen ones. Woe unto those who are so clever at net laying; they who tempt others shall be destroyed themselves.

"For thou art my strength." What an inexpressible sweetness is to be found in these few words! How joyfully may we encounter toils and how cheerfully may we endure sufferings when we can lay hold upon celestial strength. Divine power will rend asunder all the toils of our enemies, confound their politics, and frustrate their knavish tricks; he is a happy man who has such matchless might engaged upon his side. Our own strength would be of little service when embarrassed in the nets of base cunning, but the Lord's strength is ever available; we have but to invoke it, and we shall find it near at hand. If by faith we are depending alone upon the strength of the mighty God of Israel, we may use our holy reliance as a plea in supplication.

> Lord, evermore your face we seek:
>
> Tempted we are, and poor, and weak;
>
> Keep us with lowly hearts, and meek.
>
> Let us not fall. Let us not fall.

REMEMBER THE WORD UNTO THY SERVANT

"Remember the word unto thy servant, upon which thou hast caused me to hope." (Psalm 119:49)

Whatever your special need may be, you may readily find some promise in the Bible suited to it. Are you faint and feeble because your way is rough and you are weary? Here is the promise: "He giveth power to the faint" (Isaiah 40:29). When you read such a promise, take it back to the great Promiser, and ask Him to fulfill His own Word.

Are you seeking after Christ, and thirsting for closer communion with Him? This promise shines like a star upon you: "Blessed are they which do hunger and thirst after righteousness: for they shall be filled" (Matthew 5:6). Take that promise to the throne continually; do not plead anything else, but go to God over and over again with this, "O LORD God, the word that thou hast spoken ... do as thou hast said" (2 Samuel 7:25).

Are you distressed because of sin and burdened with the heavy load of your iniquities? Listen to these words: "I, even I, am he that blotteth out thy transgressions for mine own sake, and will not remember thy sins" (Isaiah 43:25). You have no merit of your own to plead why He should pardon you, but plead His written words and He will perform them.

Are you afraid lest you should not be able to hold on to the end, lest, after having thought yourself a child of God, you should prove a castaway? If that is your state, take this word of grace to the throne and plead it: "For the mountains shall depart, and the hills be removed; but my kindness shall not depart from thee, neither shall the covenant of my peace be removed, saith the LORD that hath mercy on thee" (Isaiah 54:10).

If you have lost the sweet sense of the Savior's presence, and are seeking Him with a sorrowful heart, remember the promises: "Return unto me, and I will return unto you" (Malachi 3:7). "For a small moment have I forsaken thee, but with great mercies will I gather thee" (Isaiah 54:7). Bank your faith upon God's own Word, and whatever your fears or wants, repair to the Bank of Faith with your Father's note in hand, saying, "Remember the word unto thy servant, upon which thou hast caused me to hope."

RENEW YOUR STRENGTH THROUGH PRAYER

"Let the people renew their strength." (Isaiah 41:1)

All things on Earth need to be renewed. No created thing continues by itself. "Thou renewest the face of the earth," was the Psalmist's utterance. (See Psalm 104:30.) Even the trees, which wear not themselves with care, nor shorten their lives with labor, must drink of the rain of Heaven and suck from the hidden treasures of the soil. The cedars of Lebanon, which God has planted, only live because day by day they are full of sap, fresh drawn from the earth. Neither can man's life be sustained without renewal from God.

As it is necessary to replace the waste of the body by the frequent meal, so we must replace the waste of the soul by feeding upon the Book of God, or by listening to the preached Word, or by the soul-fattening table of the ordinances. How depressed are our graces when means are neglected! What poor starvelings some saints are who live without the diligent use of the Word of God and secret prayer! If our piety can live without God, it is not of divine creating; it is but a dream, for if God had begotten it, it would wait upon Him as the flowers wait upon the dew.

Without constant restoration we are not ready for the perpetual assaults of hell or the stern afflictions of Heaven or even for the strifes within. When the whirlwind shall be loosed, woe to the tree that has not sucked up fresh sap, and grasped the rock with many intertwined roots. When tempests arise, woe to the mariners that have not strengthened their mast, nor cast their anchor, nor sought the haven. If we suffer the good to grow weaker, the evil will surely gather strength and struggle desperately for the mastery over us; and so, perhaps, a painful desolation, and a lamentable disgrace may follow. Let us draw near to the footstool of divine mercy in humble entreaty, and we shall realize the fulfillment of the promise, "They that wait upon the LORD shall renew their strength" (Isaiah 40:31).

SAUL PRAYED

"Behold, he prayeth." (Acts 9:11)

Prayers are instantly noticed in Heaven. The moment Saul began to pray the Lord heard him. Here is comfort for the distressed, but praying soul. Oftentimes a poor, brokenhearted one bends his knee, but can only utter his wailing in the language of sighs and tears; yet that groan has made all the harps of Heaven thrill with music; that tear has been caught by God and treasured in the lachrymatory of Heaven. "Put thou my tears into thy bottle" (see Psalm 56:8) implies that they are caught as they flow.

The suppliant, whose fears prevent his words, will be well understood by the Most High. He may only look up with misty eye, but "prayer is the falling of a tear." Tears are the diamonds of Heaven; sighs are a part of the music of Jehovah's court and are numbered with "the most sublime strains that reach the majesty on high."

Think not that your prayer, however weak or trembling, will be disregarded. Jacob's ladder is lofty, but our prayers shall lean upon the angel of the covenant and so climb its starry rounds. Our God not only hears prayer but also loves to hear it. "He forgetteth not the cry of the humble" (Psalm 9:12). True, He regards not high looks and lofty words; He cares not for the pomp and pageantry of kings; He listens not to the swell of martial music; He regards not the triumph and pride of man; but wherever there is a heart big with sorrow, or a lip quivering with agony, or a deep groan, or a penitential sigh, the heart of Jehovah is open; He marks it down in the registry of His memory; He puts our prayers, like rose leaves, between the pages of His book of remembrance, and when the volume is opened at last, there shall be a precious fragrance springing up therefrom.

> *Faith asks no signal from the skies,*
> *To show that prayers accepted rise,*
> *Our Priest is in His holy place*
> *And answers from the throne of grace.*

SIMON'S MOTHER LAY SICK

"But Simon's wife's mother lay sick of a fever, and anon they tell him of her." (Mark 1:30)

Very interesting is this little peep into the house of the apostolic fisherman. We see at once that household joys and cares are no hindrance to the full exercise of ministry, because they furnish an opportunity for personally witnessing the Lord's gracious work upon one's own flesh and blood; they may even instruct the teacher better than any other earthly discipline. Papists and other sectaries may decry marriage, but true Christianity and household life agree well together.

Peter's house was probably a poor fisherman's hut, but the Lord of glory entered it, lodged in it, and wrought a miracle in it. Should our little book be read this morning in some very humble cottage, let this fact encourage those living there to seek the company of King Jesus. God is oftener in little huts than in rich palaces. Jesus is looking round your room now, and is waiting to be gracious to you.

Into Simon's house sickness had entered, fever in a deadly form had prostrated his mother-in-law, and as soon as Jesus came they told Him of the sad affliction, and He hastened to the patient's bed. Have you any sickness in the house this morning? You will find Jesus to be by far the best physician; go to Him at once and tell Him all about the matter. Immediately lay the case before Him. It concerns one of His people, and, therefore, will not be trivial to Him. Observe, that at once the Savior restored the sick woman; none can heal as He does.

We may not always be sure that the Lord will at once remove all disease from those we love, but we may know that believing prayer for the sick is far more likely to be followed by restoration than anything else in the world; and where this avails not, we must meekly bow to His will by whom life and death are determined. The tender heart of Jesus waits to hear our griefs, let us pour them into His patient ear.

SINKING TIMES ARE PRAYING TIMES

"Beginning to sink, he cried, saying, Lord, save me."
(Matthew 14:30)

Sinking times are praying times with the Lord's servants. Peter neglected prayer when he started upon his venturous journey, but when he began to sink, his danger made him a supplicant, and his cry, though late, was not too late. In our hours of bodily pain and mental anguish, we find ourselves as naturally driven to prayer as the wreck is driven upon the shore by the waves. The fox hastens to its hole for protection; the bird flies to the wood for shelter; and even so the tried believer hurries to the mercy seat for safety. Heaven's great harbor of refuge is *all-prayer*; thousands of weather-beaten vessels have found a haven there, and the moment a storm comes on, it is wise for us to make for it with all sail.

Short prayers are long enough. There were but three words in the petition that Peter gasped out, but they were sufficient for his purpose. Not length but strength is desirable. A sense of need is a mighty teacher of brevity. If our prayers had less of the tail feathers of pride and more wing they would be all the better. Verbiage is to devotion as chaff is to the wheat. Precious things lie in small compass, and all that is real prayer in many a long address might have been uttered in a petition as short as that of Peter.

Our extremities are the Lord's opportunities. Immediately a keen sense of danger forces an anxious cry from us that the ear of Jesus hears, and with Him ear and heart go together, and the hand does not long linger. At the last moment we appeal to our Master, but His swift hand makes up for our delays by instant and effectual action. Are we nearly engulfed by the boisterous waters of affliction? Let us then lift up our souls unto our Savior, and we may rest assured that He will not suffer us to perish. When we can do nothing Jesus can do all things; let us enlist His powerful aid upon our side, and all will be well.

TAKE HEED WHAT YOU ASK

"And he requested for himself that he might die."
(1 Kings 19:4)

It was a remarkable thing that the man who was never to die, for whom God had ordained an infinitely better lot, the man who should be carried to Heaven in a chariot of fire, and be translated, that he should not see death—should thus pray, "O LORD, take away my life; for I am not better than my fathers" (1 Kings 19:4). We have here a memorable proof that God does not always answer prayer in kind, though He always does in effect. He gave Elijah something better than that which he asked for, and thus really heard and answered him. Strange was it that the lionhearted Elijah should be so depressed by Jezebel's threat as to ask to die, and blessedly kind was it on the part of our heavenly Father that He did not take His desponding servant at his word.

There is a limit to the doctrine of the prayer of faith. We are not to expect that God will give us everything we choose to ask for. We know that we sometimes ask, and do not receive, because we ask amiss. If we ask for that which is not promised—if we run counter to the spirit which the Lord would have us cultivate—if we ask contrary to His will, or to the decrees of His providence—if we ask merely for the gratification of our own ease, and without an eye to His glory, we must not expect that we shall receive.

Yet, when we ask in faith, nothing doubting, if we receive not the precise thing asked for, we shall receive an equivalent, and more than an equivalent, for it. As one remarks, "If the Lord does not pay in silver, He will in gold; and if He does not pay in gold, He will in diamonds." If He does not give you precisely what you ask for, He will give you that which is tantamount to it and that which you will greatly rejoice to receive in lieu thereof. Be then, dear reader, much in prayer, and make this evening a season of earnest intercession, but take heed what you ask.

THE IRON SHALL SWIM

"The iron did swim." (2 Kings 6:9)

The axe head seemed hopelessly lost, and as it was borrowed, the honor of the prophetic band was likely to be imperiled, and so the name of their God to be compromised. Contrary to all expectation, the iron was made to mount from the depth of the stream and to swim, for things impossible with man are possible with God.

I knew a man in Christ but a few years ago who was called to undertake a work far exceeding his strength. It appeared so difficult as to involve absurdity in the bare idea of attempting it. Yet he was called thereto, and his faith rose with the occasion; God honored his faith, unlooked for aid was sent, and the iron did swim.

Another of the Lord's family was in grievous financial straits, he was able to meet all claims, and much more if he could have realized a certain portion of his estate, but he was overtaken with a sudden pressure; he sought for friends in vain, but faith led him to the unfailing Helper, and lo, the trouble was averted, his footsteps were enlarged, and the iron did swim.

A third had a sorrowful case of depravity to deal with. He had taught, reproved, warned, invited, and interceded, but all in vain. Old Adam was too strong for young Melancthon, the stubborn spirit would not relent. Then came an agony of prayer, and before long a blessed answer was sent from Heaven. The hard heart was broken, and the iron did swim.

Beloved reader, what is your desperate case? What heavy matter have you in hand this evening? Take it to the Lord. The God of the prophets lives, and the lives to help His saints. He will not suffer you to lack any good thing. Believe in the Lord of hosts! Approach Him, pleading the name of Jesus, and the iron shall swim; you too shall see the finger of God working marvels for His people. According to your faith be it unto you, and yet again the iron shall swim.

WAIT ON THE LORD

"Wait on the LORD." (Psalm 27:14)

It may seem an easy thing to wait, but it is one of the postures that a Christian soldier learns through years of teaching. Marching and quick-marching are much easier to God's warriors than standing still. There are hours of perplexity when the most willing spirit, eagerly desirous to serve the Lord, knows not what part to take. Then what shall it do? Vex itself by despair? Fly back in cowardice, turn to the right hand in fear, or rush forward in presumption? No, but simply wait. Wait in prayer, however. Call upon God, and spread the case before Him; tell Him your difficulty, and plead His promise of aid.

In dilemmas between one duty and another, it is sweet to be as humble as a child, and wait with simplicity of soul upon the Lord. It is sure to be well with us when we feel and know our own folly, and are heartily willing to be guided by the will of God. But wait in faith. Express your unwavering confidence in Him; for unfaithful, untrusting waiting is but an insult to the Lord. Believe that if He will keep you tarrying even till midnight, yet He will come at the right time; the vision shall come and shall not tarry. Wait in quiet patience, not rebelling because you are under the affliction, but blessing your God for it.

Never murmur against the second cause, as the children of Israel did against Moses; never wish you could go back to the world again, but accept the case as it is and put it as it stands, simply and with your whole heart, without any self-will, into the hand of your covenant God, saying, "Now, Lord, not my will, but yours be done. I know not what to do; I am brought to extremities, but I will wait until you shall hold back the floods, or drive back my foes. I will wait, if you keep me many a day, for my heart is fixed upon you alone, O God, and my spirit waits for you in the full conviction that you will yet be my joy and my salvation, my refuge and my strong tower."

WHEN YOU HEAR THE SOUND

*"When thou hearest the sound of a going in the tops of the
mulberry trees, that then thou shalt bestir thyself."
(2 Samuel 5:24)*

The members of Christ's Church should be very prayerful,
always seeking the unction of the Holy One to rest upon
their hearts, that the Kingdom of Christ may come, and that
His "will be done on earth, even as it is in heaven;" but there
are times when God seems especially to favor Zion, such
seasons ought to be to them like "the sound of a going in
the tops of the mulberry trees." We ought then to be doubly
prayerful, doubly earnest, wrestling more at the throne than
we have been wont to do. Action should then be prompt and
vigorous. The tide is flowing—now let us pull manfully for
the shore. O for Pentecostal outpourings and Pentecostal
labors.

Christian, in yourself there are times "when thou hearest
the sound of a going in the tops of the mulberry trees." You
have a peculiar power in prayer; the Spirit of God gives you
joy and gladness; the Scripture is open to you; the promises
are applied; you walk in the light of God's countenance;
you have peculiar freedom and liberty in devotion and more
closeness of communion with Christ than you are accustomed
to. Now, at such joyous periods when you hear the "sound
of a going in the tops of the mulberry trees," is the time to
bestir yourself; now is the time to get rid of any evil habit,
while God the Spirit helps your infirmities. Spread your sail,
but remember what you sometimes sing:

I can only spread the sail;

Thou! Thou! must breathe the auspicious gale.

Only be sure you have the sail up. Do not miss the gale for want of preparation for it. Seek the help of God, that you may be more earnest in duty when made more strong in faith, that you may be more constant in prayer when you have more liberty at the throne, that you may be more holy in your conscience while you live more closely with Christ.

PART 2

SPURGEON'S
SERMONS
ON PRAYER

A GOLDEN PRAYER

"Father, glorify thy name." (John 12:28)

In the first part of my discourse this morning I shall strictly keep to my text, the words of our Lord Jesus Christ, and endeavor to show what it teaches us with regard to Him. These are His own words, and it would be robbery to borrow them until first we have seen what they meant as they fell from His lips. Their most golden meaning must be seen in the light of His sacred countenance. Then, in the second part of my sermon, I shall try to point out how the petition before us may be used by ourselves, and I pray that divine grace may be given us, that it may be engraved upon our hearts, and that each one of us may be taught by the Holy Spirit daily to say for himself, "Father, glorify thy name."

I would suggest that these words should be to all the Lord's people in this church their motto for another year, and, indeed, their prayer throughout life. It will as well fit the beginner in grace as the ripe believer; it will be proper both at the wicket gate of faith and at the portals of glory. Like a lovely rainbow let the prayer, "Father, glorify thy name," overarch the whole period of our life on Earth. I cannot suggest a better petition for the present moment, nor, indeed, for any moment of our pilgrimage. Let us close the old year with it and open the door of the new to the same note. As for the past, "Father, glorify thy name in the present. Fulfill this desire unto your servants, and in the future do it yet more abundantly."

I. Let us look, then, at the words, first of all, *in respect to our Lord Jesus Christ*. They occur in the following connection. He had wrought a notable miracle in the raising of Lazarus from the dead. The fame of the miracle had attracted many to hear Him; enthusiastic crowds had gathered, and He had become so extremely popular that the Pharisees said, "The world is gone after him" (John 12:19). The people were willing to have made Him a king, and a great concourse met him with branches of palm trees and cried, "Hosanna: Blessed is the King of Israel that cometh in the name of the Lord" (John 12:13). Our Lord passed in royal but humble pomp through the streets of Jerusalem, riding upon a colt, the foal of an ass. This public manifestation, the renown of the miracle, and the general talk of the populace, led to strangers hearing of Him and enquiring about Him, so that certain intelligent Greeks of a very respectable order—for their mode of address to Philip shows their superior behavior—asked to be introduced to Him. They would "see Jesus" (John 12:21); not, of course, merely see Him in the street, for that they could do if they pleased without applying to Philip, but they would have an interview with Him, and learn more about His teaching and His claims.

I suppose that the sight of these Greeks greatly gladdened the heart of the Savior, for He delighted to see men coming to the light. He seemed to say within himself, "Behold, the nations come to me; the Gentiles arise and seek their Savior." He saw in those Greeks the advance guard of the Gentile world. He looked upon the strangers with delight, regarding them as representative men, the first of myriads who from the ends of the Earth and the islands of the sea should come flocking to Him, to behold the glory of God in the face of Jesus Christ. Our Lord rejoiced in spirit; His heart was glad within Him, and He began to address himself to the people round about, and to the Greeks, who mingled with the throng.

At that very moment the thought may have flashed across the Savior's mind, "But these nations who are to be born unto me, and to be saved by me, cannot be so born without birth-pangs, nor saved except I endure unspeakable suffering as their Redeemer." This fact came vividly before our Lord's mind, and it rushed over His spirit like a raging torrent. He saw that He could not become the seed corn of a great harvest unless first of all He should fall into the ground and die. He was the one grain of wheat upon whom all depended, and He must lose comfort and life, and be buried in the earth, or else He would abide alone, and bring forth no fruit. He saw the vicarious suffering which lay in His way, and His soul was troubled.

Do not imagine that our Savior dreaded death in itself. He was far superior in sacred courage and strength of mind to any of His servants, and yet many of them have welcomed death, and others of them, such as the martyrs, have endured it in its most terrible forms without fear, even expressing a holy delight in glorifying the name of God by their mortal agony. Our Lord was not less brave than these in prospect of His departure. But never let it be forgotten that the death of Christ was a very peculiar one, and, in fact, stands by itself alone. His death was the vindication of justice, it was the death of the sin bearer, it was a sacrificial, substitutionary, expiatory death, and this is very different from the death of a pardoned and justified believer, who passes out of the world resting on the atonement, and supported by a sense of having been reconciled to God by the great sacrifice.

Our Lord was called to bear the enormous load of man's transgressions; over His holy soul the dark shadow of human guilt must pass, and on His sensitive spirit must be made to meet the iniquity of us all. His saints' deaths are blessed in the sight of the Lord, but He must be made a curse for us, that we might be blessed in Him: and, as the mind of Christ perceived this clearly lying in the way of that triumph among the Gentiles which gave Him joy, there was a struggle in His soul, and before the assembled people that struggle was manifested.

The Greeks desired to see Jesus, and they did see Him in a very remarkable matter, so that they must have been astounded at the sight. If they expected to see a king, they did indeed behold a royal soul, but they saw Him in such grief as falls not to the lot of common men. If they wished to see somewhat of His greatness of spirit and power of mind, they did see it, but it was a power that did not transfigure His face with glory, but filled it with an agony marring all its beauty.

I shall not be too bold if I say that Gethsemane was rehearsed in public upon the occasion before us. Our Lord's soul was troubled, so He says. He felt a sort of foreshadowing of that midnight among the olives, in which his soul was "exceeding sorrowful, even unto death" (Matthew 26:38). It was out of that conflict that our text came: in fact, our text is to His suffering in the midst of the crowd what "nevertheless not as I will, but as thou wilt" (Matthew 26:39) was to the agony of Gethsemane, or what "It is finished" (John 19:30) was to the passion upon Calvary. It was the culminating point, the climax, and the conquest of a great mental battle; and when He had thus spoken He seemed to shake himself clear of the agony and to emerge from it with the memorials of it still upon Him, but with His face set like a flint to go forward to the bitter and the glorious end, this being now His watchword, "Father, glorify thy name."

I shall want to call your attention, dear friends, briefly here, first, to the trouble of the Redeemer's soul. I always tremble within myself when I try to speak of the inner conflicts of our blessed Lord, for it is so easy to make a mistake and darken counsel by words without knowledge. His person is complex and, therefore, we readily get confused, yet He himself is but one, and it is equally dangerous to make overly nice distinctions. Loving jealousy of our Lord's honor makes us feel that we scarcely know how to speak of Him. I remember an earnest admirer of art who, in pointing with his walking stick to the beauties of a famous picture, pushed his cane through the canvas and ruined it; and it is possible that in our enthusiasm to point out the beauties and points of interest in the life and death of our Lord we may spoil it all. I fear lest in my ignorance I should make sorrow for myself by dishonoring Him for whose honor I would gladly lie down and die. Help me, O divine Spirit!

This much is clear, that our Savior's heart was full of trouble. He who could still the sea and bid the storms retreat was tempest-tossed in His own soul and cast about Him for anchorage. He who could drive the fever from its lair, or send a legion of demons into the deep, was nevertheless troubled in spirit and cried, "What shall I say?" (John 12:27). Master of all worlds, supreme amongst the angels, and adored at

His Father's right hand, yet He confesses, "Now is my soul troubled." Lord of all, yet learned He obedience by the things which He suffered. (See Hebrews 5:8.) How near akin it makes Him to us! How human! How compassed with infirmity!

You worship Him, and rightly so, but still He is a man and a mourner. You call Him Master and Lord, and you do well, yet He not only washed His disciples' feet, but His own feet trembled in the rough places of the way. He felt those same commotions of spirit that make our hearts sad within us and cause us to pour out our souls within us. Do not think of the Lord Jesus otherwise than as of a dear brother born for adversity, or a faithful husband sharing all our lot, being bone of our bone and flesh of our flesh. Did you cry out in anguish, "Now is my soul troubled"? Then remember that your Lord has used the same words. Are you half distracted? Are you tossed to and fro in your thoughts? Do you ever ask, "What shall I say?" Jesus also understands by sympathy what you mean. Do you look around you and feel that you know not what to do, and does your trembling heart suggest that you should pray, "Father, save me from this hour"? In all this, you may see the well-beloved's footprints—you are not upon a new and strange track; He leads you through no darker rooms than He went through before.

With like afflictions He has been afflicted; there is nothing in them novel or surprising to His sympathetic heart. Beloved friends, let me invite you to consider that not only did our Lord thus suffer, but it is joyful to reflect that He suffered all this without sin. Hence it follows that mental conflict is not in itself sinful; even the shrinking back of the flesh from suffering is not necessarily evil; and the question "What shall I say?" and the apparent distraction of the spirit for the moment as to what shall be its course, are not in themselves criminal. There could be no sin in the Lord Jesus, and consequently there is not of necessity sin in our inward struggles, though I am very far from venturing to hope that in any one of them we are quite clear of fault. Our Lord's nature was so pure that however much it was stirred it remained clear; but in our case, though the stirring is not sinful, it sets in motion the sin that dwelleth in us, and we are defiled.

Yet I do not believe that all those depressions of spirit that come of sickness, that all those wanderings of mind in the heat of fever, that all those shrinkings and drawing back from pain, which are essential to our humanity, are by our heavenly Father set down as sin, though sin is doubtless mixed with them. If they are sinful in themselves, yet surely the sins are blotted out as soon as they are written down, for "like as a father pitieth his children, so the LORD pitieth them that fear him" (Psalm 103:13). He pities rather than censures or condemns.

You do not judge your children harshly for what they say when they are racked with pain or prostrated by weakness; you bear with their little fancies and peevishness, and the like, and you never taunt them with their follies afterwards; neither can I think that our heavenly Father would have us doubt our interest in Christ because in our semi-delirium we could not realize His love. Nor would He have us question the grace that is in us because our feverish thoughts were akin to despair. When the true heart struggles to love and trust and obey, but the poor brain is tortured with dark thoughts, the conflict is not all sinful, nor any of it necessarily so. There may be an awful struggle in the soul and yet the Father may be glorified; the sin lies not in the conflict but in the defeat, if defeat there be. The guilt is not in the shrinking from pain, but in permitting that natural feeling to hinder us from duty or to lead us to rebel against chastisement. "If it be possible, let this cup pass from me," is not a sinful utterance if it be followed by "nevertheless not as I will, but as thou wilt" (Matthew 26:39).

I feel so glad to think our Lord, when He was passing through this inward conflict, spoke out His feelings. It is instructive that He should have done so, for with His strength of mind He was quite capable of preserving a self-contained attitude and keeping His agony to himself; yet you notice that neither here, in which case He spoke so that others heard Him, nor at Gethsemane, in which case He took three of His disciples to be with Him and went to them again and again for sympathy, nor even on the Cross, in which case He cried aloud: "My God, my God, why hast thou forsaken me?" (Matthew 27:46) did He endeavor to conceal His emotion from others. It may be that by this He intended to teach us wisdom; He would show us by His own example that it is well for us not to be too much shut up within ourselves.

Smother not your sorrow; tell it out, or it may gather an ungovernable heat. That is the worst of grief which cannot weep or moan. Draw up the sluices, give a vent to pent-up feeling: even though it be but a child who hears your tale, it will relieve your mind to tell it. Anything is better than banking up the fires and concentrating all the heat within the soul. Act not the stoic's part; be not ashamed to let it be known that you are a man, a man who can grieve and be troubled even as others. It may sometimes be well to follow the poet's advice who says, "Bear and still bear and silent be, Tell no man your misery," but I question if the occasions are very frequent. At any rate, such is not the command of our Lord, nor does His example point in that direction.

In speaking out, our Lord gives us a full permit to speak too. We might have said, "No, I will not tell what is going on within, lest my weakness should seem to dishonor God." Now, we know that our Lord did not dishonor the Father by saying, "Now is my soul troubled," and by revealing the inward conflict of His soul; neither will the fact of our speaking out our grief necessarily dishonor our God. Jesus wept, and we may weep. Jesus told out His sorrow to His friends, and you may do the same. In thus speaking, our Lord affords us the best of help, for His fellow-feeling is a grand support. Did He say, "Now is my soul troubled," and did He scarce know what to ask? But did He at the last still triumph and resign himself into the Father's hands? Then, girded about by the selfsame power, we also will encounter the same sorrow after our measure, and endure until we triumph as He did. Even though in the triumph there should be clear evidence of our personal weakness, yet we will not regret it, since by that means our God shall be the more surely glorified by the more distinct revelation of His power.

I will say no more about the trouble of our Redeemer, because I would now ask you to fix your thoughts for a minute upon the firm resolve which the text sets forth. There is a battle, but from the very first moment to the last of it there is really no question in the Savior's mind about what He means to do; His purpose was settled beyond disturbance. The surface of His mind was ruffled, but deep down in His heart the current of the Redeemer's soul flowed on irresistibly in the ordained channel. He was even straitened till He had been baptized with the appointed baptism. Observe the question raised, and see how really it was answered in His heart before He asked it. "Now is my soul troubled; and what shall I say? Father, save me from this hour" (John 12:27). Must men be unsaved and Jesus be delivered from the lowering storm? If so, yonder Greeks need not ask to see Him, for there will be no life by looking unto Him. The disciples round about need not cling to Him as their helper, for there is no help in Him, unless He dies to redeem the sons of men.

Shall men, then, be unredeemed? Shall the blood of atonement be unspilled, and no man be ransomed from going down to the pit? Shall He remain alone, the grain of wheat unsown? If He does, He will be happy enough and glorious enough, for Heaven is all His own. Does He need men to make Him blessed? Does He require worms of the dust to make Him glorious? Should He remain alone, He will still be God and Lord. But shall the death penalty be left to be borne by men, guilty men, who deserve to bear it? Shall there be no Cross, no Calvary, no open tomb, no resurrection, no gates of Heaven set wide open for coming souls?

There is the question, and you see in the text how resolutely Jesus had settled it. He says in effect, "Father, glorify your name by my death—for this purpose have I come to this hour, that by my agony and bloody sweat, by my Cross and passion, I may redeem the sons of men. Redeemed they must and shall be, cost me what it may. I have resolved to bear the penalty, and magnify your law, and I will perform it, though hell itself be let loose against me and all its waves of fire dash over me. I will endure the Cross, and despise the shame, to honor you, my Father."

Observe right well that the text indicates the deep intent that steadied our Lord's resolve. Why is Christ resolved to die? Is it to save men? Yes, but not as the chief reason. His first prayer is not, "Father, save my people," but "Father, glorify thy name." The glory of God was the chief end and object of our Savior's life and death. It is that the Father's name may be illustrious that Jesus would have souls redeemed. His passion had for its main intent the exhibition of the attributes of God. And, brethren, how completely He has glorified Jehovah's name! Upon the Cross we see the divine justice in the streaming wounds of the great substitute, for the Son of God must needs die when sin is laid upon Him. There also you behold infinite wisdom, for what but infallible wisdom could have devised the way whereby God might be just and yet the justifier of him that believeth. (See Romans 3:26.)

There, too, is love, rich, free, boundless love—never so conspicuous as in the death of man's Redeemer. Till this day it still remains a question concerning the Atonement as to which of the attributes is best displayed: the justice, the wisdom, or the love. In the Atonement the divine attributes are all so perfectly glorified that no one crowds out the other; each one has its full display without in the least degree diminishing the glory of any other. Our blessed Lord, that the Father might be glorified, pushed on to the end that He had set before Him. Whatever conflict might be within His spirit, His heart was fixed upon bearing to the death our load and suffering to the end our penalty.

Now, brethren, I will detain you here with but one other thought—it is this: the grand result that came of it was that God was in very deed greatly glorified, and to this fact special testimony was given. A voice was heard out of Heaven saying,

"I have both glorified it and will glorify it again" (John 12:28). That voice speaks of the past; the Incarnation of Christ had glorified the name of God. I am unable to describe to you how much luster the love of God receives from the fact of the Word being made flesh and dwelling among us. It is the mystery of mysteries, the marvel of all marvels, that the Creator should espouse the nature of His creature, and that He should be found in fashion as a man.

Oh, Bethlehem, you have exceedingly magnified the condescension of God. Angels might well sing, "Glory to God in the highest, and on earth peace, good will toward men" (Luke 2:14). Not Bethlehem alone, but Nazareth, and the thirty years that our Lord spent on Earth all illustrate the condescension, the pity, the longsuffering of God. Did God dwell among us thirty years? Did He abide in humility in the carpenter's shop for the best part of that time, and did He afterwards come forth to be a poor man, a teacher of peasants, a friend of sinners, a man of sorrows, despised and rejected of men? Could the holy and the just, the infinite and the glorious thus, as it were, compress infinity into so small a space, and marry deity to such poverty and shame? It was so. Then tune your harps anew, you seraphs, to tell the amazing love and condescension of "Immanuel, God with us" (Isaiah 7:14). Well spoke that voice, "I have glorified it." But hearken yet again, for it adds, " and will glorify it again."

To my mind that word "again" sounds like certain voices I have heard in the Alps. The horn is sounded and then follows an echo; not just once, but perhaps fifty times the music is distinctly repeated, the voices following each other in gradually melting strains. The metaphor is not complete, for in this case the echoes increase in volume; instead of diminishing, they wax louder and louder. Lo, Jesus hangs upon the Cross and dies, and God is glorified, for justice has its due. He lies in the grave till the third morning, but He bursts the bonds of death. Lo, God's great name is glorified again, since the divine power, truth, and faithfulness are all seen in the Resurrection of Christ, Yet a few more days and He ascends into Heaven, the Man, the God, and a cloud hides Him from our sight—and then He glorified the Father's name again by leading captivity captive.

Then comes Pentecost, and the preaching of the gospel among the heathen, and then is the name of God glorified by the outpouring of the Spirit. Every conversion of a sinner, and every sanctification of a believer, is a fresh glorifying of the name of the Father, and every reception of a perfected one into Heaven—and surely they are entering Heaven every day, troops of them climbing the celestial hills, drawn upward by almighty love—everyone, I say, in entering into Paradise glorifies Jehovah's name again. And, brethren, by-and-by, when the whole Earth shall be filled with His glory, then will the Father glorify His own name again. When in His own time the Lord shall descend from Heaven with a shout, with the trump of the archangel and the voice of God, and when He shall reign amongst His ancients gloriously, and we shall hear the gladsome acclamation, "Alleluia, for the Lord God omnipotent reigneth" (Revelation 19:6), and when comes the end, and He shall have delivered up the Kingdom to God, even the Father, and God shall be all in all, then shall the eternal echoes roll along the glories of the great Father God. The glorious name of the one Jehovah shall through all space and all eternity be magnified, and the prayer of our once suffering but now exalted Savior shall be fully answered, "Father, glorify thy name."

II. Now, brothers and sisters, we will use our text *in reference to ourselves*. May the Holy Ghost direct us in so doing. I pray that this text may be our prayer from this time forth, "Father, glorify thy name." Have you, dear hearers, ever prayed this prayer? I trust I am addressing many to whom it is a very familiar desire, and yet I question if any here have ever presented it so earnestly as those from whom it has been forced by suffering and grief. God's birds often sing best in cages; at any rate, when they have been loose a little while, and their notes grow somewhat dull, He tunes their pipes again if He puts them away awhile and clips their wings.

Now this text, as far as we are concerned, whenever we can use it, indicates conflict ended. Sometimes we are in such a condition that we do not know which way to turn. We are in great affliction; it may not be so much outward trouble as distress of mind, which is worst of all. The water has leaked into the ship, and that is worse than an ocean outside. The vessel begins to fill, you use the pumps, but cannot keep it under. At such times you cry, "What shall I do? What shall I say? Where can I look? I am oppressed and overwhelmed." But there is an end of the conflict when you turn round and cry, "Father! Father!" A child may have lost its way and it may be sobbing its heart out in its distress; but the moment it sees its father it is lost no longer; it has found its way, and is at rest. Though there may be no difference in your position, nor change in your circumstances, yet if you catch a sight of your heavenly Father, it is enough; you are a lost child no more. When you can pray, "Father, glorify thy name," then there is no more question about "What shall I say?" You have said the right thing, and there let it end.

Now, brethren, concerning this next year upon which we are entering, I hope it will be a year of happiness to you—I very emphatically wish you all a Happy New Year—but nobody can be confident that it will be a year free from trouble. On the contrary, you may be pretty confident that it will not be so, for man is born to trouble as the sparks fly upward. We have each, beloved friends, some dear faces in which we rejoice, may they long smile upon us; but remember each one of these may be an occasion of sorrow during the next year, for we have neither an immortal child, nor an immortal husband, nor an immortal wife, nor an immortal friend, and, therefore, some of these may die within the year.

Moreover, the comforts with which we are surrounded may take to themselves wings before another year shall fulfill its months. Earthly joys are as if they were all made of snow, they melt even as the hoar frost, and are gone before we conclude our thanksgiving for their coming. It may be that you will have a year of drought and shortness of bread; years lean and ill favored may be your portion. Yes, and yet more, perhaps during the year that has almost dawned you may have to gather up your feet in the bed and die, to meet your God.

Well now, concerning this approaching year and its mournful possibilities, shall we grow gloomy and desponding? Shall we wish we had never been born or ask that we may die? By no means. Shall we on the other hand grow frivolous and laugh at all things? No, that is not becoming in the heirs of God. What shall we do? We will breathe this prayer, "Father, glorify thy name." That is to say, if I must lose my property, glorify your name by my poverty; if I must be bereaved, glorify your name in my sorrows; if I must die, glorify your name in my departure.

Now, when you pray in that fashion, your conflict is over, no outward fright nor inward fear remains if that prayer rises from the heart, you have now cast aside all gloomy forebodings, and you can thoughtfully and placidly pursue your way into the unknown tomorrow. Pass on, O caravan, into the trackless desert! Still proceed into the wilderness of the future, which no mortal eye has seen, for yonder fiery pillar of cloud leads the way and all is well. "Father, glorify thy name," is our pillar of cloud, and, protected by its shade, we shall not be smitten by the heat of prosperity; "Father, glorify thy name," is our pillar of fire by night, nor shall the darkness of adversity destroy us, for the Lord shall be our light. March on, you pilgrims, without a moment's delay because of fear. Tarry not for a single instant, this being your banner and your watchword, "Father, glorify thy name." Torturing doubts and forebodings of the future all end when the glorious name is seen over all.

Also, our text breathes a spirit that is the surrender of self. When a man can truly say, "Father, glorify thy name," he begins to understand that saying of our Savior concerning the corn of wheat falling into the ground and dying, for that prayer means, "Lord, do what you will with me. I will make no stipulations, but leave all to you. Remember that I am dust, and deal tenderly with me, but still glorify your name. Do not spare me, if thereby you would be less glorious. Act not according to my foolish wishes or childish desires, but glorify your name in me by any means and by all means." The prayer means I am willing to be made nothing of so that your will may be done. I am willing to be as one dead and buried, forgotten, and unknown if you may be magnified. I am ready to be buried and sown because I believe this is the way by which I shall grow and bring forth fruit to your praise. This surrender includes obedient service, for our great Master goes on to say, "If any man serve me, let him follow me." True self-renunciation shows itself in the obedient imitation of Christ. "Father, glorify thy name" means waiting for the Lord's bidding and running in His ways. If the petition be written out at length it runs thus: "Help me to copy my Savior's example; help me to follow in His blessed footsteps! This is my desire, passively to honor my heavenly Father by bearing His will and actively to glorify Him by doing His will. Lord, help me to do both of these, and never let me be forgetful that I am not my own, but wholly my Lord's."

The prayer appears to me to be most properly used when it is made a personal one: "Father, glorify thy name in me. I am the recipient of so much mercy; get some glory out of me, I pray." Beloved, I think you must have noticed in this world that the man who really lives is the man who more than his fellows has learned to live for others and for God. You do not care for the preacher whose object is to display his own powers; you go away dissatisfied after hearing his bravest orations, but if any man shall only desire your soul's good and God's glory, you will put up with much eccentricity from him, and bear with many infirmities, because instinctively you love and trust the man who forgets himself. Now, what you thus see in preachers I beg you to try and consider in yourselves. If any of you are living for yourselves, you will be unlovable; if you even act under the ambition to be loved, you will miss your mark; but if you will love for love's sake, if you will seek to be Christlike, if you will lay yourselves out to glorify God, to increase His kingdom, and to bless your fellow men, you will live in the highest and noblest sense. Seek not your own greatness, but labor to make Jesus great, and you will live. Christians live by dying. Kill self and Christ shall live in you, and so shall you, yourself, most truly live. The way upward in true life and honor is to go downward in self-humiliation.

Renounce all, and you shall be rich; have nothing, and you shall have all things. Try to be something, and you shall be nothing; be nothing, and you shall live; that is the great lesson that Jesus would teach us, but that we are slow to learn. "Father, glorify thy name" means let the corn of wheat be buried out of sight, to lose itself in its outgrowth. O self, you are a dead thing; be laid deep in the sepulcher. You rotten carcass, for such you have become since Jesus died for me, you are an offense unto me! Away with you! Do not poison my life, mar my motives, spoil my intents, hinder my self-denials, and defile the chastity of my heart. You prompt me to make provision for the flesh: away with you, away with you! "Father, glorify thy name."

In our text, in the next place, a new care is paramount. The man has forgotten self, and self is buried like a grain of wheat, but now he begins to care for God's glory. His cry is, "Father, glorify thy name." Oh, if you can get rid of self you will feel in your heart a daily intensified longing to have the name of God glorified. Do you not sometimes feel sick at heart as you gaze upon this present generation? My soul is pained within me often when I see how everything is out of joint. Everything is now denied which from our youth we have regarded as sacred truth. The infallibility of Scripture is denied; the authenticity of one portion is challenged, and the inspiration of another called in question, and the good old Book is torn to pieces by blind critics. Eternal verities, against which only blaspheming infidels used to speak, are now questioned by professed ministers of Christ. Doctrines which our sires never thought of doubting are now trailed in the mire, and that by those who profess to be teachers of God's Word. "Father, glorify thy name" comes leaping to our lips because it is burning in our hearts—burning there in holy wrath against the treachery of men. Indignation arises from our jealousy, and our eager spirits cry, "Oh, that God would glorify His name!" To many of us this is our heaviest care.

Brethren, we desire the Lord to glorify that name in ourselves by preventing our impatience in suffering, and keeping us from faintness in labor. We beseech our heavenly Father to destroy our selfishness, to cast out our pride, and to overcome every evil propensity that would prevent His getting glory out of us. Our soul is even as the clusters of the vine that belong to the owner of the vineyard: our whole nature is as the fruit for which the great vinedresser waits. Here fling me into the wine vat; let every cluster and every grape be gathered and pressed. Great Lord, cast me into the wine vat of your service, and then express from me every drop of the essence of life. Let my whole soul flow forth to you; let the ruddy juice burst forth on the right and on the left; and when the first rich liquor of my life is gone, then even to the utmost lees let me be pressed, till the last drop of the living juice that may bring glory to you shall have come forth from me. Fling all away that will not turn into your glory, but use all that can be used. To the utmost glorify your name. O thou great Father of my spirit, the care of your child is to glorify you. If you are a father, you should have honor from your children. "Honor your father" is the first commandment with promise, and it is precious in our eyes. From our inmost hearts we pray, "Our Father which art in heaven, hallowed be thy name, thy kingdom come."

Now, see how that care is divested of all sorrow by our casting it upon God. The prayer is not "Father, help me to glorify thy name," but it is "Father, glorify thy name" yourself. Your glory is too much for me to compass, so do glorify your own self. In your providence so arrange my position and condition as to glorify your name. By your grace so sustain me and sanctify me, that I may glorify you. I cannot do it, but you can, and the care which I was glad to feel I am glad also to bring by faith to you. "Father, glorify thy name."

And now, brethren, if you can pray in that fashion, your confidence will come back to you; if you have been greatly distracted, calm peace will visit you again, for now you will say, "I will bear the Lord's will, and will be content therewith. I cannot quarrel with my Master's dealings any more, for I have asked Him to glorify His name, and as I know that He is doing it, I cannot murmur. How can I struggle against that which is really glorifying my Father? Your heart will cease to question and to quake, and nestle down beneath the eternal wings, in deep and happy peace. Filled with patience, you will take the cup which stood un-tasted, and grasp it with willingness, if not with eagerness. "It is to glorify God," you say, "Every drop of this cup is for His glory"; and, therefore, you put the chalice to your lips and drink straight on and on and on till you have drained the last drop, and find that "It is finished." I know you will not fail to do this if your soul has really felt the power of this prayer, "Father, glorify thy name."

Sometimes it seems to me that it is worthwhile to pray to be burned at a stake, quick to the death, if by martyrdom we could glorify God. I could not desire such a death, and yet from one point of view I have often envied martyrs those ruby crowns that they cast at the feet of their dear Lord. How honorable in them to have glorified God by so much suffering. Surely he is the grandest creature God has made who glorifies Him most. And who is he? Not the tall archangel of whom Milton sings, whose wand might make a mast for some great admiral, but the most insignificant nobody who has laid long upon her bed of weariness, and there has praised the Lord by perfect patience. She, though apparently the least, may be the greatest glorifier of the Father. Perhaps the tiniest creature God has made will bring Him more glory than leviathan, who makes the deep to be hoary and causes the waters to boil like a pot. That which most thoroughly yields itself to God, that which most completely annihilates itself into the eternal All is most glorifying to Him. May God of His infinite mercy bring us to this self-annihilation, this care for His glory only. Strive after it, beloved, by the power of the Holy Ghost.

One word to those of you who will have no sympathy with this sermon. You know that hymn in which the enquirer asks "If I find Him, if I follow, what reward is here?" and the answer is, "Many a labor, many a sorrow, many a tear."

This is very discouraging, is it not? You who look for mirth and selfish pleasure turn away in disgust. Yet the lines are very true. Jesus himself said, "Whosoever doth not bear his cross, and come after me, cannot be my disciple" (Luke 14:27). But know this, the day will come when those who were willing to suffer for Christ will be counted to be the only sane persons who ever lived, and when those who looked to the main chance, and cared for self, and disregarded God and faith in Christ and love for their fellow men, will be regarded as having been mere idiots and drivellers.

Hear this parable. It is spring time, and yonder is a farmer walking the furrows and sowing his seed. Those who know nothing of husbandry mock at him for his wastefulness with his grain. He is far too prodigal of good food. He is the wise man, is he not, who locks his granary door and preserves his corn? Why should he go and fling it into the cold, thankless mould? Wait till the end of June, when the bloom is on the wheat. Wait till July and August have brought the months of harvest, and you shall see that he who gave his wheat to die shall, amidst the shouts of "harvest home," be reckoned to have been wise and prudent; while he who kept the door of his granary bolted, through his sluggishness and selfishness, shall then be seen to be only fit for Bedlam, for he has no harvest, save a mass of tangled weeds. Scatter yourselves, scatter your lives for others! Give yourselves up to Jesus. He who in this respect hates his life shall find it, but he that keeps it shall lose it.

Still, O you ungodly, if you live to yourselves, God will yet have glory, and even glory out of you. You shall not rob Him of His honor, nor tear a jewel from His throne. God will be glorified by you and in you in some form or other. Your everlasting lamentations, because of your great selfish mistakes, will vindicate the wisdom and the justice of God to all eternity. In a future state, though you gnaw the flesh of your right arms for very anguish and sorrow and passion, you will be obliged to own that the warnings of the gospel were true, and that God is just. Your well-deserved griefs shall help to make up the burden of that song that shall eternally celebrate the wisdom and goodness of God, for you will have to confess that Jesus was right and you were wrong; that to believe in Him and to be His disciple was the right thing; and that to despise Him, and to live unto yourself was what He told you it would be—namely, destruction and ruin.

God grant His blessing for Jesus' sake. Amen.

HOW TO CONVERSE WITH GOD

*"Then call thou, and I will answer: or let me speak,
and answer thou me." (Job 13:22)*

Job might well have been driven frantic by his miserable comforters; it is wonderful that he did not express himself far more bitterly than he did. Surely Satan found better instruments for his work in those three ungenerous friends than in the marauding Sabeans or the pitiless whirlwind. They assailed Job remorselessly, and seemed to have no more bowels of compassion than so many flint stones. No wonder that he said to them many things which otherwise he would never have thought of uttering, and a few which I dare say he afterwards regretted. Possibly the expression of our text is one of those passages of too forcible speech.

The tormented patriarch did what none but a man of the highest integrity could have done so intensely as he did; he made his appeal from the false judgment of man to the bar of God, and begged to be forthwith summoned before the tribunal of the Judge of all, for he was sure that God would justify him. "Though he slay me, yet will I trust in him: but I will maintain mine own ways before him. He also shall be my salvation: for an hypocrite shall not come before him" (Job 13:15-16). He was ready to appear at the Judgment Seat of

God, there to be tried as to his sincerity and uprightness. He says, "Only do not two things unto me: then will I not hide myself from thee. Withdraw thine hand far from me: and let not thy dread make me afraid" (Job 13:20-21). He offers in the words of our text to come before the righteous Judge in any way which He might appoint—either he will be the defendant and God shall be the plaintiff in the suit—"Call thou and I will answer," or else he will take up the part of the plaintiff and the Lord shall show cause and reason for His dealings towards him, or convict him of falsehood in his pleas—"Let me speak, and answer thou me." He feels so sure he has not been a hypocrite that he will answer to the all-seeing there-and-then without fear of the result.

Now, brethren, we are far from condemning Job's language, but we would be quite as far from imitating it. Considering the circumstances in which Job was placed, considering the hideous libels that were brought against him, considering how he must have been stung when accused so wrongfully at such a time, we do not wonder that he thus spoke. Yet it may be that he spoke unadvisedly with his lips; at any rate it is not for us to employ his language in the same sense, or in any measure to enter upon self-justification before God. On the contrary, let our prayer be, "Enter not into judgment with thy servant: for in thy sight shall no man living be justified" (Psalm 143:2). How shall man be just with God? How can we challenge His judgment before whom the heavens are not pure, and who charged His angels with folly? (See Job 4:18.) Unless, indeed, it be in a gospel sense, when, covered with the righteousness of Christ, we are made bold by faith to cry, "Who shall lay anything to the charge of God's elect? It is God that justifieth, who is he that condemneth? it is Christ that died, yea rather, that hath risen again, who is even at the right hand of God, who also maketh intercession for us" (Romans 8:33-34).

I am going to use the words of Job in a different sense from that in which he employed them, and shall apply them to the sweet communion we have with our Father, God. We cannot use them in reference to our appearance before His judgment seat to be tried; but they are exactly suitable when we speak of those blessed approaches to the mercy seat when we draw near to God to be enriched and sanctified by sacred communion. The text brings out a thought that I wish to convey to you: "Call thou, and I will answer: or let me speak, and answer thou me." May the Holy Spirit bless our meditation.

The three points this morning will be two methods of secret converse: first, "Call thou, and I will answer: or let me speak, and answer thou me"; second, the method of combining the two, and here we shall try to show how the two modes of converse should be united in our communion with God; and third, we shall show how these two modes of fellowship are realized to the full in the person of our Lord Jesus Christ, who is our answer to God, and God's answer to us.

1. First, then, here are *two methods of sacred converse between God and the soul*: sometimes the Lord calls to us and we reply, and at other times we speak to God and He graciously deigns to answer us. A missionary some years ago, returning from South Africa, gave a description of the work that had been accomplished there through the preaching of the gospel, and among other things he pictured a little incident of which he had been an eyewitness. He said that one morning he saw a converted African chieftain sitting under a palm tree with his Bible open before him. Every now and then he cast

his eyes on his Book and read a passage, and then he paused and looked up a little while, and his lips were seen to be in motion. Thus he continued alternately to look down on the Scriptures and to turn his eyes upward towards Heaven. The missionary passed by without disturbing the good man, but a little while after he mentioned to him what he had seen, and asked him why it was that sometimes he read, and sometimes he looked up. The African replied, "I look down to the Book, and God speaks to me, and then I look up in prayer, and speak to the Lord, and in this way we keep up a holy talk with each other." I would set this picture before you, as being the mirror and pattern of conversation with Heaven—the heart hearkening to the voice of God and then replying in prayer and praise.

We will begin with the first method of communion. Sometimes it is well in our converse with God that we should wait till our heavenly Father has spoken—"Call thou, and I will answer." In this way the Lord communed with his servant Abraham. If you refer to those sacred interviews with which the patriarch was honored, you will find that the record begins with words similar to, "The Lord spoke unto Abraham and said." After a paragraph or two you hear Abraham speaking to the Lord, and then comes the Lord's reply, and another word from the patriarch, but the conversation generally began with the Lord himself. So was it with Moses. While he kept his flock in the wilderness he saw a bush that burned and was not consumed, and he turned aside to gaze upon it, and then the Lord spoke to him out of the bush. The Lord called first, and Moses answered. Notably was this the case in the instance of the holy child Samuel. While he lay asleep the Lord sai to him, "Samuel, Samuel," and he said, "Here am I," a yet a second and a third time the voice of God commence sacred intercourse. (See 1 Samuel 3:1-11.) No doubt the Lord had heard the voice of the child in prayer at other times, but upon this notable occasion the Lord first called Samuel, and Samuel answered, "Speak, Lord, for thy servant heareth." So was it with Elijah. There was a still small voice, and the Lord said to the prophet, "What doest thou here, Elijah?" Then Elijah replied, "I have been very jealous for the God of Hosts: because the children of Israel have forsaken thy covenant, thrown down thine altars, and slain thy prophets with the sword" (1 Kings 19:13-14). To which complaint his great Master gave a comfortable answer.

Now, as it was with these saints of old, so has it been with us. The Lord our God has spoken to us by His Spirit, and our spiritual ears have listened to His words, and thus our intercourse with Heaven has commenced. If the Lord wills to have the first word in the holy conversation that He intends to hold with His servants, God forbid that any speech of ours should interpose. Who would not be silent to hear Jehovah speak?

How does God speak to us then, and how does He expect us to answer? He speaks to us in the written Word. This "more sure word of prophecy, whereunto ye do well if ye take heed, as unto a light that shineth in a dark place" (2 Peter 1:19). He speaks to us also in the ministry of His Word, when things new and old that are in Holy Scripture are brought forth His chosen servants, and are applied with power to our 's by the Holy Spirit. The Lord is not dumb in the midst family, though, alas, some of His children appear to f hearing. Though the Urim and Thummim are no e seen upon the breasts of mortal men, yet the silent. O that we were always ready to hear the loving voice of the Lord. The Lord's voice has many tones, all equally divine. Sometimes He uses the voice of awakening, and then we should give earnest heed. We are dead and He quickens us. We are sluggish and need to be bestirred, and the Lord, therefore, cries aloud to us, "Awake thou that sleepest" (Ephesians 5:14). We are slow to draw near to Him, and, therefore, lovingly He says, "Seek ye my face." What a mercy it is if our heart at once answers, "Thy face, LORD, will I seek" (Psalm 27:8). When He arouses us to duty there is true communion in our hearts if we at once reply "Here am I; send me" (Isaiah 6:8).

Our inmost souls should reply to the Lord's call as the echo answers to the voice. I fear it is sometimes far otherwise, and then our loving Lord has His patience tried. Remember how He says, "Behold I stand at the door and knock" (Revelation 3:20). He knocks because He finds that door closed that should have been wide open. Alas, even His knocks are for a while in vain, for we are stretched upon the bed of ease and make idle excuses for remaining there—"I have put off my coat, how shall I put it on? I have washed my feet; how shall I defile them?" (Song of Solomon 5:3). Let us no longer treat Him in this ungenerous manner, lest He take it amiss and leave us, for if He goes away from us we shall seek Him but find Him not, we shall call Him but He will give us no answer. If we will not arise at His call, it may be He will leave us to slumber like sluggards till our poverty comes as one that travels, and our want as an armed man. If our Beloved cries, "Rise up my love, my fair one, and come away" (Song of Solomon 2:10), let us not linger for an instant. If He cries, "Awake, awake; put on thy strength, O Zion" (Isaiah 52:1), let us arise in the power of His call and shake ourselves from the dust. At the first sound of Heaven's bugle in the morning, let us quit the bed of carnal ease and go forth to meet our Lord and King. Herein is communion: the Lord draws us and we run after Him, He arouses us and we wake to serve Him, He restores our soul and our hearts praise Him.

Frequently the voice of God is for our instruction. All Scripture is written for that purpose, and our business is to listen to its teachings with open ear and willing heart. Well did the Psalmist say, "I will hear what God the LORD will speak: for he will speak peace unto his people" (Psalm 85:8). God's own command of mercy is, "Incline your ear and come unto me: hear and your soul shall live" (Isaiah 55:3). This is the very gospel of God to the unsaved ones, and it is an equally important message to those who have through grace believed, for they also need to receive of His words. "Man shall not live by bread alone, but by every word which proceedeth out of the mouth of God" (Matthew 4:4). Hence, one of the saints cried out, "Thy words were found, and I did eat them" (Jeremiah 15:16), and another said, "How sweet are thy words unto my taste! yea, sweeter than honey to my mouth!" (Psalm 119:103).

God's Word is the soul's manna and the soul's water of life. How greatly we ought to prize each word of divine teaching. But, dear brethren, do you not think that many are very neglectful of God's instructive voice? In the Bible we have precious doctrines, precious promises, precious precepts, and above all a precious Christ, and if a man would really live upon these choice things, he might rejoice with joy unspeakable and full of glory. But how often is the Bible left unread! And so God is not heard. He calls and we give no heed. As for the preaching of the Word when the Holy Spirit is in it, it is the "power of God unto salvation" (Romans 1:16), and the Lord is pleased "by the foolishness of preaching to save them that believe" (1 Corinthians 1:21); but all believers do not hear the voice of the Lord by His ministers as they should. There is much carping criticism, much coldness of heart, much glorying in man, and a great lack of teachableness of spirit, and thus the Word is shut out of our hearts. The Lord would gladly teach us by His servants, but our ears are dull of hearing.

Is it any wonder, therefore, that those professors cannot pray who are forever grumbling that they cannot hear? God will be deaf to us if we are deaf to Him. If we will not be taught we shall not be heard. Let us not be as the adder which is deaf to the charmer's voice. Let us be willing, yea, eager to learn. Did not our Lord Jesus say, "Take my yoke upon you, and learn of me"? And is there not a rich reward for so doing in His sweet assurance, "Ye shall find rest unto your souls"? (Matthew 11:29). Search the Scriptures, that no Word from the Lord may be inadvertently slighted by you; hear the Word attentively and meditate on it in your heart, and daily make this your prayer, "What I know not, teach me, Lord." "Open thou mine eyes, that I may behold wondrous things out of thy law" (Psalm 119:18). Let us strive against prejudice, and never let us dream that we are so wise that we need learn no more. Jesus Christ would have us be teachable as little children and ready to receive with meekness the engrafted Word that is able to save our souls.

You will have a blessed fellowship with your Lord if you will sit at His feet and receive His words. O for His own effectual teaching. Call, O Lord, and I will answer. The Lord also speaks to His servants with the voice of command. Those who trust Christ must also obey Him. In the day when we become the Lord's children we come under obligations to obey. Does He not himself say, "If I be a father, where is mine honor?" Dear friends, we must never have a heavy ear towards the precepts. I know some who drink in the promises as Gideon's fleece did the dew, but as for the commands, they refuse them, as a man turns from wormwood. But the child of God can say, "Oh, how I love thy law! it is my meditation all the day" (Psalm 119:97): "I will delight myself in thy commandments, which I have loved" (Psalm 119:47). The will of God is very sweet to His children; they long to have their own wills perfectly conformed to it.

True Christians are not pickers and choosers of God's Word; the part that tells them how they should live in the power of the Spirit of God is as sweet to them as the other portion that tells them how they are saved by virtue of the redeeming sacrifice of Jesus Christ. Dear brethren, if we shut our ears to what Jesus tells us, we shall never have power in prayer, nor shall we enjoy intimate communion with the well-beloved. "If ye keep my commandments, ye shall abide in my love," says He, "even as I have kept my Father's commandments, and abide in his love" (John 15:10). If you will not hear God, you cannot expect Him to hear you, and if you will not do what He bids you, neither can you expect Him to give you what you seek at His hands. An obedient heart is needful if there is to be any happy converse between God and the soul.

The Lord sometimes speaks to His servants in the tone of rebuke, and let us never be among those who harden their necks against Him. It is not a pleasant thing to be told of our faults, but it is a most profitable thing. Brethren, when you have erred, if you are on good terns with God, He will gently chide you. His voice will sound in your conscience, "My child, was this right? My child, was this as it ought to be? Is this becoming in one redeemed with precious blood?" When you open the Bible, many a text will be like a mirror showing you yourself, and the spots upon your face, and conscience looking thereon will say, "Do not so, my son, this is not as your Lord would have it." "Surely it is good to be said unto God, I have borne chastisement, I will not offend any more. That which I see not teach me; if I have done iniquity, I will do no more." If we do not listen to God's rebuking voice in His Word, He will probably speak in harsher tones by some difficult circumstance. Perhaps He will hide from us the light of His countenance and deny us the consolations of the Spirit. Before this is the case, it will be wise to turn our hearts unto the Lord, or if it has already come to that, let us say, "Show me where you contend with me. Make me to know my faults, my Father, and help me to purge myself from them." Brethren, be not as the horse, or as the mule, but pray to be made tender in spirit. Let this be your prayer:

Quick as the apple of an eye,

Oh, God, my conscience make,

Awake, my soul, when sin is nigh,

And keep it still awake.

Oh, may the least omission pain

My well-instructed soul;

And drive me to the blood again,

Which makes the wounded whole!

Let us hear Nathan as kindly when he rebukes us as when he brings a promise, for in both cases the prophet speaks his

Master's own sure Word. Let us thank the Lord for chiding us and zealously set about destroying the idols against which His anger is set. It is due to the Lord, and it is the wisest course for ourselves. But blessed be His name, the Lord "will not always chide, neither will he keep his anger for ever" (Psalm 103:9).

Very frequently the Lord speaks to us in consolatory language. How full the Bible is of comforts, how truly has God carried out His own precept to the prophet: "Comfort ye, comfort ye my people, saith your God" (Isaiah 40:1). What more, indeed, could God have said than He has said for the consolation of His own beloved? Be not slow to hear when God is swift to cheer you. Alas, our mischief sometimes turns a deaf ear even to the sweetest note of Jehovah's love. We cannot think that all things will work together for our good; we cannot believe that the providence that looks so evil can really be a blessing in disguise. Blind unbelief is sure to err, and it errs principally in stopping its ear against those dulcet tones of everlasting loving-kindness that ought to make our hearts leap within us for joy. Beloved, be not hard to comfort, but when God calls be ready to answer Him, and say, "I believe You, Lord, and rejoice in your Word, and therefore my soul shall put away her mourning, and gird herself with delight." This is the way to keep up fellowship with God, to hear His consolations and to be grateful for them.

And last of all upon this point, God speaks to His people sometimes in the tones that invite to innermost communion. I cannot tell now how they sound; your ear must itself have heard them to know what they are. Sometimes He calls His beloved one to come away to the top of Amana, to ascend above the world and all its cares, and to come to the Mount of Transfiguration. "There," says He, "will I show you my loves." There the Lord seems to lay bare His heart to His child, and to tell him all the heights and depths of unsearchable love, and let him understand his eternal union with Christ, and the safety that comes of it, and the mystical covenant with all its treasures; "For the secret of the LORD is with them that fear him; and he will show them his covenant" (Psalm 25:14). It is a sad thing when the Lord calls us into the secret chamber, where none may approach but men who are greatly beloved, and we are not prepared to enter. That innermost heart-to-heart communion is not given to him who is unclean. God said even to Moses, "Put off thy shoes from off thy feet, for the place whereon thou standest is holy ground" (Exodus 3:5). There is no enjoying that extraordinary nearness to God with which He sometimes favors His choice ones, unless the feet have been washed in the brazen laver, and the hands have been cleansed in innocence. "Blessed are the pure in heart, for they shall see God" (Matthew 5:8). He that is of clean hands and a pure heart, he shall dwell on high; and only he, for God will not draw those who are inconsistent in their profession of faith in Him and those who are dallying with sin into close contact with himself. "Be ye clean, that bear the vessels of the LORD" (Isaiah 52:11), and especially be clean, you who hope to stand in His holy place and to behold His face, for that face is only to be beheld in righteousness.

Brethren, it is clear that the voice of God speaks to us in different tones, and our business, as His children, is to answer at once when He speaks to us. This is one form of holy fellowship.

The second and equally common form is that we speak to God and He graciously replies to us. How should we speak to the Most High? I answer, first, *we ought constantly to speak to Him in the tone of adoration.* We do not, I fear, adore and reverently magnify God one hundredth part as much as we should. The general frame of a Christian should be such that whenever his mind is taken off from the necessary thoughts of his calling he should at once stand before the throne, blessing the Lord, if not in words, yet in heart. I was watching the lilies the other day as they stood upon their tall stalks with flowers so fair and beautiful; they cannot sing, but they seemed to me to be offering continual hymns to God by their very existence. They had lifted themselves as near to Heaven as they could; indeed, they would not commence to flower till they had risen as far from the Earth as their nature would permit, and then they just stood still in their beauty and showed to all around what God can do, and as they poured out their sweet perfume in silence they said by their example, "Bless the Lord, as we also do by pouring out our very souls in sweetness." Now, you may not be able to preach, and it would not be possible to be always singing, especially in some company; but your life, your heart, your whole being should be one perpetual discourse of the loving-kindness of the Lord, and your heart, even if the Lord be silent, should carry on fellowship by adoring His blessed name.

Coupled with adoration, the Lord should *always hear the voice of our gratitude.* One of our brethren in prayer last Monday night commenced somewhat in this fashion. He said, "Lord, you do so continuously bless us, that we feel as if we could begin to praise you now and never leave off anymore. We are half ashamed to ask for anything more, because you always give so promptly and so bountifully." In this spirit let us live. Let us be grateful unto Him and bless His name, and come into His presence with thanksgiving! The whole life of the Christian man should be a psalm of which the contents should be summed up in this sentence, "Bless the LORD, O my soul, and all that is within me bless his holy name" (Psalm 103:1). Now, adoration and thanksgiving, if rendered to God with a sincere heart through Jesus Christ, will be acceptable to God, and we shall receive an answer of peace from Him, so that we shall realize the second half of our text, "I will speak, and answer thou me."

But, my brethren, it would not suffice for us to come before God with adoration only, for we must remember what we are. Great is He and therefore to be adored, but sinful are we, and, therefore, when we come to Him there must always be confession of sin upon our lips. I never expect, until I get to Heaven, to be able to cease confessing sin every day and every time I stand before God. When I wander away from God I may have some idea of being holy, but when I draw near to Him I always feel as Job did when he said, "I have heard of thee by the hearing of the ear: but now mine eye seeth thee. Wherefore I abhor myself, and repent in dust and ashes" (Job 42:5-6). If you would have the Lord hear, be sure you speak to Him in humble notes. You have rebelled against Him, you are a sinner by nature, and though forgiven and accepted, and, therefore, freed from dread of wrath, you can never forget that you were a rebel, and if it had not been for sovereign grace, you would have been so still; therefore, speak with lowliness and humility before the Lord if you would receive an answer.

Beloved friends, we should also speak to God *with the voice of petition*, and this we can never cease to do, for we are always full of wants. "Give us this day our daily bread" (Matthew 6:11) must be our prayer as long as we are in the land where daily needs require daily supplies. We shall always need to make request for physicals and for spirituals, for ourselves and for others, too. The work of intercessory prayer must never be allowed to cease. Speak to the Lord, you that have His ear; speak for us, His servants, who are His ambassadors to men, speak for the Church also, plead for rebellious sinners, and ask that unnumbered blessings may be given from above. We should also speak to Him sometimes in the language of resolution. If the poor prodigal was right in saying, "I will arise and go to my father" (Luke 15:18), so are Christians right in saying, "Therefore will I call upon him as long as I live" (Psalm 116:2), or in saying, "As long as I live, I will bless the Lord." (See Psalm 104:33.) Sometimes when a duty is set before you very plainly, which you had for a while forgotten, it is very sweet to say unto the Lord, "Lord, your servant will rejoice to do this, only help me." Register the secret vow before the Lord and honorably fulfill it.

We should often use the language *of intimate communion.* "What language is that?" you ask; and I answer, "I cannot tell you." There are times when we say to the blessed Bridegroom of our souls love words that the uncircumcised ear must not hear. Why, even the little that is unveiled before the world in the Song of Solomon has made many a man raise trivial objections, for the carnal mind cannot understand such spiritual secrets. You know how the Church cries out concerning her Lord: "Let him kiss me with the kisses of his mouth, for thy love is better than wine" (Song of Solomon 1:2). There are many love passages and love words between sanctified souls and their dear Lord and Master, which it is not lawful for a man to utter in a mixed assembly, it is like the casting of pearls before swine, or reading one's love letters in the public streets. Oh, you chosen, speak to your Lord. Keep nothing from Him. He has said, "If it were not so, I would have told you" (John 14:2). He has told you all that He has seen with the Father; now tell Him everything that is in your heart, and when you speak with sacred childlike confidence, telling Him everything, you will find Him answering you with familiar love, and sweet will be the fellowship thus created. So now I have shown you that there are two forms of the believer's communion with God.

2. Let us now consider the *method of the combination of the two*. With regard to this subject, I would say that they must be united. Brethren, we sometimes go to prayer, and we want God to hear us, but we have not heard what God has to say. This is wrong. Suppose a person neglects the hearing of the Word, but is very fond of prayer. I feel certain that his prayer will soon become flat, stale, and unprofitable, because no conversation can be very lively that is all on one side. The man speaks, but he does not let God speak, and, therefore, he will soon find it hard to maintain the conversation. If you are earnest in regular prayer, but do not as regularly read or hear the Scriptures, your soul gives out without taking in and is very apt to run dry. Not only thoughts and desires will be lifeless, but even the expressions will become monotonous. If you consider how it is that your prayer appears to lack vivacity and freshness, the probable reason is that you are trying to maintain a maimed fellowship. When conversation is all one sided, do you wonder that it's somewhat boring? If I have a friend at my house tonight, and we wish to have fellowship with each other, I must not do all the talking, but I must wait for him to answer me, or to suggest new topics, as he may please; and if he be wiser than I am, there is the more reason why I should play second in the conversation, and leave its guidance very much to him.

It is such a condescension on God's part to speak with us that we ought eagerly to hear what He has to say. Let Him never have to complain that we turned away our ear from Him. At the same time we must not be silent ourselves; for to read the Scriptures, to hear sermons, and never to pray would not bring fellowship with God. That would be a lame conversation. Remember how Abraham spoke with God again and again, though he felt himself to be but dust and ashes; how Moses pleaded; and how David sat before the Lord and then spoke with his tongue. Above all, remember how Jesus talked with His Father as well as hearkened to the voice from Heaven. Let both forms of converse unite, and all will be well.

Again, it will be well sometimes to *vary the order*. Dear Mr. Miller, who is a man living near to God, whose every word is like a pearl, said the other day, "Sometimes when I go into my closet to pray, I find I cannot pray as I would. What do I then? Why, since I cannot speak to the Lord, I beg the Lord to speak to me, and, therefore, I open the Scriptures and read my portion; and then I find the Lord gives me matter for prayer." Is not this a suggestion of much weight? Does it not commend itself to your spiritual judgment? Have you not observed that when somebody calls to see you, you may not be in a fit condition to start a profitable conversation; but if your friend will lead, your mind takes fire, and you have no difficulty in following him. Frequently it will be best to ask the Lord to lead the sacred converse, or wait awhile till He does so. It is a blessed thing to wait at the posts of His doors, expecting a word of love from His throne. It is generally best in communion with God to begin with hearing His voice, because it is due to His sacred majesty that we should first hear what He has to say to us; and it will especially be best for us to do so when we feel out of order for communion. If the flesh in its weakness hampers the spirit, then let the Bible reading come before the praying, that the soul may be awakened thereby.

Still, there are times when it will be better to speak to our heavenly Father at once. For instance, if a child has done wrong, it is very wise of him to run straight away to his father, before his father has said anything to him, and say, "Father, I have sinned." The prodigal had the first word, and so should our penitence seek for speedy audience, and pour itself out like water before the Lord. Sometimes, too, when our heart is very full of thankfulness, we should allow praise to burst forth at once. When we have received a great favor we ought not to wait till the giver of it speaks to us, but the moment we see him we should at once acknowledge our indebtedness. When the heart is full of either prayer or praise, and the presence of Jesus is felt by the power of the Holy Spirit, we begin addressing the Lord with all our hearts. The Lord has spoken, and it is for us to reply at once.

On the other hand, when for wise reasons our Lord is silent unto us, it is well to take with us words and come unto Him. If you have read your Bible, and have felt no visit from the Holy Spirit, or if you have heard a sermon and found no dew from the Lord attending it, then turn at once to prayer. Tell the Lord your condition, and entreat Him to reveal himself unto you. Pray first and read afterwards, and you will find that your speaking with God will be replied to by His speaking to you through the Word. Take the two methods—common sense and your own experience will guide you, and let sometimes one come first and sometimes the other. But let there be a reality about both. Mockery in this matter is deadly sin. Do not let God's Word be before you as a mass of letterpress, but let the book speak to your soul.

Some people read the Bible through in a set time, and in great haste, and they might just as well never look at it at all. Can a man understand a country by merely tearing through it at a railway pace? If he desires to know the character of the soil and the condition of the people, he walks leisurely through the land and examines with care. God's Word needs digging, or its treasures will lie hidden. We must put our ear down to the heart of Scripture and hear its living throbs. Scripture often whispers rather than thunders, and the ear must be duly trained to comprehend its language. Resolve emphatically, "I will HEAR what God the Lord shall speak." Let God speak to you, and in order that He may do so, pause and meditate, and do not proceed till you grasp the meaning of the verses as far as the Spirit enables you. If you do not understand some passages, read them again and again, and remember it is good to read even those parts of Scripture that you do not understand, even as it is good for a child to hear his father's voice whether he understands all his father has to say or not. At any rate, faith finds exercise in knowing that God never speaks in vain, even though He is not understood. Hear the Word till you do understand it. While you are listening, the sense will gradually break in upon your soul, but mind that you listen with opened ear and willing heart. When you speak to God do not let it be a dead form, for that is an insult to the Most High. If the heart be absent, it is as wicked to say a prayer as to be prayerless. If one should obtain an audience of Her Majesty and then should read a petition in which he took no interest, which was in fact a mere set of words, it would be an insult of the worst kind. Beware lest you thus insult the Majesty of Heaven!

3. The last thought is only meant to be dropped before you for you to enlarge upon it at your leisure, *the blessed realization of these two forms of communion in the person of Christ.*

"Call thou, and I will answer." Infinite majesty of God, call upon me and ask for all you can ask, and I bless you that I have an answer for you. Ask your poor servant for all you can demand of him and he will gladly reply. Brethren, do you ask in wonder—How can we answer Him? The answer is clear— By bringing Jesus to remembrance. Our Lord Jesus Christ is man's complete answer to God. Divine justice demands death as the penalty of sin. Behold the Son of God taken down from the Cross because He was surely dead, wrapped in the cerements [burial garments] of the grave and laid in Joseph's tomb. God's justice demands suffering, demands that the sinner be abandoned of God. See yonder Cross and hear the cry, "My God, my God, why hast thou forsaken me?" (Mark 15:34). Great God, you have in Jesus all the suffering your justice can ask, even to death itself. God's holiness righteously demands a life of obedience; man cannot be right before God unless he renders perfect obedience to the Law.

Behold our answer, we bring a perfect Savior's active and passive obedience and lay it down at Jehovah's feet—what can He ask for more? He requires a perfect heart and an unblemished person, and He cannot accept less than a perfect manhood. We bring the Father His only begotten, the Son of man, our brother; and here is our answer: *there is the perfect man, the sinless head of the race.*

Oh, never try to reply to God with any other answer than this. Whatever He asks of you, bring Him your Savior;

He cannot ask more. You bring before Him that which fully contents Him, for He himself has said, "This is my beloved Son, in whom I am well pleased" (Matthew 3:17). Let your answer then, to the justice of God, be Christ.

But I said that Christ fulfilled the other purpose. He is God's answer to us. What have you to ask of God this morning? Are you so far away from Him that you enquire, "How can I be saved?" No answer comes out of the excellent glory except Christ on the Cross; that is God's answer. Believe in Him and live. By those wounds, by that bloody sweat, by that sacrificial death, you must be saved; look you there! Do you say unto the Lord, "I have trusted Christ, but am I secure of salvation?" No answer comes but Christ risen from the dead to die no more. Death has no more dominion over Him, and He has said, "Because I live ye shall live also" (John 14:19). The risen Christ is the Lord's assurance of our safety for eternity. Do you ask the Lord, "How much do you love me?" You have asked a large question, but there is a large answer for you. He gives His Son, behold what manner of love is born! Do you enquire, "Lord, what will you give me?" His Son is the answer to that question, also. Behold these lines written on His bleeding person, "He that spared not his own Son, but delivered him up for us all, how shall he not with him also freely give us all things?" (Romans 8:32). Would you know more? Do you say, "What sign do you show that all these things are so?" He gives you Christ in Heaven. Yea, if you ask, "Lord, what shall your servant be when you have completed your work of grace upon me?" He points you to Jesus in the glory, for you shall be like Him. If you ask what is to be your destiny in the future, He shows you Christ coming a second time without a sin-offering unto salvation.

Dear friend, you can ask nothing of your God but what He gives you at once—a reply in Jesus. Oh, What blessed talk is that when the Christian's heart says Jesus, and the Christian's God says Jesus, and how sweet it is when we come to Jesus and rest in Him, and God is in Jesus and makes Him His rest forever. Thus do believers and their God rest together in the same Beloved One.

May the Lord add His blessing to our meditation, and make this kind of communion common among us for Jesus' sake. Amen.

INTERCESSORY PRAYER

"And the LORD turned the captivity of Job,
when he prayed for his friends." (Job 42:10)

"The LORD turned the captivity of Job." So, then, our longest sorrows have a close, and there is a bottom to the profoundest depths of our misery. Our winters shall not frown forever; summer shall soon smile. The tide shall not eternally ebb out; the floods retrace their march. The night shall not hang its darkness forever over our souls; the sun shall yet arise with healing in his wings. (See Malachi 4:2.)

"The LORD turned the captivity of Job." Our sorrows shall have an end when God has gotten His end in them. The ends in the case of Job were these, that Satan might be defeated, foiled with his own weapons, blasted in his hopes when he had everything his own way. God, at Satan's challenge, had allowed Satan to touch all that Job had and in his bone and in his flesh (Job 1:12, 2:7), and yet the tempter could not prevail against him, but received his rebuff in those conquering words, "Though he slay me, yet will I trust in him" (Job 13:15). When Satan is defeated, then shall the battle cease. The Lord aimed also at the trial of Job's faith. Many weights were hung upon this palm tree, but it still grew uprightly. The fire had been fierce enough, the gold was undiminished, and only the dross was consumed.

Another purpose the Lord had was His own glory. And God was glorified abundantly. Job had glorified God on his dunghill; now let him magnify his Lord again upon his royal seat in the gate. God had gotten unto himself eternal renown through that grace by which He supported His poor, afflicted servant under the heaviest troubles which ever fell to the lot of man. God had another end and that also was served. Job had been sanctified by his afflictions. His spirit had been mellowed. That small degree of tartness towards others, which may have been in Job's temper, had been at last removed, and any self-justification that once had lurked within was fairly driven out.

Now God's gracious designs are answered, he removes the rod from His servant's back, and takes the melted silver from the midst of the glowing coals. God does not afflict willingly, nor grieve the children of men for nothing, and He shows this by the fact that He never afflicts them longer than there is need for it, and never suffers them to be one moment longer in the furnace than is absolutely requisite to serve the purposes of His wisdom and His love.

"The Lord turned again the captivity of Job." Beloved brother in Christ, you have had a long captivity in affliction. God has sold you into the hand of your adversaries, and you have wept by the waters of Babylon, hanging your harp upon the willows. (See Psalm 137:1-2.) Despair not! He that turned the captivity of Job can turn yours as the streams in the south. He shall make again your vineyard to blossom, and your field to yield her fruit. You shall again come forth with those that make merry, and once more shall the song of gladness be on your lips. Let not despair rivet his cruel fetters about your soul. Hope yet, for there is hope. Trust still, for there are glimpses of confidence. So shall He bring you up again rejoicing, from the land of your captivity, and you shall say of Him, "He has turned for me my mourning into dancing" (Psalm 30:11).

The circumstance that attended Job's restoration is that to which I invite your particular attention. "The LORD turned the captivity of Job, when he prayed for his friends." Intercessory prayer was the omen of his returning greatness. It was the bow in the cloud, the dove bearing the olive branch, the voice of the turtle announcing the coming summer. When his soul began to expand itself in holy and loving prayer for his erring brethren, then the heart of God showed itself to him by returning to him his prosperity without, and cheering his soul within. Brethren, it is not fetching a laborious compass, when from such a text as this I address you upon the subject of prayer for others. Let us learn today to imitate the example of Job, and pray for our friends, and peradventure if we have been in trouble, our captivity shall be turned.

Four things I would speak of this morning, and yet but one thing. I would speak upon intercessory prayer thus: first, by way of commending the exercise; second, by way of encouraging you to enlist in it; third, by way of suggestion, as to the persons for whom you should especially pray; and fourth, by way of exhortation to all believers to undertake and persevere in the exercise of intercessions for others.

1. First then, by way of *commending the exercise*. Let me remind you that intercessory prayer has been practiced by

all the best of God's saints. We may not find instances of it appended to every saint's name, but beyond a doubt, there has never been a man eminent for piety personally, who has not always been preeminent in his anxious desires for the good of others, and in his prayers for that end. Take Abraham, the father of the faithful. How earnestly did he plead for his son Ishmael! "O that Ishmael might live before thee!" (Genesis 17:18). With what importunity did he approach the Lord on the plains of Mamre, when he wrestled with Him again and again for Sodom; how frequently did he reduce the number, as though, to use the expression of the old Puritan, "He were bidding and beating down the price at the market. Peradventure there be fifty righteousness within the city, peradventure there lack five of the fifty righteousness, peradventure there shall be twenty found there, peradventure ten shall be found there. And He said, I will not destroy it for ten's sake." (See Genesis 18:16-33).

Well did Abraham wrestle, and if we may sometimes be tempted to wish he had not paused when he did, yet we must commend him for continuing so long to plead for that doomed and depraved city. Remember Moses, the most royal of men, whether crowned or uncrowned, how often did he intercede? How frequently do you meet with such a record as this —"Moses and Aaron fell on their faces before God!" (See Numbers 20:6.) Remember that cry of his on the top of the mount, when it was to his own personal disadvantage to intercede, and yet when God had said, "Let me alone, ... I will make of thee a great nation" (Exodus 32:10), how he continued, how he thrust himself in the way of the axe of justice, even after the Israelites worshiped the golden calf and sinned grievously against God, and cried, "Yet now, if thou wilt forgive their sin," (and here he reached the very climax of agonizing earnestness), "and if not, blot me, I pray thee, out of thy book which thou hast written" (Exodus 32:32). Never was there a mightier prophet than Moses and never one more intensely earnest in intercessory prayer.

Or pass on, if you will, to the days of Samuel. Remember his words, "God forbid that I should sin against the LORD, in ceasing to pray for you" (1 Samuel 12:23). Or think of Solomon, and of his earliest intercession at the opening of the Temple, when, with outstretched hands, he prayed for the assembled people. Or if you want another royal example, turn to Hezekiah with Sennacherib's letter spread out before the Lord, when he prayed not only for himself but for God's people of Israel in those times of great difficulties. Think, too, of Elijah, who for Israel's sake would bring down the rain, that the land would not perish; as for himself, miracles gave him his bread and his water, it was for others that he prayed, and he said to his servant, "Go again seven times" (1 Kings 18:43). Forget not Jeremiah, whose tears were prayers—prayers coming too intensely from his heart to find expression in any utterance of the lip. He wept himself away, his life was one long shower, each drop a prayer, and the whole deluge a flood of intercession.

And if you would have an example taken from the times of Christ and His apostles, remember how Peter prays on the top of the house and Stephen amidst the falling stones. Or think, if you will, of Paul, of who even more than of others it could be said, that he never ceased to remember the saints in his prayers: "Cease not to give thanks for you, making mention of you in my prayers" (Ephesians 1:16). Then stopping in the very midst of the epistle he says, "For this cause I bow my knees unto the Father of our Lord Jesus Christ" (Ephesians

3:14). As for the cloud of holy witnesses in our own time, I will hazard the assertion that there is not a single child of God who does not plead with God for his children, his family, the Church at large, and for the poor ungodly perishing world. I deny his saintship if he does not pray for others.

But further, while we might commend this duty by quoting innumerable examples from the lives of eminent saints, it is enough for the disciple of Christ if we say that Christ in His holy gospel has made it your duty and your privilege to intercede for others. When He taught us to pray He said, "Our Father," and the expressions that follow are not in the singular but in the plural: "Give us this day our daily bread ... Forgive us our debts ... Lead us not into temptation." By these He evidently intended to set forth that none of us are to pray for ourselves alone. While we may have sometimes prayers so bitter that they must be personal like the Savior's own: "If it be possible, let this cup pass from me" (Matthew 26:39), as a rule our prayers should be public prayers. Though offered in private, and even in secret, we should not forget the Church of the living God.

By the mouth of Paul how frequently does the Holy Ghost exhort us to pray for ministers! "Brethren," says Paul, "pray for us" (1 Thessalonians 5:25). And in Ephesians 6:18, after exhorting them to offer prayers and supplications for all classes and conditions of men, he adds, "And for me, that utterance may be given unto me, that I may open my mouth boldly, to make known the mystery of the gospel, for which I am an ambassador in bonds: that therein I may speak boldly, as I ought to speak" (Ephesians 6:19-20).

James, who is ever a practical apostle, bids us pray for one another; in that same verse, where he says, "Confess your faults one to another," he says "and pray for another," and adds the privilege, "that ye may be healed" (James 5:16), as if the healing would not only come to the sick person for whom we pray, but to us who offer the prayer, thereby indicating that we receive some special blessing when our hearts are enlarged for the people of the living God.

But, brethren, I shall not continue to quote the texts in which the duty of praying for others is definitely laid down. Permit me to remind you of the high example of your Master; He is your pattern, so follow His leadership. Was there even one who interceded as He did? Remember that golden prayer of His, where He cried for His own people, "I pray not that thou shouldest take them out of the world, but that thou shouldest keep them from the evil!" (John 17:15). Oh, what a prayer was that! He seems to have thought of all their wants, of all their needs, of all their weaknesses, and in one long stream of intercession, He pours out His heart before His Father's throne. Think how even in the agonies of His crucifixion, He did not forget that He was still an intercessor for man. "Father, forgive them; for they know not what they do" (Luke 23:34).

Oh, remember, brethren, it is your Savior's example to you today, for there before the throne, with outstretched hands, He prays not for himself, for He has attained His glory; not for himself, for He rests from His labors, and has received His everlasting recompense; but for you, for the purchase of His blood, for as many as are called by His grace; yea, and for those who shall believe on Him through our word:

For all that come to God by Him,

Salvation He demands;

Points to the wounds upon His heart,

And spreads His bleeding hands.

Come, brethren, with such an example as this, we are truly guilty if we forget to plead for others.

But I will go a little further. If in the Bible there were no example of intercessory supplication, if Christ had not left it upon record that it was His will that we should pray for others, and even if we did not know that it was Christ's practice to intercede, yet the very spirit of our holy religion would constrain us to plead for others. Do you go up into your closet, and in the face and presence of God think of none but yourself? If so, surely the love of Christ cannot be in you, for the spirit of Christ is not selfish. No man lives unto himself when he has the love of Christ in him, I know there are some whose piety is comfortably tethered within the limits of their own selfish interests. It is enough for them if they hear the Word, if they are saved, if they get to Heaven. Ah, miserable spirit, you shall not get there! It would need another Heaven for you, for the Heaven of Christ is the Heaven of the unselfish, the temple of the large hearted, the bliss of loving spirits, the Heaven of those who like Christ, those who are calling to become poor, that others may he rich. I cannot believe—it is a libel upon the Cross of Christ; it is a scandal upon the doctrine He taught—if I could ever believe that the man whose prayers are selfish has anything of the Spirit of Christ within him.

Brethren, I commend intercessory prayer, because it opens a man's soul, gives a healthy play to his sympathies, constrains him to feel that he is not everybody, and that this wide world and this great universe were not after all made that he might be its petty lord, that everything might bend to his will, and all creatures crouch at his feet. It does him good, I say, to make him know that the Cross was not uplifted alone for him, for its far reaching arms were the means to drop blessings upon millions of the human race. You lean and hungry worshiper of self, this is an exercise that would make another man of you, a man more like the Son of Man, and less like Nabal, the churl.

But again, I commend the blessed privilege of intercession, because of its plain brotherly nature. You and I may be naturally hard, harsh, and unlovely of spirit, but praying much for others will remind us we have indeed a relationship to the saints, that their interests are ours, and that we are jointly concerned with them in all the privileges of grace. I do not know anything which, through the grace of God, may be a better means of uniting us the one to the other than constant prayer for each other. You cannot harbor enmity in your soul against your brother after you have learned to pray for him. If he has done you ill, when you have taken that ill to the mercy seat and prayed over it, you must forgive. Surely you could not be such a hypocrite as to invoke blessings on his head before God and then come forth to curse him in your own soul. When these have been complaints brought by brother against brother, it is generally the best way to say, "Let us pray before we enter into the matter." Wherever there is a case to be decided by the pastor, he ought always say to any of the brethren who contend, "Let us pray first," and it will often happen that through prayer the differences will soon be forgotten. They will become so slight, so trivial, that when the brethren rise from their knees they will say, "They are gone; we cannot contend now after having been one in heart before the throne of God."

I have heard of a man who had made complaints against his minister, and his minister wisely said to him, "Well, don't talk to me in the street; come to my house, and let us hear it all." He went and the minister said, "My brother, I hope that what you have to say to me may be greatly blessed to me, no doubt I have my imperfections as well as another man and I hope I shall never be above being told of them, but in order that what you have to say to me may be blessed to me, let us kneel down and pray together." So our quarrelsome friend prayed first and the minister prayed next, both briefly. When they rose from their knees, he said, "Now, my brother, I think we are both in a good state of mind; tell me what it is that you have to find fault with." The man blushed, stammered, and stuttered, and said that he did not think there was anything at all, except in himself. "I have forgotten to pray for you, sir," said he, "and of course I cannot expect that God will feed my soul through you when I neglect to mention you at the throne of grace." Ah well, brethren, if you will exercise yourselves much in supplication for your brethren, you will forgive their tempers, you will overlook their rashness, you will not think of their harsh words, but knowing that you also may be tempted and are men of like passions with them, you can cover their fault and bear with their infirmities.

Shall I need to say more in commendation of intercessory prayer except it be this, that it seems to me that when God gives any man much grace, it must be with the design that he may use it for the rest of the family. I would compare you who have near communion with God to courtiers in the king's palace. What do courtiers do? Do they not avail themselves of their influence at court to take the petitions of their friends and present them where they can be heard? This is what we call patronage—a thing with which many find fault when it is used for political ends, but there is a kind of heavenly patronage that you ought to use right diligently. I ask you to use it on my behalf. When it is well with you, then think of me. I pray you use it on the behalf of the poor, the sick, the afflicted, the tempted, the tried, the desponding, the despairing; when you have the King's ear, speak to Him for us. When you are permitted to come very near to His throne, and He says to you, "Ask, and I will give you what you will." When your faith is strong, your eye is clear, your access is near, your interest is sure, and the love of God is sweetly shed abroad in your heart—then take the petitions of your poor brethren who stand outside at the gate and say, "My Lord, I have a poor one, a poor child of yours, who has desired me to ask of you this favor. Grant it unto me; it shall be a favor shown unto myself; grant it unto him, for he is one of yours. Do it for Jesus' sake!"

To come to an end in this matter of commendation, it is utterly impossible that you should have a large measure of grace unless it prompts you to use your influence for others. Soul, if you have grace at all, and are not a mighty intercessor, that grace must be but as a grain of mustard seed—a shriveled, uncomely, puny thing. You have just enough grace to float your soul clear from the quicksand, but you have no deep floods of grace, or else you would carry in your joyous skiff a rich cargo of the wants of others up to the throne of God, and you would bring back for them rich blessings, which but for you they might not have obtained. If you be like an angel with your foot upon the golden ladder that reaches to Heaven, if you are ascending and descending, know that you will ascend with prayers for others and descend with blessings for others, for it is impossible for a full-grown saint to live or to pray for himself alone.

2. We turn to our second point, and endeavor to say something *by way of encouragement*, that you may cheerfully offer intercessory supplications. First, remember that intercessory prayer is the sweetest prayer God ever hears. Do not question it, for the prayer of Christ is of this character. In all the incense which now our great High Priest puts into the censor, there is not a single grain that is for himself. His work is done; His reward has been obtained. Now you do not doubt but that Christ's prayer is the most acceptable of all supplications. Very well, my brethren, the more your prayer is like Christ's, the more sweet it will be, and while petitions for yourself will be accepted, yet your pleadings for others, having in them more of the fruits of the spirit—more love, perhaps more faith, certainly more brotherly kindness—they will be as the sweetest oblation you can offer to God, the very fat of your sacrifice.

Remember, again, that intercessory prayer is exceedingly prevalent. What it has wrought! Intercessory prayer has stayed plagues. It removed the darkness that rested over Egypt, it drove away the frogs that leaped upon the land; it scattered the lice and locusts that plagued the inhabitants of Zoan; it removed the pestilence, and the thunder, and the lightning; it stayed all the ravages that God's avenging hand did upon Pharaoh and his people. Intercessory prayer has healed diseases—we know it did in the early church. We have evidence of it in Mosaic times. When Miriam was struck with leprosy, Moses prayed, and the leprosy was removed. It has restored withered limbs. When the king's arm was withered, he said to the prophet, "Pray for me," and his arm was restored as it was before. (See 1 Kings 13:6.) Intercessory prayer has raised the dead, fair Elisha stretched himself twice upon the child, and the child sneezed seven times, and the child's soul returned. (See 2 Kings 4:33-35.)

As to how many souls intercessory prayer has instrumentally saved, recording angel, you can tell! Eternity, you shall reveal! There is nothing that intercessory prayer cannot do. Oh, believer, you have a mighty engine in your hand, so use it. Use it constantly, use it now with faith, and you shall surely prevail. But perhaps you have a doubt about interceding for someone who has fallen far into sin. Brethren, did you ever hear of men who have been thought to be dead while yet alive? Have you never heard by the farmer's fire some old-fashioned story of one who was washed and laid out, and wrapped up in his shroud to be put into his coffin, and yet he was but in a trance and not dead? And have you not heard old legends of men and women who have been burled alive? I cannot vouch for the accuracy of those tales, but I can tell all of you that spiritually there has been many a man given up for dead who was still within reach of grace. There has been many a soul that has been put into the winding sheet even by Christian people, given up to damnation even by the ministers of Christ, consigned to perdition even by their own kinfolk. But yet into perdition they did not come, but God found them, and took them out of the horrible pit and out of the miry clay, and set their living feet upon His living rock. (See Psalm 40:2.) Oh, give up nobody; still pray, lay none out for spiritually dead until they are laid out for dead naturally.

But perhaps you say, "I cannot pray for others, for I am so weak, so powerless." You will get strength, my brethren, by the exertion. Besides, the prevalence of prayer does not depend upon the strength of the man who prays, but upon the power of the argument he uses. Now, brethren, if you sow seed, you may be very feeble, but it is not your hand that puts the seed into the ground that produces the harvest; it is the vitality in the seed. And so in the prayer of faith. When you can plead the promise and drop that prayer into the ground with hope, your weakness shall not make it miscarry; it shall still prevail with God and bring down blessings from on high.

Job, you came from your dunghill to intercede, and so may I come from my couch of weakness; you came from your poverty and your desertion to intercede for others, and so may we. Elijah was a man of like passions—sweet word!—of like passions, like infirmities, like tendencies to sin, but he prevailed, and so shall you. Only do see to it that you be not negligent in these exercises, but that you pray much for others, even as Job prayed for his friends.

Now that the air is very hot, and the atmosphere heavy and becalmed, our friends find it difficult to listen, more difficult even than the speaker finds it to preach. Now that I may have your attention yet once again—and a change of position may do you all good—will you stand up and put the text into use by offering an intercessory prayer, and then I will go on again. It shall be this one:

Pity the nations, O our God,

Constrain the Earth to come;

Send thy victims word abroad,

And bring the strangers home!

(The congregation here rose, and sang the verse.)

3. The third point is *a suggestion as to the persons for whom we should more particularly pray.* It shall be but a suggestion, and I will then turn to my last point. In the case of Job, he prayed for his offending friends. They had spoken exceedingly harshly of him. They had misconstrued all his previous life, and that there had never been a part of his character that deserved censure—for the Lord witnessed concerning him, that he was a perfect and an upright man—yet they accused him of hypocrisy, and supposed that all he did was for the sake of gain. Now, perhaps there is no greater offense which can be given to an upright and a holy man, than to his face to suspect his motives and to accuse him of self-seeking. And yet, shaking off everything, as the sun pushes away the darkness that has hidden its glory, and scatters it by its own beams, Job comes to the mercy seat and pleads. He is accepted himself and be begs that his friends may be accepted, too. Carry your offending ones to the throne of God; it shall be a blessed method of proving the trueness of your forgiveness. Do not do that, however, in a threatening way.

I remember having to deal faithfully with a hypocrite, who told me, by way of threatening that he should pray for me. It was a horrid threat, for who would wish to have his name associated with a prayer that would be an abomination to the Lord? Do not do it in that sense, as though like a supercilious hypocrite, you would make your prayer itself a stalking horse for your vainglory, but do it when you are alone before God, and in secret, not that you may gratify your revenge by telling the story again, for that is abominable indeed, but that you may remove from your erring brother any sin that may have stained his garments by asking the Lord to forgive him.

Again, be sure you take there your argumentative friends. These brethren had been arguing with Job, and the controversy dragged its weary length along. Brethren, it is better to pray than it is to argue. Sometimes you think it would be a good thing to have a public discussion upon a doctrine. It would be a better thing to have prayer over it.

You say, "Let two good men, on different sides, meet and fight the matter out."

I say, "No! let the two good men meet and pray the matter out."

He that will not submit his doctrine to the test of the mercy seat, I should suspect is wrong. I can say that I am not afraid to offer prayer, that my brethren who do not see "believers' baptism," may be made to see it. If they think it is wrong, I wish that they would pray to God to set us right, but I have never heard them do that. I have never heard them say to the Lord to convince us of the truth of infant sprinkling—I wish they would if they believe it to be scriptural, and I am perfectly willing to put it to the old test, the God that answers by fire. Let Him be God, and whichever shall prevail, when prayed, shall be the ultimate arbiter; let that stand.

Carry your dear friends who are wrong in practice, not to the discussion room, or to the debating club, but carry them before God, and let this be your cry, "Oh, you who teaches us to our profit, teach me if I am wrong, and teach my friend wherein he errs, and make him right." This is the thing we ought also to do with our haughty friends. Eliphaz and Bildad were very high and haughty—how they looked down upon poor Job! They thought he was a very great sinner, a very desperate hypocrite; they stayed with him, but, doubtless, they thought it to be a very great condescension. Now, you sometimes hear complaints made by Christians about other people being proud. It will not make them humble for you to grumble about that. What if there be a Mrs. So-and-so who wears a very rustling dress, and never takes any notice of you because you cannot rustle too! What if there be a brother who can afford to wear creaking boots, and will not notice you in the street because you happen to be poor! Tell your Father about it; that is the best way.

Why, you would not be angry I suppose, with a man for having the gout or a torpid liver or a cataract in the eye; indeed, you would pity him. Why be angry with your brother because of his being proud? It is a disease, a very bad disease, that scarlet fever of pride; go and pray the Lord to cure him. Your anger will not do it; it may puff him up and make him worse than ever he was before, but it will not set him right. Pray him down, brother, pray him down; have a duel with him, and have the choice of weapons yourself, and let that be the weapon of all-prayer, and if he is proud, I know this, if you prevail with God, God will soon take the pride out of his own child and remake him humble, as he should be.

But particularly let me ask you to pray most for those who are disabled from praying for themselves. Job's three friends could not pray for themselves because the Lord said he would not accept them if they did. He said he was angry with them, but as for Job, He said, "Him will I accept" (Job 42:8). Do not let me shock your feelings when I say there are some, even as God's people, who are not able to pray acceptably in certain seasons. When a man has just been committing sin, repentance is his first work, not prayer; he must first set matters right between God and his own soul before he may go and intercede for others. And there are many poor Christians that cannot pray; doubt has come in, sin has taken away their confidence, and they are standing outside the gate with their petitions; they dare not enter within the veil. There are many tried believers, too, that are so desponding that they cannot pray with faith, and, therefore, they cannot prevail.

Now, my dear brethren, if you can pray, take their sins into court with you, and when you have had your own hearing, then say, 'But, my Lord, inasmuch as you have honored me, and made me to eat of your bread and drink from your cup, hear me for your poor people who are just now denied the light of your countenance." Besides, there are millions of poor sinners who are dead in sin and they cannot pray, so pray for them; it is a blessed thing—that vicarious repentance and vicarious faith that a saint may exert towards a sinner. "Lord, that sinner does not feel; help me to feel for him because he will not feel; Lord, that sinner will not believe in Christ; he does not think that Christ can save him, but I know He can, and I will pray believingly for that sinner and I will repent for him, and though my repentance and my faith will not avail him without his personal repentance and faith, yet it may come to pass that through me he may be brought to repentance and led to prayer."

4. Now, lest I should weary you, let me come to the closing part of my discourse. And, O God, lend us your strength now, that this duty may come forcibly home to our conscience, and we may at once engage in this exercise! Brethren, I have to *exhort you to pray for others.* Before I do it, I will ask you a

personal question. Do you always pray for others? Are you guilty or not guilty here? Do you think you have taken the case of your children, your church, your neighborhood, and the ungodly world before God as you ought to have done? If you have, I have not. For I stand here a chief culprit before the Master to make confession of the sin, and while I shall exhort you to practice what is undoubtedly a noble privilege, I shall be most of all exhorting myself. I begin thus, by saying, "Brethren, how can you and I repay the debt we owe to the Church unless we pray for others? How was it that you were converted? It was because somebody else prayed for you." I, in tracing back my own conversion, cannot fail to impute it, through God's Spirit, to the prayers of my mother. I believe that the Lord heard her earnest cries when I knew not that her soul was exercised about me. There are many of you that were prayed for when you were asleep in your cradles as unconscious infants. Your mothers' liquid prayers fell hot upon your infant brows, and gave you what was a true christening while you were still but little ones.

There are husbands here who owe their conversion to their wives' prayers; brothers who must acknowledge that it was a sister's pleading; children who must confess that their Sabbath school teachers were wont to pray for them. Now, if by the prayers of others, you and I were brought to Christ, how can we repay this Christian kindness, but by pleading for others? He who has not a man to pray for him may write himself down a hopeless character. During one of the revivals in America, a young man was going to see the minister but he did not, because the minister had avoided him with considerable coldness. A remark was made to the minister about what he had done, and he said, "Well, I did not want to see him; I knew he had only come to mock and scoff. What should I ask him for? You do not know him as well as I do, or else you would have done the same." A day or two after there was a public meeting, where the preaching of the Word was to be carried on in the hope that the revival might be continued. A young man who had been lately converted through the prayers of another young man was riding to worship on his horse, and as he was riding along, he was overtaken by our young friend whom the minister thought was so godless. He said to him, "Where are you going today, William?"

"Well, I am going to the meeting, and I hear that you have been converted."

"I thank God that I have been brought to a knowledge of the truth," he answered.

"Oh!" said the other, "I shall never be; I wish I might." His friend was surprised to hear him whom the minister thought to be so hard say that, and he said, "But why cannot you be converted?"

"Why?" said the other, "you know you were converted through the prayers of Mr. K — ."

"Yes, so I was."

"Ah," said the other "there is nobody to pray for me; they have all given me up long ago."

"Why," said his friend, "it is very singular, but Mr. K — , who prayed for me, has been praying for you too; we were together last night, and I heard him."

The other threw himself back in his saddle, and seemed as if he would fall from his horse with surprise. "Is that true?" said he.

"Yes, it is."

"Then blessed be God, there is hope for me now, and if he has prayed for me, that gives me a reason why I should now pray believingly for myself." And he did so, and that meeting witnessed him confessing his faith in Christ!

Now, let no man of your acquaintance say that there is nobody to pray for him; but as you had somebody to plead for you, find a person and plead for them.

Then, again, permit me to say, how are you to prove your love to Christ or to His Church if you refuse to pray for men? "We know that we have passed from death unto life, because we love the brethren" (1 John 3:14). If we do not love the brethren, we are still dead. No man loves the brethren who does not pray for them. It's the very least thing you can do, and if you do not perform the least, you certainly will fail in the greater. You do not love the brethren unless you pray for them, and then it follows you are dead in trespasses and sins. Let me ask you again how is it that you hope to get your own prayers answered if you never plead for others? Will not the Lord say, "Selfish wretch, you are always knocking at my door, but it is always to cry for your own welfare and never for another's; inasmuch as you never asked for a blessing for one of the least of these my brethren, neither will I give a blessing to you. You love not the saints, you love not your fellowmen, how can you love me whom you have not seen, and how shall I love you and give you the blessing which you ask at my hands?"

Brethren, again I say I would earnestly exhort you to intercede for others, for how can you be Christians if you do not? Christians are priests, but how can they be priests if they offer no sacrifice? Christians are lights, but how can they be lights unless they shine for others? Christians are sent into the world even as Christ was sent into the world, but how are they sent unless they are sent to pray? Christians are meant not only to be blessed themselves, but in them shall all the nations of the Earth be blessed. But how can this happen if you refuse to pray? Give up your profession; cast down, I pray you, the ephod of a priest if you will not burn the incense; renounce your Christianity if you will not carry it out; make not a mock and sport of solemn things. And you must do so if you still refuse selfishly to give to your friends a part and a lot in your supplication before the throne.

O brethren, let us unite with one heart and with one soul to plead with God for this neighborhood! Let us carry "London" written on our breasts just as the high priest of old carried the names of the tribes. Mothers, bear your children before God! Fathers, carry your sons and your daughters! Men and brethren, let us take a wicked world and the dark places thereof that are full of the habitations of cruelty! Let us cry aloud and keep no silence, and give to the Lord no rest till He establish and make His Church a praise in the Earth. Evoke, you watchmen upon Zion's walls, and renew your shouts! Wake, you favorites of Heaven, and renew your prayers! The cloud hangs above you; it's yours to draw down its sacred floods in genial showers by earnest prayers.

God has put high up in the mountains of His promise springs of love; it is yours to bring them down by the divine channel of your intense supplications. Do it, I pray you, lest inasmuch as you have shut your bowels of compassion and have refused to plead with God for the conversion of others, He should say in His wrath, "These are not my children. They have not my spirit. They are not partakers of my love, neither shall they enter into my rest." Why, there are some of you that have not prayed for others for months, I am afraid, except it be at a prayer meeting. You know what your night prayers are. It is, "Lord, take care of my family." You know how some farmers pray. "Lord, send fair weather in this part of the country. Lord, preserve the precise fruits of the field all around this neighborhood. Never mind about their being spoilt anywhere else, for that will send the markets up." And so there are some who make themselves special objects of supplication, and what care they for the perishing crowd? This is the drift of some men's wishes, "Lord, bless the Church, but don't send another minister into our neighborhood, lest he should take our congregations from us. Lord, send laborers into the vineyard, but do not send them into our corner, lest they should take any of our glory from us." That is the kind of supplication. Let us have done with such. Let us be Christians; let us have expanded souls and minds that can feel for others. Let us weep with them that weep and rejoice with them that rejoice, and as a Church and as private persons, we shall find the Lord will turn our captivity when we pray for our friends. God, help us to plead for others! And as for you that have never prayed for yourselves, God help you to believe in the Lord Jesus!

LET US PRAY

"But it is good for me to draw near to God."
(Psalm 73:28)

There are many ways by which the true believer draws near to God. The gates of the King's palace are many, and through the love of Jesus and the rich grace of His Spirit, it is our delight to enter and approach our heavenly Father. First and foremost among these is communion, that sweet converse that man holds with God, that state of nearness to God, in which our mutual secrets are revealed—our hearts being open unto Him, His heart being manifested to us. Here we see the invisible and hear the unutterable. The outward symbol of fellowship is the sacred Supper of the Lord at which, by means of simple emblems, we are divinely enabled to feed, after a spiritual sort, upon the flesh and blood of the Redeemer. This is a pearly gate of fellowship, a royal road that our feet delight to tread.

Moreover, we draw near to God even in our sighs and tears, when our desolate spirits long for His sacred presence, crying, "Whom have I in heaven but thee, and there is none upon earth that I desire beside thee" (Psalm 73:25). And as often as we read the promise written in the Word, and are enabled to receive it and rest upon it as the very words of a covenant God, we do truly "draw near to God."

Nevertheless, prayer is the best used means of drawing near to God. You will excuse me, then, if in considering my text this morning, I confine myself entirely to the subject of prayer. It is in prayer mainly that we draw near to God, and certainly it can be said emphatically of prayer that it is good for every man who knows how to practice that heavenly art, to use it to draw near to God. To assist your memories, that the sermon may abide with you in future days, I shall divide my discourse this morning in a somewhat singular manner; first, I shall look upon my text as being a touchstone by which we may try our prayers, aye, and try ourselves, too. Then I shall take the text as a whetstone to sharpen our desires, to make us more earnest and more diligent in supplication, because "it is good to draw near to God" and then, I shall have the solemn task in the last place of using it as a tombstone, with a direful epitaph upon it for those who do not know what it is to draw near to God, for "A prayerless soul is a Christless soul."

1. First, then, regard my text as *a touchstone* by which you may test your prayers, and thus try yourselves.

That is not prayer of which it cannot be said that there was in it a drawing near unto God. Come hither then with your supplications. I see one coming forward who says, "I am in the daily habit of using a form of prayer both at morning and at evening. I could not be happy if I went abroad before I had first repeated my morning prayer, nor could I rest at night without again going over the holy sentence appointed for use at eventide. Sir, my form is the very best that could possibly be written; it was compiled by a famous bishop, one who was glorified in martyrdom and ascended to his God in a fiery chariot of flame."

My friend, I am glad to hear, if you use a form, that you use the best. If we must have forms at all, let them be of the most excellent kind. So far so good. But let me ask you a question, I am not about to condemn you for any form you may have used, but tell me now, and tell me honestly from your inmost soul, have you drawn near to God while you have been repeating those words? If you have not—O solemn thought!—all the prayers you have ever uttered have been an idle mockery. You have *said* prayers, but you have never *prayed* in your life. Imagine not that there is any enchantment in any particular set of words. You might as well repeat the alphabet backwards, or the "abracadabra" of a wizard, as to go over the best form in the world, unless there is something more than form in it. Have you drawn near to God?

Suppose that one of us should be desirous of presenting a petition to the House of Commons. We wisely ask in what manner the petition should be worded. We procure the exact phrases and suppose that in the morning we rise and read this form, or repeat it to ourselves, and conclude with, "And your petitioners will ever pray" and the like. We do the same again at night, the same the next day, and for months we continue the practice. One day meeting some member of the House, we accost him and astonish him by saying, "Sir, I wonder I have never had an answer from the House, I have been petitioning these last six months, and the form I used was the most accurate that could be procured."

"But," says he, "how was your petition presented?"

"Presented! I had not thought of that; I have repeated it."

"Yes," he would say, "and you may repeat it many a long day before any good comes from it! It is not the repeating it, but the presenting of the petition, and having it pleaded by some able friend that will get you the boon you desire."

And so it may be, my friend, that you have been repeating collects and prayers; and have you ignorantly imagined that you have prayed? Why, your prayer has never been *presented*. You have not laid it before the bleeding Lamb of God, and have not asked Him to take it for you into the sacred place where God abides, and there to present the petition with His own merits before His Father's throne. I will not bid you cease from your form, but I do beseech you by the living God, either cease from it, or else beg the Holy Spirit to enable you to draw near to God in it. Oh, I beseech you, take not what I may say for any censoriousness; I speak now as God's own messenger in this matter. Your prayer has not been heard, and it neither can nor will be answered unless there be in it a true and real desire to draw near to God.

"Ah," says another, "I am pleased to hear these remarks, for I am in the habit of offering extempore prayer every morning and evening, and at other times; besides, I like to hear you speak against the form, sir."

Note, I did not speak against the form, that is not my business upon this occasion. One class of sinners is always pleased to hear another class of sinners found fault with. You say you offer an extempore supplication. I bring your prayer to the same touchstone as the former. What is there in the form that you can extemporize, that it should be so much better than that which was composed by some holy man of God?

Possibly your extempore form is not worth a farthing, and if it could be written, might be a disgrace to prayer writers. I bring you at once to the test—have you in your prayer drawn near to God? When you have been on your knees in the morning, have you thought that you were talking to the King of Heaven and Earth? Have you breathed your desires, not to the empty winds, but into the ear of the Eternal? Have you desired to come to Him and tell Him your wants, and have you sought at His hands the answer to your requests? Remember, you have not prayed successfully or acceptably unless you have in prayer endeavored to draw near to God.

Suppose now, to take a case, that I should desire some favor of a friend. I shut myself up alone, and I commence delivering an oration, pleading earnestly for the boon I need. I repeat this at night, and so on month after month. At last I meet my friend and tell him that I have been asking a favor of him, and that he has never heard my prayer. "Nay," says he, "I have never seen you, you never spoke to me."

"Ah, but you should have heard what I said; if you had but heard it, surely it would have moved your heart."

"Ah," says he, "but then you did not address it to me. You wrote a letter, you tell me, in moving strains, but did you post the letter? Did you see it was delivered to me?"

"No, no," you say, "I kept the letter after I had written it. I never sent it to you."

Now mark, it is just the same with extempore prayer. You plead; but if you are not pleading with God, to what effect is your pleading? You talk, but if you are not talking to a manifestly present God, to what effect is all your talking? If you do not seek to come near to Him, what have you done? You have offered sacrifice, perhaps, but it has been upon your own high places, and the sacrifice has been an abomination. You have not brought it up to God's one altar; you have not come up to the mercy seat, where is His own visible presence! You have not drawn near to God, and consequently your prayers, though they be multiplied by tens of thousands, are utterly valueless to your soul's benefit. Drawing near to God is an indispensable requisite in accepted prayer.

But, now, lest I should be misunderstood as to this drawing near to God, let me attempt to describe it in degrees, for all men cannot draw near to God with the same nearness of access. When first the life of grace begins in the soul you will draw near to God, but it will be with great fear and trembling. The soul conscious of guilt, and humbled thereby, is overawed with the solemnity of its position; it is cast to the Earth with the grandeur of that God in whose presence it stands. I remember the first time I ever sincerely prayed in my life; but the words I used I remember not. Surely there were few enough words in that petition. I had often repeated a form. I had been in the habit of continually repeating it. At last I came really to pray; and then I saw myself standing before God, in the immediate presence of the heart-searching Jehovah, and I said within myself, "I have heard of thee by the hearing of the ear: but now mine eye seeth thee. Wherefore I abhor myself, and repent in dust and ashes" (Job 42:5-6).

I felt like Esther when she stood before the king, faint and overcome with dread. I was full of penitence of heart, because of His majesty and my sinfulness. I think the only words I could utter were something like these: "Oh!—Ah!" And the only complete sentence was, "God, be merciful to me, a sinner!" The overwhelming splendor of His majesty, the greatness of His power, the severity of His justice, the immaculate character of His holiness, and all His dreadful grandeur—these things overpowered my soul, and I fell down in utter prostration of spirit. But there was in that a true and real drawing near to God. Oh, if some of you when you are in your churches and chapels, did but realize that you are in God's presence, surely you might expect to see scenes more marvelous than any of the convulsions of the Irish Revival. If you knew that God was there, that you were speaking to Him, that in His ear you were uttering that often-repeated confession, "We have done the things that we ought not to have done, we have left undone the things that we ought to have done"—ah, my friends, there would be then a deep humility and a solemn abasement of spirit. May God grant to us all, as often as we offer prayer of any sort, that we may truly and really draw near to Him, even if it be only in this sense.

Later in life, as the Christian grows in grace, although he will never forget the solemnity of his position, and never will lose that holy awe that must overshadow a gracious man, when he is in the presence of a God who can create or can destroy, that fear has all its terror taken out of it; it becomes a holy reverence, and no more a slavish abject dread. Then the man of God, walking amid the splendors of deity, and veiling his face like the glorious cherubim, with those twin wings, the blood and righteousness of Jesus Christ, will, reverent and bowed in spirit, approach the throne, and seeing there a God of love, goodness, and mercy, he will realize rather the covenant character of God than His absolute deity. He will see in God His goodness rather than His greatness and more of His love than of His majesty. Then will the soul, bowing again as reverently as before, enjoy a sacred liberty of intercession; for while humbled in the presence of the infinite God, it is yet sustained by the divine consciousness of being in the presence of mercy and of love in infinite degree. This is a state to which men reach after they have had their sins forgiven, after they have passed from death unto life; then they come to rejoice in God, and draw near to Him with confidence.

There is yet a third and higher stage, which I fear too few among us ever arrive at. It is when the child of God, awed by the splendor, and delighting in the goodness of God, sees something which is more enchanting to him than either of these, namely, the fact of his relationship to God. He sees on the throne, not simply goodness; but his Father's goodness, not merely love, but love that has from all eternity been set upon him—love that has made him its darling, that has written his name upon its breast, love that for his sake did even deign to die. Then the child of God comes near to the throne, then he takes hold of his Father's knees, and though conscious of the greatness of the God, yet is he still more alive to the loveliness of the Father, and he cries, "My Father, hear my prayer and grant me my request, for Jesus' sake."

In this position, it sometimes happens that the child of God may pray in such a way that others cannot understand him at all. If you had heard Martin Luther pray, some of you would have been shocked, and perhaps it would have been presumption if you had prayed as he did, because Martin Luther was God's own son, and you, alas, are destitute of sonship. He had a liberty to talk to God as another man had not. If you are not the son of God, if you have no realization of your adoption, the utmost you can do is to come into the King's court as a humble beggar. May God give you grace to get further; may you come there, not simply as a petitioner, but as a follower of the Son of God—a servant. But happy is the man who has received his full adoption, and knows himself to be a son. It is rudeness for anyone to do to a king what a king's son may do. A king's own child may talk familiarly to his own parent, and there are love-doings and words of high and hallowed familiarity, and of close and sacred communing, between God and His own adopted child that I could not tell you. They are things that are something like what Paul heard in Paradise; it is scarcely lawful for a man to utter them in public, though in private he knows their sweetness.

Ah, my dear hearers, some of you, I doubt not, know more about this than I do, but this I know, it is the happiest moment in one's life when we can go up to our Father and our God in Christ Jesus, and can know and feel of a surety that His infinite love is set on us, and that our love is gone forth to Him. There is a sweet embrace that is not to be excelled. No chariots of Amminadab can describe the heavenly rapture. Even Solomon's Song itself, glowing though its figures be, can scarcely reach the mystery—the length, the breadth, the height of the embracing of God by the creature, and the embracing of the creature by its God.

Now, I repeat, it is not essential to the success of your prayers that you should come up to this last point. Possibly you never may attain to this eminence of grace. I do not even think that it is absolutely necessary that your prayer should come to the second point to be prayer. It should be so, and it will be, as you grow in grace. But, remember this, you must draw near to God in one of these three grades either in a lowly sense of His majesty, or in a delightful consciousness of His goodness, or in a ravishing sense of your own relationship to Him, or else your prayer is as worthless as the chaff, it is but as whispering to the wind, or the uttering of a cry to the desert air, where no ear can hear nor hand can help. Bring your prayers, then, to these touchstones and God help you to examine them, and be honest with yourselves, for your own soul's sake.

2. I have thus concluded *the touchstone*. I now come to the second head of the discourse, which was *the whetstone*, to whet your desires, to make you more eager to be much in prayer, and to be more earnest in it.

"It is good for me to draw near to God." Now, first and foremost, let us remark that the goodness of prayer does not lie in any merit that there is in prayer itself. There is no merit whatever in prayer; and wherever the idea of the merit of prayer could come from, one is at a loss to know, except that it must have come from a near relative of the *father of lies*. If a beggar should be always on your doorstep, or should be always meeting you in the street, or stopping you on your journeys, and asking you to give him help, I suppose the last thing you would understand would be the merit of his prayers. You would say, "I can understand their impudence, I can allow their earnestness, I can comprehend their importunity, but as for merit, what merit can there be in a beggar's cry?" Remember, your prayers at the best are nothing but a beggar's cry. You still stand as beggars at the gate of mercy, asking for the dole of God's charity, for the love of Jesus. And He gives freely. But He gives, not because of your prayers, but because of *Christ's blood and Christ's merit*. Your prayers may be the sacred vessel in which He puts the alms of His mercy; but the merit by which the mercy comes is in the veins of Christ, and nowhere else. Remember that there can be no merit in a beggar's cry.

But, now, let us note that it nevertheless is good, practically good, for us to pray and draw near to God; and the first thing that would whet our desires in prayer is this: prayer explains mysteries. I utter that first because it is in the Psalm. Poor Asaph had been greatly troubled. He had been trying to untie that Gordian Knot concerning the righteousness of a providence that permits the wicked to flourish and the godly to be tried, and because he could not untie that knot, he tried to cut it, and he cut his own fingers in the act, and became greatly troubled. He could not understand how it was that God could be just and yet give riches to the wicked while His own people were in poverty. At last Asaph understood it all, for he went into the house of his God, and there he understood their end. And he says—looking back upon his discovery of a clue to this great labyrinth—"It is good for me to draw near to God."

And now, my dear hearers, if you would understand the Word of God in its knotty points, if you would comprehend the mystery of the Gospel of Christ, remember, Christ's scholars must study upon their knees. Depend upon it, that the best commentator upon the Word of God is its author, the Holy Ghost, and if you would know the meaning, you must go to Him in prayer. Often when a Psalm has staggered me in reading it, and I have not understood it, if I have knelt down and tried to read it over in that position, and see if I could realize the meaning in my own heart, some one word in the text has glistened, and that one word has been the key to the whole. John Bunyan says that he never forgot the divinity he taught, because it was burnt into him when he was on his knees. That is the way to learn the gospel. If you learn it upon your knees you will never unlearn it. That which men teach you, men can un-teach you. If I am merely convinced by reason, a better reasoner may deceive me. If I merely hold my doctrinal opinions because they seem to me to be correct, I may be led to think differently another day. But if God has taught them to me—He who is himself pure truth—I have not learned amiss, but I have so learned that I shall never unlearn, nor shall I forget.

Behold, believer, you are this day in a labyrinth; whenever you come to a turning place, where there is a road to the right or to the left, if you would know which way to go, fall on your knees, then go on; and when you come to the next turning place, on your knees again, and so proceed again. The one clue to the whole labyrinth of providence, and of doctrinal opinion, and of sacred thought, is to be found in that one hallowed exercise—prayer. Continue much in prayer, and neither Satan nor the world shall much deceive you. Behold, before you is the sacred ark of truth. But where is the key? It hangs upon the silver nail of prayer; go take it down, unlock the casket, and be rich.

A second whetstone for your prayers shall be this: *Prayer brings deliverance*. In an old author, I met with the following allegory; as I found it, so I tell it to you.

Once upon a time, the king of Jerusalem left his city in the custody of an eminent captain, whose name was Zeal. He gave unto Zeal many choice warriors, to assist him in the protection of the city. Zeal was a right-hearted man, one who never wearied in the day of battle, but would fight all day, and all night, even though his sword did cleave to his hand, as the blood ran down his arm. But it happened upon this time, that the king of Arabia, getting unto himself exceeding great hosts and armies, surrounded the city, and prevented any introduction of food for the soldiers, or of ammunition to support the war. Driven to the last extremity, Captain Zeal called a council of war, and asked of them what course they should take. Many things were proposed, but they all failed to effect the purpose, and they came to the sad conclusion that nothing was before them but the surrender of the city, although upon the hardest terms. Zeal took the resolution of the council of war, but when he read it, he could not bear it. His soul abhorred it. "Better," said he, "to be cut in pieces, than surrender. Better for us to be destroyed while we are faithful, than to give up the keys of this royal city."

In his great distress, he met a friend of his who was called Prayer. Prayer said to him, "Oh, captain, I can deliver this city." Now, Prayer was not a soldier, at least he did not look as if he was a warrior, for he wore the garments of a priest. In fact he was the king's chaplain, and was the priest of the holy city of Jerusalem. Nevertheless, this Prayer was a valiant man, and wore armor beneath his robes. "Oh, captain," said he, "give me three companions and I will deliver this city—their names must be Sincerity, Importunity, and Faith." Now these four brave men went out of the city at the dead of night when the prospects of Jerusalem were the very blackest; they cut their way right through the hosts that surrounded the city. With many wounds and much smuggling they made their escape and traveled all that night long as quickly as they could across the plain, to reach the camp of the King of Jerusalem. When they slowed a little, Importunity would hasten them on; and when at any time they grew faint, Faith would give them a drink from his bottle, and they would recover. They came at last to the palace of the great king. The door was shut, but Importunity knocked long, and, at last it was opened. Faith stepped in; Sincerity threw himself on his face before the throne of the great king; and then Prayer began to speak. He told the king of the great straits in which the beloved city was now placed, the dangers that surrounded it, and the almost certainty that all the brave warriors would be cut in pieces by the morrow. Importunity repeated again and again the wants of the city. Faith pleaded hard the royal promise and covenant.

At last the king said to Captain Prayer, "Take soldiers with you and go back; lo, I am with you to deliver this city." At the morning light, just when the day broke—for they had returned more swiftly than could have been expected, for though the journey seemed long in going there, it was very short in coming back, in fact they seemed to have gained time on the road—they arrived early in the morning, fell upon the hosts of the king of Arabia, took him prisoner, slew his army, and divided the spoil, and then entered the gates of the city of Jerusalem in triumph. Zeal put a crown of gold upon the head of Prayer, and decreed that henceforth whenever Zeal went forth to battle, Prayer should be the standard-bearer, and should lead the vanguard.

The allegory is full of truth; let him that heareth understand. If we would have deliverance in the hour, "Let us pray." Prayer shall soon bring sweet and merciful deliverances from the throne of our faithful God. This is the second sharpening of your desires upon the whetstone. And now a third. It was said of faith, in that mighty chapter of the Hebrews, that faith stopped the mouth of lions and the like. But one singular thing faith did, which is as great a miracle as any of them, was this: *faith obtained promises.* Now the like can be said of prayer. Prayer obtains promises; therefore, "it is good for me to draw near to God." We read a story in the *History of England*, whether true or not we cannot tell, that Queen Elizabeth gave to the Earl of Essex a ring, as a token of her favor. "When you are in disgrace," she said, "send this ring to me. When I see it I will forgive you, and accept you again to favor." You know the story of that ill-fated noble, how he sent the ring by a faithless messenger, and it was never delivered, and, therefore, he perished at the block.

Ah! God has given to each one of His people the sacred ring of promise. And He says, "As often as you are in need, or in sorrow, show it to me, and I will deliver you." Take heed then, believer, that you have a faithful messenger. And what messenger can you employ so excellent as true, real, earnest prayer? But, take heed that it be real prayer, for if your messenger miscarry, and the promise is not brought to God's eye, who knows, you may never obtain the blessing. Draw near to God with living, loving prayer; present the promise, and you shall obtain the fulfillment.

Many things might I say of prayer; our old divines are full of glowing praise concerning it. The early fathers speak of it as if they were writing sonnets. Chrysostom [John Chrysostom (347–407), archbishop of Constantinople] preached of it as if he saw it incarnate in some heavenly form. And the choicest metaphors were gathered together to describe in rapturous phrase the power, nay, the omnipotence of prayer.

Would to God that we loved prayer as our fathers did of old. It is said of James the Less, that he was so much in prayer that his knees had become hard and knobby like those of a camel. It was doubtless but a legend, but legends often are based on truths. And certain it is that Hugh Latimer, that blessed saint and martyr of our God, was accustomed to pray so earnestly in his old age when he was in his cell, that he would often pray until he had no strength left to use, and the prison attendants had to lift him from his knees. Where are the men like these? Oh, angels of the covenant, where can you find them? When the Son of Man comes shall He find prayer on the Earth? Ours are not worthy of the name of supplication. Oh, that we had learned that saved art, that we could draw near to God and plead His promise.

Watts has put several things together in one verse.

Prayer clears the sky: "Prayer makes the darkened cloud withdraw."

Prayer is a heaven climber: "Prayer climbs the ladder Jacob saw."

Prayer makes even Satan quake: "For Satan trembles when he sees,

The weakest saint upon his knees."

– Isaac Watts

I have thus given you three reasons why we should be diligent in prayer. Let me add yet another, for we must not leave this part of the whetstone until we have thoroughly entered into the reasons why "it is good for us to draw near unto God." Let me remark that prayer has a mighty power to sustain the soul in every season of its distress and sorrow. Whenever the soul becomes weak, use the heavenly strengthening plaster of prayer. It was in prayer that the angel appeared unto the Lord and strengthened Him. That angel has appeared to many of us, and we have not forgotten the strength we received when on our knees. You remember in the ancient mythology the story of him who as often as he was thrown down, recovered strength because he touched his mother Earth. It is so with the believer. As often as he is thrown down upon his knees he recovers himself, for he touches the great source of his strength—the mercy seat. If you have a burden on your back, remember prayer, for you shall carry it well if you can pray.

Once on a time Christian had upon his back a terrible burden that crushed him to the ground, so that he could not carry it; he crept along on his hands and knees. There appeared to him a fair and comely damsel, holding in her hand a wand, and she touched the burden. It was there; it was not removed, but strange to say, the burden became weightless. It was there in all its outward shape and features, but without weight. That which had crushed him to the ground, had become now so light that he could leap and carry it. Beloved, do you understand this? Have you gone to God with mountains of troubles on your shoulders, unable to carry them, and have you seen them, not removed, but still remaining in the same shape, but of a different weight? They became blessings instead of curses; what you thought was an iron cross suddenly turned out to be a wooden one, and you carried it with joy, following your Master.

I will give but one other reason, lest I should weary you, and that certainly is not my desire, but to quicken you rather than to weary you. Beloved, there is one reason why we should pray, those of us who are engaged in the Lord's work in any way, because it is prayer that will ensure success. Two laborers in God's harvest met each other once upon a time, and they sat down to compare notes. One was a man of sorrowful spirit, and the other joyous, for God had given him the desire of his heart. The sad brother said, "Friend, I cannot understand how it is that everything you do is sure to prosper: You scatter seed with both your hands very diligently, and it springs up, and so rapidly too, that the reaper treads upon the heels of the sower, and the sower himself again upon the heels of the next reaper. I have sown," said he, "as you have done, and I think I can say I have been just as diligent; I think too the soil has been the same, for we have labored side by side in the same town. I hope the seed has been of the same quality, for I have found mine where you get yours—the common granary. But alas, my seed, friend, never springs up. I sow it. It is as if I sowed upon the waves, for I never see a harvest. Here and there a sickly blade of wheat I have discovered with great and diligent search, but I can see but little reward for all my labors." They talked long together, for the brother who was successful was one of a tender heart, and, therefore, he sought to comfort this mourning brother. They compared notes, they looked through all the rules of husbandry, and they could not solve the mystery, why one was successful and the other labored in vain. At last one said to the other, "I must retire."

"Wherefore?" said the other.

"Why, this is the time," said he, "when I must go and steep my seed."

"Steep your seed?" said the other.

"Yes, my brother, I always steep my seed before I sow it. I steep it till it begins to swell and germinate, and I can almost see a green blade springing from it, and then you know it speedily grows after it is sown."

"Ah," said the other, "but I understand not what you mean. How do you steep your seed, and in what mysterious mixture?"

"Brother," said he, "it is a composition made of one part of the tears of agony for the souls of men, and the other part of the tears of a holy agony that wrestles with God in prayer. This mixture if you drop your seed in it, has a transcendent efficacy to make every grain full of life, so that it is not lost."

The other rose and went on his way, and forgot not what he had learned, but he began to steep his seed too; he spent less time in his study, more time in his closet; he was less abroad, more at home, less with man, and more with God. And he went abroad and scattered his seed, and he too, saw a harvest, and the Lord was glorified in them both.

Brethren, I do feel with regard to myself, and therefore, when I speak of others I speak not uncharitably, that the reason of the nonsuccess of the ministry in these years (for compared with the Day of Pentecost, I cannot call our success a success) lies in our want of prayer. If I were addressing students in the college, I think I should venture to say to them, set prayer first in your labors; let your subject be well prepared; think well of your discourse, but best of all, pray over it, study on your knees. And now in speaking to this assembly, containing Sabbath-school teachers and others who in their way are laboring for Christ, let me beseech you whatever you do, go not about your work except you have first entreated that the dew of Heaven may drop on the seed you sow. Steep your seed and it shall spring up. We are demanding in our days more laborers—it is a right prayer; we are seeking that the seed should be of the best sort—it is a right demand, but let us not forget another that is even more necessary than this, let us ask, let us plead with God, that the seed be steeped, that men may preach agonizing for souls. I like to preach with a burden on my heart—the burden of other men's sins, the burden of other men's hard-heartedness, the burden of their unbelief, the burden of their desperate estate, which must before long end in perdition. There is no preaching, I am persuaded, like that, for then we preach as though, "We never might preach again, as dying men to dying men."

And, oh, may each of you labor after the latter fashion in your own sphere, ever taking care to commit your work to God. I will tell you here an incident of the revival. It is one I know to be correct. It is told by a good brother who would not add a word thereunto, I am sure. It happened, not long ago, that in a school that is sustained by the Corporation of the City of London, in the north of Ireland, one of the bigger boys had been converted to God; and one day, in the midst of school, a younger youth was greatly oppressed by a sense of sin, and so overwhelmed did he become that the master plainly perceived that he could not work, and, therefore, he said to him, "You had better go home, and plead with God in prayer in private." He said, however, to the bigger boy, who was all rejoicing in hope, "Go with him; take him home and pray with him." They started together: on the road they saw an empty house; the two boys went in and there began to pray; the plaintive cry of the young one, after a little time changed into a note of joy, when, suddenly springing up, he said, "I have found rest in Jesus, I have never felt as I do now; my sins, which are many, are all forgiven." The proposal was to go home; but the younger lad forbade this. No, he must go and tell the master of the school that he had found Christ. So hurrying back, he rushed in and said, "Oh! I have found the Lord Jesus Christ." All the boys in the school, who had seen him sitting sad and dull upon the form, remarked about the joy that flashed from his eye, when he cried, "I have Christ," The effect was electric. The boys suddenly and mysteriously disappeared; the master knew not where they were gone; but looking over into the playground, he saw by the wall a number of boys, one by one, in prayer asking for mercy. He said to the elder youth, "Cannot you go and tell these boys the way of salvation—tell them what they must do to be saved?"

He did so, and silent prayer was suddenly changed into a loud, piercing shriek—the boys in the school understood it, and, impelled by the great Spirit, they all fell on their knees, and began to cry aloud for mercy through the blood of Christ. But this was not all. There was a girls' schoolroom in the same building overhead. The ear had been well tutored to understand what that cry meant and soon interpreted it, and the girls, too, affected by the same Spirit, fell down and began to cry aloud for the forgiveness of their sins. Here was an interruption of the school! Was ever such a thing known before in a schoolroom? Classes are all put aside, books forgotten, everything cast to the winds, while poor sinners are kneeling at the foot of the Cross seeking for pardon. The cry was heard throughout the various offices attached to this large school, and it was heard also across the street, and passersby were attracted—men of God, ministers and clergymen of the neighborhood were brought in—the whole day was spent in prayer, and they continued until almost midnight; but they separated with songs of joy, for that vast mass of girls and boys, men and women, who had crowded the two schoolrooms, had all found the Savior.

Our good brother, Dr. Arthur, says that he met with a youth while travelling in Ireland, and he said to him, "Do you love the Savior?"

And he said, "I trust I do."

"How did you come to love Him?"

"Oh," said he, "I was converted in the big schoolroom that night. My mother heard that there was a revival going on there, and she sent me to fetch my little brother; she did not want him, she said, to get convinced; and I went to fetch my brother, and he was on his knees crying, 'Lord, have mercy upon me, a sinner.' I stopped and I prayed, too, and the Lord saved us both."

Now to what are we to attribute this? I know many of the brethren there—the Presbyterians and others—and I do not think there is any difference or any superiority in their ministry over anything we can see or hear in London, and I think they themselves would subscribe to the truth of what I assert. The difference is this: there has been prayer there; living, hearty prayer has been offered continually, perhaps by some who did not live in Ireland. God alone knows where that revival really began. Some woman on her bed may have been exercised in her soul for that district and may have been wrestling with God in prayer; and then the blessing descended. And if God will help you and help me to lay near to the heart of the neighborhood in which we live, the family over which we preside, the congregation we have to address, the class we have to teach, the laborers we employ, or any of these, surely then by mighty prayer we shall bring down a great blessing from high; for prayer is never lost; preaching may be, but prayer never is. Praying breath can never be spent in vain. If the Lord sends to all the churches of Great Britain the power of prayer, then shall there come conversions of multitudes of souls through the outpoured energy of the Holy One of Israel!

3. I shall have little time to close up the third point, further than to remark that while I have been preaching I do hope there have been some here who have heard for themselves. Ah, my hearers, religion is more solemn work than some men think of. I am often shocked with the brutality of what are called the lower classes of society, and with their coarse blasphemies; but there is one thing—and I speak honestly to you now, as fearing no man—there is one thing that is to me more shocking still, and that is the frivolous way in which the mass of our higher classes spend all their time. What are your morning calls but pretenses for wasting your time? What are your amusements but an attempt to kill the time that hangs laboriously on your hands? And what are many of your employments but an industrious idleness, spinning and knitting away the precious hours that God knows will be few enough when you come to look back upon them from a dying bed. Oh, if you did but know what you are made for, and your high destiny, you would not waste your time in the paltry things that occupy your hands and your souls. God Almighty forgive those wasted hours that, if you be Christians, ought to be employed for the good of others. God, forgive those moments of frivolity that ought to have been occupied in prayer. If such a congregation as this could but be solemnly alive to the interests of this land and the poverty of it, to its miseries, to its wickedness: if but such a host as I have here could solemnly feel this matter, how much good would certainly come to us! This would be the best missionary

society; so many hearts of tenderness and affection, all beating high with an eager desire to see sinners brought to Christ.

Ah, we cannot approve of the doctrines of the Roman Church, but still sometimes we have to be abashed at their zeal. Would to God that we had sisters of mercy who were merciful, indeed; not dressed in some fanciful garb, but going from house to house to comfort the sick and help the needy! Would that you all were brothers of the heart of Jesus, and all of you sisters of Him, whose mother's heart was pierced with agony, when He died that we might be saved. Oh, my dear hearers, this I speak with an earnest anxiety, that the words may be prophetic of a better age. But now, there are some of you here, perhaps, that never prayed in your lives, toying like glittering insects, wasting your little day. You know not that death is near you; and, oh, if you have never sought and have never found the Savior. However bright those eyes, if they have never seen the wounds of Christ, if they have never looked to Christ, they shall not simply be sealed in death, but they must behold sights of fearful woe eternally. Oh, may God grant you grace to pray; may He lead you home to your houses, to fall on your knees, and for the first time to cry, "Lord, have mercy upon me!" Remember, you have sins to confess, and if you think you have not, you are in a sad state of heart, it proves that you are dead in trespasses and sins—dead in them. Go home and ask the Lord to give you a new heart and a right spirit, and may He who dictates the prayer graciously hear; and may you, and I, and all of us, when this life has passed away and time is exchanged for eternity, stand before the throne of God at last. I have to preach continually to a congregation in which I know there are many drunkards, swearers, and the like—with these men I know how to deal, and God has given me success; but I sometimes tremble for you amiable, excellent, upright daughters, who make glad your father's house, and wives that train up your children well. Remember, if you have not the root of the matter in you: "Except a man be born again, he cannot see the kingdom of God" (John 3:3).

And as we must be honest with the poor, so must we be with the rich; and as we must lay the axe to the root of the tree with the drunkard and the swearer, so must we with you. You are as much lost as they are, and shall as surely perish as they do, unless you be born again. There is but one road to Heaven for you all alike. As a minister of the gospel, I know no rich men and no poor men; I know no working classes and no gentlemen; I know simply God's sinful creatures, bidden to come to Christ and find mercy through His atonement. He will not reject you. Put the black thought away. He is able to save; doubt Him not. Come to Him; come and be welcome. God help you to come.

God Almighty bless you for Jesus' sake. Amen.

PAUL'S FIRST PRAYER

"For behold he prayeth." (Acts 9:11)

God has many methods of quenching persecution. He will not suffer His Church to be injured by its enemies or overwhelmed by its foes; and He is not short of means for turning aside the way of the wicked, or of turning it upside down. In two ways He usually accomplishes His end; sometimes by the confusion of the persecutor, and at others in a more blessed manner, by His conversions. Sometimes, He confuses and confounds His enemies; He makes the diviner mad; He lets the man who comes against Him be utterly destroyed, allows him to drive on to his own destruction, and then at last turns round in triumphant derision upon the man who hoped to have said aha! aha! to the Church of God. But at other times, as in this case, He converts the persecutor. Thus, He transforms the foe into a friend; He makes the man who was a warrior against the gospel a soldier for it. Out of darkness He brings forth light; out of the eater He gets honey; yea, out of stony hearts He raises up children unto Abraham.

Such was the case with Saul. A more furious bigot it is impossible to conceive. He had been bespattered with the blood of Stephen, when they stoned him to death; so officious was Saul in his cruelty, that the men left their clothes in his charge. Living at Jerusalem, in the college of Gamaliel, he constantly came in contact with the disciples of the man of Nazareth; he laughed at them, he reviled them as they passed along the street; he procured enactments against them and put them to death; and now, as a crowning point, this werewolf, having tasted blood, becomes exceeding mad, determines to go to Damascus, that he may glut himself with the gore of men and women; that he may bind the Christians, and bring them to Jerusalem, there to suffer what he considered to be a just punishment for their heresy and departure from their ancient religion. But, oh, how marvelous was the power of God! Jesus stays this man in his mad career; just as with his lance in rest he was dashing against Christ. Christ met him, unhorsed him, threw him on the ground, and questioned him, "Saul, Saul, why persecutest thou me?" (Acts 9:4). He then graciously removed his rebellious heart—gave him a new heart and a right spirit—turned his aim and object—led him to Damascus—laid him prostrate for three days and nights—spoke to him—made mystic sounds go murmuring through his ears—set his whole soul on fire; and when at last he started up from that three-day trance, and began to pray, then it was that Jesus from Heaven descended, came in a vision to Ananias, and said, "Arise, and go into the street which is called Straight, and inquire in the house of Judas for one called Saul of Tarsus; for, behold, he prayeth."

First, our text was an announcement; "Behold, he prayeth." Second, it was an argument; "For, behold, he prayeth." Then, to conclude, we will try to make an application of our text to your hearts. Though application is the work of God alone, we will trust that He will be pleased to make that application while the Word is preached this morning.

First, here was an announcement; "Go to the house of Saul of Tarsus; for behold, he prayeth." Without any preface, let me say, that this was the announcement of a fact that was noticed in Heaven; that was joyous to the angels; that was astonishing to Ananias, and that was a novelty to Saul himself.

It was the announcement of *an effect that was noticed in Heaven*. Poor Saul had been led to cry for mercy, and the moment he began to pray, God began to hear. Do you not notice, in reading the chapter, what attention God paid to Saul? He knew the street where he lived; "Go to the street that is called *Straight*." He knew the house where he resided; "*Inquire at the house of Judas.* " He knew his name; it was *Saul*. He knew the place where he came from; "Inquire for Saul of *Tarsus*." And He knew that he had prayed.

"Behold, *he prayeth*." Oh, it is a glorious fact that prayers are noticed in Heaven. The poor, broken-hearted sinner, climbing up to his bedroom, bends his knee, but can only utter his wailing in the language of sighs and tears. Lo! that groan has made all the harps of Heaven thrill with music; that tear has been caught by God, and put into the lachrymatory [tear bottle] of heaven, to be perpetually preserved. The suppliant, whose fears prevent his words, will be well understood by the Most High. He may only shed one hasty tear, but "prayer is the falling of a tear." Tears are the diamonds of Heaven; sighs are a part of the music of Jehovah's throne; for though prayers be "the simplest form of speech that infant lips can try," so are they likewise the "sublimest strains that reach the majesty on high."

Let me expand on this thought a moment. Prayers are noticed in Heaven. Oh! I know what is the case with many of you. You think, "If I turn to God, if I seek Him, surely I am so inconsiderable a being, so guilty and vile, that it cannot be imagined He would take any notice of me." My friends, harbor no such heathenish ideas. Our God is not a god who sits in one perpetual dream; nor does He clothe himself in such thick darkness that He cannot see; He is not like Baal who hears not. True, He may not regard battles; He cares not for the pomp and pageantry of kings; He listens not to the swell of martial music; He regards not the triumph and the pride of man; but wherever there is a heart big with sorrow, wherever there is an eye suffused with tears, wherever there is a lip quivering with agony, wherever there is a deep groan, or a penitential sigh, the ear of Jehovah is wide open; He marks it down in the registry of His memory; He puts our prayers, like rose leaves, between the pages of His book of remembrance, and when the volume is opened at last, there shall be a precious fragrance springing up. Oh, poor sinner, of the blackest and vilest character, your prayers are heard, and even now God has said of you, "Behold, he prayeth." Where was it? In a barn? Where was it? In the closet? Was it at your bedside this morning, or in this hall ? Are you now turning your eye to Heaven? Speak, poor heart; did I hear your lips just now mutter, "God, have mercy upon me, a sinner?" I tell you, sinner, there is one thing that does outstrip the telegraph. You know, we can now send a message and receive an answer in a few moments, but I read of something in the Bible more swift than an electric current: "Before they call I will answer, and while they are speaking I will hear." So, then, poor sinner, you are noticed; yes, you are heard by Him who sits on the throne.

Again, this was the announcement of a *fact joyous to Heaven*. Our text is prefaced with "Behold," for doubtless, our Savior himself regarded it with joy. Once only do we read of a smile resting upon the countenance of Jesus, when, lifting up His eyes to Heaven, He exclaimed, "I thank thee, O Father, Lord of Heaven and Earth, because thou hast hid these things from the wise and prudent, and hast revealed them unto babes: even so, Father; for so it seemed good in thy sight" (Luke 10:21). The Shepherd of our souls rejoices in the vision of His sheep securely folded; He triumphs in spirit when He brings a wanderer home. I conceive that when He spoke these words to Ananias, one of the smiles of Paradise must have shone from His eyes. "Behold," I have won the heart of my enemy; I have saved my persecutor; even now he is bending the knee at my footstool, "Behold, he prayeth."

Jesus himself led the song, rejoicing over the new convert with singing. Jesus Christ was glad, and rejoiced more over that lost sheep than over ninety and nine that went not astray. And angels rejoiced, too. Why? When one of God's elect is born, angels stand around his cradle. He grows up, and runs into sin. Angels follow him, tracking him all his way. They gaze with sorrow upon his many wanderings. The fair Peri drops a tear whenever that loved one sins. Presently the man is brought under the sound of the gospel. The angel says, "Behold, he begins to hear." He waits a little while, the Word sinks into his heart, a tear runs down his cheek, and at last he cries from his inmost soul, "God, have mercy upon me! "See! The angel claps his wings; up he flies to Heaven, and says, "Brethren angels, listen to me, "Behold, he prays." Then they set Heaven's bells ringing; they have a jubilee in glory; again they shout with gladsome voices, for truly I tell you, "There is joy in the presence of the angels of God over one sinner that repenteth" (Luke 15:10). They watch us till we pray, and when we pray, they say, "Behold, he prays."

Moreover, my dear friends, there may be other spirits in Heaven that rejoice besides the angels. Those persons are our friends who have gone before us. I have not many relations in Heaven, but I have one whom I dearly love, who, I doubt not, often prayed for me, for she nursed me when I was a child and brought me up during part of my infancy, and now she sits before the throne in glory—suddenly snatched away. I fancy she looked upon her darling grandson, and as she saw him in the ways of sin, vice, and folly, she could not look with sorrow, for there are no tears in the eyes of glorified ones; she could not look with regret, because they cannot know such a feeling before the throne of God, but, ah, that moment when, by sovereign grace, I was constrained to pray, when all alone I bent my knee and wrestled, methinks I see her as she said, "Behold, he prays; behold, he prays." Oh! I can picture her countenance. She seemed to have two Heavens for a moment, a double bliss, a Heaven in me as well as in herself—when she could say, "Behold, he prays."

Ah, young man, there is your mother walking the golden streets. She is looking down upon you this hour. She nursed you; on her breast you lay when but a child, and she consecrated you to Jesus Christ. From Heaven, she has been watching on with that intense anxiety that is compatible with happiness; this morning she is looking upon you. What do you say, young man? Does Christ by His Spirit say in your heart, "Come unto me?" Do you drop a tear of repentance? I think I see your mother as she cries, "Behold, he prays." Once more she bends before the throne of God and says, "I thank you, ever gracious One, that he who was my child on Earth, has now become Your child in light."

211

But, if there is one in Heaven who has more joy than another over the conversion of a sinner, it is a minister, one of God's true ministers. O my hearers, you little think how God's true ministers do love your souls. Perhaps you think it is easy work to stand here and preach to you. God knows, if that was all, it would be easy work; but when we think that when we speak to you, your salvation or damnation, in some measure, depends upon what we say—when we reflect that if we are unfaithful watchmen, your blood will God require at our hands—O good God, when I reflect that I have preached to thousands in my lifetime, many thousands, and have perhaps said many things I ought not to have said, it startles me, it makes me shake and tremble.

Martin Luther said he could face his enemies, but could not go up his pulpit stairs without his knees knocking together. Preaching is not child's play; it is not a thing to be done without labor and anxiety; it is solemn work; it is awful work, if you view it in its relation to eternity. Ah, how God's minister prays for you! If you might have listened under the eaves of his chamber window, you would have heard him groaning every Sunday night over his sermons because he had not spoken with more effect; you would have heard him pleading with God, "Who has believed our report? To whom is the arm of the Lord revealed?" Ah, when he observes you from his rest in Heaven—when he sees you praying, how will he clap his hands and say, "Behold the child you have given me! behold, he prays!"

I am sure when we see one brought to know the Lord, we feel very much like one who has saved a fellow-creature from being drowned. There is a poor man in the flood; he is going down, he is sinking, he must be drowned; but I spring in, grasp him firmly, lift him up on the shore, and lay him on the ground; the physician comes; he looks at him, he puts his hand upon him, and says, "I am afraid he is dead." We apply all the means in our power, we do what we can to restore life. I feel that I have been that man's deliverer, and, oh, how I stoop down and put my ear beside his mouth! At last I say, "He breathes! He breathes!" What pleasure there is in that thought! He breathes; there is life still. So when we find a man praying, we shout—he breathes; he is not dead, he is alive; for while a man prays he is not dead in trespasses and sins, but is brought to life, is quickened by the power of the Spirit. "Behold, he prays." This was joyful news in Heaven, as well as being noticed by God.

Then, in the next place, this was *an event most astonishing to men*. Ananias lifted up both his hands in amazement. "O my Lord, I should have thought anybody would pray but that man! Is it possible?" I do not know how it is with other ministers, but sometimes I look upon such-and-such individuals in the congregation, and I say, "Well, they are very hopeful; I think I shall have them. I trust there is a work going on, and hope soon to hear them tell what the Lord has done for their souls." Soon, perhaps, I see nothing of them, and miss them altogether; but instead thereof, my good Master sends me one of whom I had no hope—an outcast, a drunkard, a reprobate, to the praise of the glory of His grace. Then I lift up my hands in astonishment, thinking "I should have thought of anybody rather than you."

I remember a circumstance that occurred a little while ago. There was a poor man who was about sixty years old; he had been a rough sailor, one of the worst men in the village; it was his custom to drink, and he seemed to be delighted when he was cursing and swearing. He came into the chapel, however, one Sabbath day, when one nearly related to me was preaching from the text concerning Jesus weeping over Jerusalem. And the poor man thought, "What! did Jesus Christ ever weep over such a wretch as I am?" He thought he was too bad for Christ to care for him. At last he came to the minister, and said, "Sir, sixty years have I been sailing under the standard of the devil; it is time I should have a new owner; I want to scuttle the old ship and sink her altogether! Then I shall have a new one, and I shall sail under the colors of Prince Immanuel." Ever since that moment that man has been a praying character, walking before God in all sincerity. Yet, he was the very last man you would have thought of.

Somehow God does choose the last men; He does not care for the diamond, but He picks up the pebble stones, for He is able, out of "stones, to raise up children unto Abraham." God is wiser than the chemist: He not only refines gold, but He transmutes base metal into precious jewels; He takes the filthiest and the vilest, and fashions them into glorious beings, makes them saints, whereas they have been sinners and sanctifies them, whereas they have been unholy.

The conversion of Saul was a strange thing; but, beloved, was it stranger than that you and I should have been Christians? Let me ask you if anybody had told you, a few years ago, that you would belong to a church and be numbered with the children of God, what would you have said? "Stuff and nonsense! I am not one of your canting Methodists ; I am not going to have any religion; I love to think and do as I like." Did not you and I say so? Then how on Earth did we get here? When we look at the change that has passed over us, it appears like a dream. God has left many in our families who were better than we were, and why has He chosen us? Oh, is it not strange? Might we not lift up our hands in astonishment, as Ananias did, and say, "Behold, behold, behold: it is a miracle on Earth, a wonder in Heaven?"

The last thing I have to say here, is this—this fact was a novelty to Saul himself. "Behold, he prayeth." What is there novel in that? Saul used to go up to the Temple twice a day, at the hour of prayer. If you could have accompanied him, you would have heard him speak beautifully, in words like these: "Lord, I thank you I am not as other men are; I am not an extortioner, nor a publican; I fast twice in the week, and give tithes of all I possess" and so on. Oh, you might have found him pouring out a fine oration before the throne of God. And yet it says, "Behold, he prayeth." What! had he never prayed before? No, never. All he had ever done before went for nothing; it was not prayer.

I have heard of an old gentleman, who was taught when he was a child to pray, "Pray, God, bless my father and mother," and he kept on praying the same thing for seventy years, when his parents were both dead. After that it pleased God, in His infinite mercy, to touch his heart, and he was led to see that notwithstanding his constancy to his forms, he had not been praying at all; he often said his prayers, but never prayed.

So it was with Saul. He had pronounced his magniloquent orations, but they were all good for nothing. He had prayed his long prayers for a pretense; it had all been a failure. Now comes a true petition, and it is said by the Lord, "Behold, he prayeth."

See a man trying to obtain a hearing from his Maker. How he stands! He speaks Latin and blank verse before the

215

Almighty's throne; but God sits in calm indifference, paying no attention. Then the man tries a different style; he procures a book, and bending his knee again, prays in a delightful form the best old prayer that could ever be put together; but the Most High disregards his empty formalities. At last the poor creature throws the book away, forgets his blank verse and formalities, and says, "O Lord, hear, for Christ's sake."

"Hear him," says God, "I have heard him." There is the mercy you have sought. One hearty prayer is better than ten thousand forms. One prayer coming from the soul is better than a myriad of cold readings. As for prayers that spring from the mouth and head only, God abhors them; he loves those that come deep from the heart. Perhaps I should be impudent if I were to say that there are hundreds here this morning who never prayed once in their lives. There are some of you who never did. There is one young man over there, who told his parents when he left them, that he should always go through his form of prayer every morning and night. But he is ashamed, and he has left it off. Well, young man, what will you do when you come to die? Will you have "the watchword at the gates of death?" Will you "enter Heaven by prayer?" No, you will not; you will be driven from His presence, and be cast away.

Second, we have here *an argument*. "For, behold, he prayeth." It was an argument, first of all, *for Ananias' safety*. Poor Ananias was afraid to go to Saul; he thought it was very much like stepping into a lion's den. "If I go to his house," he thought, the moment he sees me, he will take me to Jerusalem at once, for I am one of Christ's disciples; I dare not go."

But God says, "Behold, he prayeth."

"Well," says Ananias, "that is enough for me. If he is a praying man, he will not hurt me; if he is a man of real devotion, I am safe."

Be sure that you may always trust a praying man. I do not know how it is, but even ungodly men always pay a reverence to a sincere Christian. A master likes to have a praying servant, after all. If he does not regard religion himself, he likes to have a pious servant, and he will trust him rather than any other. True, there are some of your professedly praying people that have not a bit of prayer in them. But whenever you find a really praying man, trust him with untold gold; for if he really prays, you need not be afraid of him. He who communes with God in secret, may be trusted in public. I always feel safe with a man who is a visitor at the mercy seat.

I have heard an anecdote of two gentlemen traveling together, somewhere in Switzerland. Presently they came into the midst of the forests; and you know the gloomy tales the people tell about the inns there, how dangerous it is to lodge in them. One of them, an infidel, said to the other, who was a Christian, I don't like stopping here at all; it is very dangerous indeed."

"Well," said the other, "let us try." So they went into a house: but it looked so suspicious that neither of them liked it; and they thought they would prefer being at home in England.

Presently the landlord said, "Gentlemen, I always read and pray with my family before going to bed; will you allow me to do so tonight?"

"Yes," they said, "with the greatest pleasure."

When they went upstairs, the infidel said, "I am not at all afraid now."

"Why?" asked the Christian.

"Because our host has prayed," the infidel replied.

"Oh!" said the Christian, "then it seems, after all, you think something of religion; because a man prays, you can go to sleep in his house."

And it was marvelous how both of them did sleep. Sweet dreams they had, for they felt that where the house had been roofed by prayer, and walled with devotion, there could not be found a man living that would commit an injury to them. This, then, was an argument to Ananias, that he might go with safety to Saul's house.

But more than this. Here was *an argument for Paul's sincerity*. Secret prayer is one of the best tests of sincere religion. If Jesus had said to Ananias, "Behold, he preacheth," Ananias could have said, "That he may do, and yet be a deceiver." If He had said, "He has gone to a meeting of the church," Ananias could have said, "He may enter there as a wolf in sheep's clothing." But when He said, "Behold, he prayeth" that was argument enough.

A young person comes and tells me about what he has felt and what he has been doing. At last I say, "Kneel down and pray."

"I would much rather not."

"Never mind, you shall." Down he falls on his knees; he has hardly a word to say; he begins groaning and crying, and there he stays on his knees till at last he stammers out, "'Lord, have mercy upon me a sinner; I am the greatest of sinners; have mercy upon me!"

Then I am a little more satisfied, and I say, "I did not mind all your talk; I wanted your prayers." But oh, if I could trace him home; if I could see him go and pray alone, then I should feel sure; for he who prays in private is a real Christian. The mere reading of a book of daily devotion will not prove you a child of God; if you pray in private, then you have a sincere religion; and a little religion, if sincere, is better than mountains of pretense. Home piety is the best piety. Praying will make you leave off sinning, or sinning will make you leave off praying. Prayer in the heart proves the reality of conversion. A man may be sincere, but sincerely wrong. Paul was sincerely right. "Behold, he prayeth," was the best argument that his religion was right. If any one should ask me for an epitome of the Christian religion, I should say it is in that one word—"prayer." If I should be asked, "What will take in the whole of Christian experience?' I should answer, "Prayer." A man must have been convinced of sin before he could pray; he must have had some hope that there was mercy for him before he could pray. In fact, all the Christian virtues are locked up in that word, "prayer." Do but tell me you are a man of prayer, and I will reply at once, "Sir, I have no doubt of the reality, as well as the sincerity of your religion."

But one more thought, and I will leave this subject. *It was a proof of this man's election*, for you read directly afterwards, "for he is a chosen vessel" (Acts 9:15). I often find people troubling themselves about the doctrine of election. Every now and then I get a letter from somebody taking me to task for preaching election. All the answer I can give is, "There it is in the Bible; go and ask my Master why He put it there. I cannot help it. I am only a serving man, and I tell you the message from above. If I were footman, I should not alter my master's message at the door. I happen to be an ambassador of Heaven, and I dare not alter the message I have received. If it is wrong, send up to headquarters. There it is, and I cannot alter it."

This much let me say in explanation. Some say, "How can I discover whether I am God's elect? I am afraid I am not God's elect."

Do you pray? If it can be said, "Behold, he prayeth," it can also be said, "He is a chosen vessel." Do you have faith? If so, you are elect. Those are the marks of election.

If you have none of those, you have no grounds for concluding that you belong to the peculiar people of God. Have you a desire to believe? Have you a wish to love Christ? Have you the millionth part of a desire to come to Christ? And is it a practical desire? Does it lead you to offer earnest, tearful supplication? If so, never be afraid of non-election; for whoever prays with sincerity is ordained of God before the foundation of the world, that he "should be holy and without blame before him in love" (Ephesians 1:4).

Third; now for the application. A word or two with you, my dear friends, before I send you away this morning. I regret that I cannot better enter into the subject, but my glorious Master requires of each of us according to what we have, not according to what we have not. I am deeply conscious that I fail in urging home the truth so solemnly as I ought; nevertheless, "My work is with God and my judgment with my God," and the last day shall reveal that my error lay in judgment, but not in sincere affection for souls.

First, allow me to address the children of God. Do you not see, my dear brethren, that the best mark of our being sons of God is to be found in our devotion?

"Behold, he prayeth." Well, then, does it not follow, as a natural consequence, that the more we are found in prayer the brighter will our evidences be. Perhaps you have lost your evidence this morning; you do not know whether you are a child of God or not; I will tell you where you lost your confidence—you lost it in your closet. Whenever a Christian backslides, his wandering commences in his closet. I speak what I have felt. I have often gone back from God—never so as to fall finally, I know, but I have often lost that sweet savor of His love which I once enjoyed. I have had to cry:

Those peaceful hours I once enjoyed,

How sweet their memory still

But they have left an aching void,

The world can never fill.

I have gone up to God's house to preach, without either fire or energy; I have read the Bible, and there has been no light upon it; I have tried to have communion with God, but all has been a failure. Shall I tell where that commenced? It commenced in my closet. I had ceased in a measure to pray. Here I stand, and do confess my faults; I do acknowledge that whenever I depart from God it is there it begins. O Christians, would you be happy? Be much in prayer. Would you be victorious? Be much in prayer.

Restraining prayer, we cease to fight,

Prayer makes the Christian's armor bright.

Mrs. Berry used to say, "I would not be hired out of my closet for a thousand worlds." Mr. Jay said, "If the twelve apostles were living near you, and you had access to them, if this intercourse drew you from the closet, they would prove a real injury to your souls."

Prayer is the ship that brings home the richest freight. It is the soil that yields the most abundant harvest. Brother, when you rise in the morning your business so presses, that with a hurried word or two, down you go into the world, and at night, jaded and tired, you give God the frayed end of the day. The consequence is that you have no communion with Him. The reason we have not more true religion now is because we have not more prayer. Sirs, I have no opinion of the churches of the present day that do not pray. I go from chapel to chapel in this metropolis, and I see pretty good congregations, but I go to their prayer meetings on a week evening, and I see a dozen persons. Can God bless us, can He pour out His Spirit upon us, while such things as these exist? He could, but it would not be according to the order of His dispensations, for He says, "When Zion travails she brings forth children."

Go to your churches and chapels with this thought, that you want more prayer. Many of you have no business here this morning. You ought to be in your own places of worship. I do not want to steal away the people from other chapels; there are enough to hear me without them. But though you have sinned this morning, hear while you are here, as much to your profit as possible. Go home and say to your minister, "Sir, we must have more prayer." Urge the people to more prayer. have a prayer meeting, even if you have it all to yourself; and if you are asked how many were present, you can say, "Four."

"Four! how so?"

"Why, there was myself, and God the Father, God the Son, and God the Holy Ghost; and we have had a rich and real communion together."

We must have an outpouring of real devotion, or else what is to become of many of our churches? O, may God awaken us all, and stir us up to pray, for when we pray we shall be victorious.

I should like to take you this morning, and as Samson did with the foxes, tie the firebrands of prayer to you, and send you in among the shocks of corn till you burn the whole up. I should like to make a conflagration by my words, and to set all the churches on fire, till the whole has smoked like a sacrifice to God's throne.

If you pray, you have a proof that you are a Christian; the less you pray, the less reason have you to believe your Christianity; and if you have neglected to pray altogether, then you have ceased to breathe, and you may be afraid that you never did breathe at all.

And now, my last word is to the ungodly. O sirs! I could gladly wish myself anywhere but here; for if it be solemn work to address the godly, how much more when I come to deal with you. We fear lest, on the one hand, we should so speak to you as to make you trust in your own strength; while, on the other hand, we should lull you into the sleep of sloth and security. I believe most of us feel some difficulty as to the most fit manner to preach to you—not that we doubt but that the gospel is to be preached—but our desire is so to do it, that we may win your souls. I feel like a watchman, who, while guarding a city, is oppressed with sleep. How earnestly does he strive to arouse himself, while infirmity would overcome him. The remembrance of his responsibility bestirs him. His is no lack of *will*, but of power; and so I hope all the watchmen of the Lord are eager to be faithful, while, at the same time, they know their imperfection. Truly, the minister of Christ will feel like the old keeper of Eddystone lighthouse; life was failing fast, but, summoning all his strength, he crept round once more to trim the lights before he died.

O may the Holy Spirit enable us to keep the beacon fire blazing, to warn you of the rocks, shoals, and quicksands that surround you, and may He ever guide you to Jesus, and not to freewill or creature merit. If my friends knew how anxiously I have sought divine direction in the important matter of preaching to sinners, they would not feel as some of them do, when they fancy I address them wrongly.

I want to do as God bids me, and if He tells me to speak to the dry bones and they shall live, I must do it, even if it does not please others. Otherwise, I should be condemned in my own conscience and condemned of God. Now, with all the solemnity that man can summon, let me say that a prayerless soul is a Christless soul. As the Lord liveth, you who never prayed are without Christ, without hope, and "aliens from the commonwealth of Israel" (Ephesians 2:12). You who never know what a groan or a falling tear are, are destitute of vital godliness. Let me ask you, sirs, whether you have ever thought in what an awful state you are? You are far from God, and, therefore, God is angry with you, for "God is angry with the wicked every day" (Psalm 7:11). O sinner, lift your eyes and behold the frowning countenance of God, for He is angry with you. And I beseech you, as you love yourself, just for one moment contemplate what will become of you, if living as you are, you should at last die without prayer.

Don't think that one prayer on your deathbed will save you. Deathbed prayer is a deathbed farce generally, and passes for nothing; it is a coin that will not ring in Heaven, but is stamped by hypocrisy and made of base metal. Take heed, sirs. Let me ask you, if you have never prayed, what will you do? It were a good thing for you if death were an eternal sleep; but it is not. If you find yourself in hell, oh, the racks and pains! But I will not harrow up your feelings by attempting to describe them. May God grant that you may never feel the torments of the lost. Only conceive that poor wretch in the flames who is saying, "O for one drop of water, to cool my parched tongue!" See how his tongue hangs from between his blistered lips! how it excoriates and burns the roof of his mouth, as if it were a firebrand. Behold him crying for a drop of water. I will not picture the scene. Suffice it for me to close up by saying, that the hell of hells will be to you, poor sinner, the thought that it is to be forever. You will look up there on the throne of God, and it shall be written, "Forever!" When the damned jingle the burning irons of their torments, they shall say, "Forever!" When they howl, the echo cries, "Forever!"

> "Forever" is written on their racks,
>
> "Forever" on their chains;
>
> "Forever" burneth in the fire,

"Forever" ever reigns.

Doleful thought! "If I could but get out, then I should be happy. If there were a hope of deliverance, then I might be peaceful; but I am here forever!" Sirs, if you would escape eternal torments, if you would be found among the numbers of the blessed, the road to Heaven can only be found by prayer—by prayer to Jesus, by prayer for the Spirit, by supplication at His mercy seat. "Say unto them, As I live, saith the Lord GOD, I have no pleasure in the death of the wicked; but that the wicked turn from his way and live: turn ye, turn ye from your evil ways; for why will ye die, O house of Israel?" (Ezekiel 33:11). "The LORD is gracious, and full of compassion" (Psalm 145:8).

Let us go unto Him and say, "He shall heal our backslidings, He shall love us freely and forgive us graciously, for His Son's name's sake." Oh, if I may but win one soul today, I will go home contented. If I may but gain twenty, then I will rejoice. The more I have, the more crowns I shall wear. Wear! No, I will take them all at once, and cast them at Jesus' feet, and say, "Not unto me, but unto thy name be all the glory, forever."

Prayer was appointed to convey

The blessings God designs to give;

Long as they live, should Christians pray,

For only while they pray, they live.

And wilt thou still in silence lie,

When Christ stands waiting for thy prayer ?
My soul, thou hast a friend on high,
Arise, and try thine interest there.

'Tis prayer supports the soul that's weak,
Though thought be broken, language lame;
Pray, if thou canst, or canst not speak,
And pray with faith in Jesus' name.

PRAYER AT THE THRONE OF GRACE

"The throne of grace" (Hebrews 4:16).

These words are found embedded in that gracious verse, "Let us therefore come boldly unto the throne of grace, that we may obtain mercy, and find grace to help in time of need;" they are a gem in a golden setting. True prayer is an approach of the soul by the Spirit of God to the throne of God. It is not the utterance of words, it is not alone the feeling of desires, but it is the advance of the desires to God, the spiritual approach of our nature towards the Lord our God. True prayer is not a mere mental exercise, nor a vocal performance, but it is deeper far than that—it is spiritual commerce with the Creator of Heaven and Earth. God is a Spirit unseen of mortal eye, and only to be perceived by the inner man. Our spirit within us, begotten by the Holy Ghost at our regeneration, discerns God, communes with Him, prefers to Him its requests, and receives from Him answers of peace. It is a spiritual business from beginning to end, and its aim and object end not with man but reach to God himself.

For such prayer, the work of the Holy Ghost himself is needed. If prayer were of the lips alone, we should only need breathe in our nostrils to pray. If prayer were of the desires alone, many excellent desires are easily felt, even by natural men. But when it is the spiritual desire, and the spiritual fellowship of the human spirit with God, then the Holy Ghost himself must be present all through it, to help infirmity, and give life and power, or else true prayer will never be presented. The thing offered to God will wear the name and have the form, but the inner life of prayer will be far from it. Moreover, it is clear from the collection of our text, that the interposition of the Lord Jesus Christ is essential to acceptable prayer. As prayer will not be truly prayer without the Spirit of God, so it will not be prevailing prayer without the Son of God. He, the great High Priest, must go within the veil for us; nay, through His crucified person the veil must be entirely taken away; for, until then, we are shut out from the living God. The man who, despite the teaching of Scripture, tries to pray without a Savior insults the deity; and he who imagines that his own natural desires, coming up before God, not sprinkled with the precious blood, will be an acceptable offering before God, makes a mistake. He has not brought an offering that God can accept, any more than if he offered an unclean sacrifice. Prayer wrought in us by the Spirit, presented for us by the Christ of God, becomes power before the Most High, but no way else.

In order, dear friends, that I may stir you up to prayer this morning, and that your souls may be led to come near to the throne of grace, I purpose to take these few words and handle them as God shall give me ability. You have begun to pray, God has begun to answer. This week has been a very memorable one in the history of this church. Larger numbers than ever before at one time have come forward to confess Christ—as plain an answer to the supplications of God's people, as though the hand of the Most High had been seen stretched out of Heaven, handing down to us the blessings for which we asked. Now, let us continue in prayer, yea, let us gather strength in intercession, and the more we succeed, the more earnest let us be to succeed yet more and more. Let us not be straitened in our own bowels, since we are not straitened in our God. This is a good day and a time of glad tidings, and seeing that we have the King's ear, I am most anxious that we should speak to Him for thousands of others; that they, also, in answer to our pleadings, may be brought nigh to Christ.

In order to explain the text this morning, I shall take it thus: First, here is a throne; then, secondly, here is grace; then we will put the two together, and we shall see grace on a throne; and putting them together in another order, we shall see sovereignty manifesting itself, and resplendent in grace.

1. Our text speaks of *a throne:* "the throne of grace." God is to be viewed in prayer as our Father; that is the aspect which is dearest to us; but still we are not to regard Him as though He were such as we are; for our Savior has qualified the expression "Our Father," with the words "who art in Heaven." And close at the heels of that condescending name, in order to remind us that our Father is still infinitely greater than ourselves, He has bidden us say, "Hallowed be thy name; thy kingdom come," so that our Father is still to be regarded as a King, and in prayer we come, not only to our Father's feet, but we come also to the throne of the great monarch of the universe. The mercy seat is a throne, and we must not forget this. If prayer should always be regarded by us as an entrance into the courts of the royalty of Heaven; if we are to behave ourselves as courtiers should in the presence of an illustrious majesty, then we are not at a loss to know the right spirit in which to pray. If in prayer we come to a throne, it is clear that our spirit should, in the first place,

be one of lovely reverence. It is expected that the subject in approaching the king should express homage and honor. The pride that will not own the king, the treason which rebels against the sovereign will should, if it be wise, avoid any near approach to the throne. Let pride bite the curb at a distance, let treason lurk in corners, for only lowly reverence may come before the king himself when He sits clothed in His robes of majesty. In our case, the king before whom we come is the highest of all monarchs, the King of kings, the Lord of lords. Emperors are but the shadows of His imperial power. They call themselves kings by divine right, but what divine right have they? Common sense laughs their pretensions to scorn. The Lord alone has divine right, and to Him only does the Kingdom belong. He is the blessed and only potentate. They are but nominal kings, to be set up and put down at the will of men, or the decree of providence, but He is Lord alone, the Prince of the kings of the Earth. "He sits on no precarious throne, Nor borrows leave to be."

My heart, be sure that you prostrate yourself in such a presence. If He be so great, place your mouth in the dust before Him, for He is the most powerful of all kings; His throne has sway in all worlds; Heaven obeys Him cheerfully, hell trembles at His frown, and Earth is constrained to yield Him homage willingly or unwillingly. His power can make or destroy. To create or to crush, either is easy enough to Him. My soul, be sure that when you draw near to the Omnipotent, who is as a consuming fire, you put your shoes from off your feet, and worship Him with lowliest humility. Besides, He is the most holy of all kings. His throne is a great white throne, unspotted and clear as crystal. "The heavens are not pure in His sight, and He charged his angels with folly" (Job 4:18). And you, a sinful creature, with what lowliness should you draw near to

Him. Familiarity there may be, but let it not be unhallowed. Boldness there should be, but let it not be impertinent. Still you are on Earth and He is in Heaven; still you are a worm of the dust, a creature crushed before the moth, and He the everlasting. Before the mountains were brought forth He was God, and if all created things should pass away again, still He is the same. My brethren, I am afraid we do not bow as we should before the eternal majesty; but, henceforth, let us ask the Spirit of God to put us in a right frame, that every one of our prayers may be a reverential approach to the infinite majesty above.

A throne, therefore, in the second place, is to be approached with devout joyfulness. If I find myself favored by divine grace to stand among those favored ones who frequent His courts, shall I not feel glad? I might have been in His prison, but I am before His throne: I might have been driven from His presence forever, but I am permitted to come near to Him, even into His royal palace, and into His secret chamber of gracious audience. Shall I not then be thankful? Shall not my thankfulness ascend into joy, and shall I not feel that I am honored, that I am made the recipient of great favors when I am permitted to pray? Wherefore is your countenance sad, O suppliant, when you stand before the throne of grace? If you were before the throne of justice to be condemned for your iniquities, your hands might well be on your loins; but now you are favored to come before the King in His silken robes of love; therefore, let your face shine with sacred delight. If your sorrows be heavy, tell them unto Him, for He can lessen them; if your sins be multiplied, confess them, for He can forgive them. O you courtiers in the halls of such a monarch, be exceeding glad and mingle praises with your prayers. It is a throne, and, therefore, in the third place, whenever it is approached, it should be with complete submission. We do not pray to God to instruct Him as to what He ought to do, neither for a moment must we presume to dictate the line of the divine procedure. We are permitted to say unto God, "This and that thing, we would like to have it," but we must evermore add, "But, seeing that we are ignorant and may be mistaken—seeing that we are still in the flesh, and, therefore, may be actuated by carnal motives—not as we will, but as you will." Who shall dictate to the throne? No loyal child of God will for a moment imagine that he is to occupy the place of the King, but he bows before Him who has a right to be Lord of all; and though he utters his desire earnestly, vehemently, importunately, and pleads and pleads again, yet it is evermore with this needful reservation: "Your will be done, my Lord; and, if I ask anything that is not in accordance therewith, my inmost will is that you would be good enough to deny your servant; I will take it as a true answer if you refuse me, if I ask that which seems not good in your sight." If we constantly remembered this, I think we should be less inclined to push certain suits before the throne, for we should feel, "I am here in seeking my own ease, my own comfort, my own advantage, and, peradventure, I may be asking for that which would dishonor God; therefore, will I speak with the deepest submission to the divine decrees." But, brethren, in the fourth place, if it be a throne, it ought to be approached with enlarged expectations. Well does our hymn put it:

Thou art coming to a king:

Large petitions with thee bring.

We do not come, as it were, in prayer, only to God's treasury where He dispenses His favors to the poor, nor do we come to the back door of the house of mercy to receive the broken scraps, though that were more than we deserve; to eat the crumbs that fall from the Master's table is more than we could claim; but, when we pray, we are standing in the palace, on the glittering floor of the great King's own reception room, and thus we are placed upon a vantage ground. In prayer we stand where angels bow with veiled faces; there, even there, the cherubim and seraphim adore, before that selfsame throne to which our prayers ascend. And shall we come there with stunted requests, and narrow and contracted faith? Nay, it becomes not a King to be giving away pence and groats [crushed grain]; He distributes pieces of broad gold; He scatters not as poor men must, scraps of bread and broken meat, but He makes a feast of fat things, of fat things full of marrow, of wines on the lees well refined.

When Alexander's soldier was told to ask what he would, he did not ask in a restrained manner after the nature of his own merits, but he made such a heavy demand that the royal treasurer refused to pay it, and put the case to Alexander, and Alexander in right kingly sort replied, "He knows how great Alexander is, and he has asked as from a king; let him have what he requests." Take heed of imagining that God's thoughts are as your thoughts, and His ways as your ways. Do not bring before God stinted petitions and narrow desires, and say, "Lord, do according to these," but, remember, as high as the heavens are above the Earth, so high are His ways above your ways, and His thoughts above your thoughts, and ask, therefore, for great things, for you are before a great throne. Oh, that we always felt this when we came before the throne of grace, for then He would do for us exceeding abundantly above what we ask or even think. (See Ephesians 3:20.)

And, beloved, I may add, in the fifth place, that the right spirit in which to approach the throne of grace is that of unwavering confidence. Who shall doubt the King? Who dares impugn the imperial Word? It was well said that if integrity were banished from the hearts of all mankind, it ought still to dwell in the hearts of kings. Shame on a king if he can lie. The worst beggar in the streets is dishonored by a broken promise, but what shall we say of a king if his word cannot be depended upon? Oh, shame upon us, if we are unbelieving before the throne of the King of Heaven and Earth. With our God before us in all His glory, sitting on the throne of grace, will our hearts dare to say we mistrust Him? Shall we imagine either that He cannot, or will not, keep His promise? Banished be such blasphemous thoughts, and if they must come, let them come upon us when we are somewhere in the outskirts of His dominions, if such a place there be, but not in prayer, when we are in His immediate presence and behold Him in all the glory of His throne of grace. There, surely, is the place for the child to trust its Father, for the loyal subject to trust his monarch; and, therefore, far from it be all wavering or suspicion. Unwavering faith should be predominant before the mercy seat.

Only one other remark upon this point. If prayer means coming before the throne of God, it ought always to be conducted with the deepest sincerity, and in the spirit that makes everything real. If you are disloyal enough to despise the King, for your own sake, at least, do not mock Him to His face, and when He is upon His throne. If anywhere you dare repeat holy words without heart, let it not be in Jehovah's palace. If a person should ask for an audience with royalty, and then should say, "I scarce know why I have come, I do not know that I have anything very particular to ask; I have no very urgent suit to press," would he not be guilty both of folly and baseness? As for our great King, when we venture into His presence, let us have an errand there. As I said the other Sabbath, let us beware of playing at praying. It is insolence towards God. If I am called upon to pray in public, I must not dare to use words that are intended to please the ears of my fellow-worshippers, but I must realize that I am speaking to God himself, and that I have business to transact with the great Lord. And, in my private prayer, if, when I rise from my bed in the morning, I bow my knee and repeat certain words, or when I retire to rest at night and go through the same regular form, I rather sin than do anything that is good, unless my very soul does speak unto the Most High. Do you think that the King of Heaven is delighted to hear you pronounce words with a frivolous tongue, and a thoughtless mind? You know Him not. He is a Spirit, and they that worship Him must worship Him in spirit and in truth. If you have any empty forms to prate, go and pour them out into the ears of fools like yourself, but not before the Lord of Hosts. If you have certain words to utter, to which you attach a superstitious reverence, go and say them in the bedizened courts of the harlot Rome, but not before the glorious Lord of Zion. The spiritual God seeks spiritual worshipers, and such He will accept, and only such; but the sacrifice of the wicked is an abomination unto the Lord, and only a sincere prayer is His delight.

Beloved, the gathering up of all our remarks is just this—prayer is no trifle. It is an eminent and elevated act. It is a high and wondrous privilege. Under the old Persian Empire a few of the nobility were permitted at any time to come in unto the king, and this was thought to be the highest privilege possessed by mortals. You and I, the people of God, have a permit, a passport to come before the throne of Heaven at any time we will, and we are encouraged to come there with great boldness; but still let us not forget that it is no mean thing to be a courtier in the courts of Heaven and Earth, to worship Him who made us and sustains us in being. Truly, when we attempt to pray, we may hear the voice saying out of the excellent glory, "Bow the knee." From all the spirits that behold the face of our Father who is in Heaven, even now, I hear a voice that says, "Oh, come let us worship and bow down, let us kneel before the LORD our maker. For he is our God, and we are the people of his pasture, and the sheep of his hand.... O worship the LORD in the beauty of holiness: fear before him, all the earth" (Psalm 95:6-7, 96:9).

2. Lest the glow and brilliance of the word "throne" should be too much for mortal vision, our text now presents us with the soft, gentle, radiance of that delightful word—"grace." We are called to the throne of grace, not to the throne of law. Rocky Sinai once was the throne of law, when God came to Paran with ten thousand of His holy ones. Who desired to draw near to that throne? Even Israel might not. Bounds were set about the mount, and if but a beast touched the mount, it was stoned or thrust through with a dart. O you self-righteous ones who hope that you can obey the Law, and think that you can be saved by it, look to the flames that Moses saw, and shrink, tremble, and despair. To that throne we do not come now, for through Jesus the case is changed. To a conscience purged by the precious blood there is no anger upon the divine throne, though to our troubled minds—

Once t'was a seat of burning wrath,

And shot devouring flame

Our God appeared consuming fire,
And jealous was His name.

And, blessed be God, we are not this morning to speak of the throne of ultimate justice. Before that we shall all come, and as many of us as have believed will find it to be a throne of grace as well as of justice; for, He who sits upon that throne shall pronounce no sentence of condemnation against the man who is justified by faith. But I have not to call you this morning to the place from whence the resurrection trumpet shall ring out so shrill and clear. Not yet do we see the angels with their vengeful swords come forth to smite the foes of God; not yet are the great doors of the pit opened to swallow up the enemies who would not have the Son of God to reign over them. We are still on praying ground and pleading terms with God, and the throne to which we are bidden to come, and of which we speak at this time, is the throne of grace. It is a throne set up on purpose for the dispensation of grace; a throne from which every utterance is an utterance of grace; the scepter that is stretched out from it is the silver scepter of grace; the decrees proclaimed from it are purposes of grace; the gifts that are scattered down its golden steps are gifts of grace; and He that sits upon the throne is grace itself. It is the throne of grace to which we approach when we pray; and let us for a moment or two think this over, by way of consolatory encouragement to those who are beginning to pray; indeed, to all of us who are praying men and women.

If in prayer I come before a throne of grace, then the faults of my prayer will be overlooked. In beginning to pray, dear friends, you feel as it you did not pray. The groanings of your spirit, when you rise from your knees are such that you think

238

there is nothing in them. What a blotted, blurred, smeared prayer it is. Never mind; you have not come to the throne of justice, else when God perceived the fault in the prayer He would spurn it—your broken words, your gasps, and stammers are before a throne of grace. When any one of us has presented his best prayer before God, if he saw it as God sees it, there is no doubt he would make great lamentation over it; for there is enough sin in the best prayer that was ever prayed to secure its being cast away from God. But it is not a throne of justice I say again, and here is the hope for our lame, limping supplications. Our condescending lying does not maintain a stately etiquette in His court like that which has been observed by princes among men, where a little mistake or a flaw would secure the petitioner's being dismissed with disgrace. Oh, no; the faulty cries of His children are not severely criticized by Him. The Lord High Chamberlain of the palace above, our Lord Jesus Christ, takes care to alter and amend every prayer before He presents it, and He makes the prayer perfect with His perfection, and prevalent with His own merits. God looks upon the prayer, as presented through Christ, and forgives all its own inherent faultiness. How this ought to encourage any of us who feel ourselves to be feeble, wandering, and unskillful in prayer. If you cannot plead with God as sometimes you did in years gone by, if you feel as if somehow or other you had grown rusty in the work of supplication, never give up, but come still; yes, and come oftener, for it is not a throne of severe criticism; it is a throne of grace to which you come.

Then, further, inasmuch as it is a throne of grace, the faults of the petitioner himself shall not prevent the success of his prayer. Oh, what faults there are in us! To come before a throne how unfit we are—we, that are all defiled with sin within and without! Dare any of you think of praying were it not that God's throne is a throne of grace? If you could, I confess I could not. An absolute God, infinitely holy and just, could not in consistency with His divine nature answer any prayer from such a sinner as I am, were it not that He has arranged a plan by which my prayer comes up no longer to a throne of absolute justice, but to a throne which is also the mercy seat, the propitiation, the place where God meets sinners, through Jesus Christ. Ah, I could not say to you, "Pray," not even to you saints, unless it were a throne of grace, much less could I talk of prayer to you sinners; but now I will say this to every sinner here, though he should think himself to be the worst sinner who ever lived, cry unto the Lord and seek Him while He may be found. A throne of grace is a place fitted for you. Go to your knees; by simple faith go to your Savior, for He it is who is the throne of grace. It is in Him that God is able to dispense grace unto the most guilty of mankind. Blessed be God, neither the faults of the prayer nor yet of the suppliant shall shut out our petitions from the God who delights in broken and contrite hearts.

If it be a throne of grace, then the desires of the pleader will be interpreted. If I cannot find words in which to utter my desires, God in His grace will read my desires without the words. He takes the meaning of His saints, the meaning of their groans. A throne that was not gracious would not trouble itself to make out our petitions; but God, the infinitely gracious one, will dive into the soul of our desires, and He will read there what we cannot speak with the tongue. Have you never seen the parent, when his child is trying to say something to him, and he knows very well what it is the little one has to say, help him over the words and utter the syllables for him, and if the little one has half-forgotten what he would say, you have been the father who would suggest the word. So the ever blessed Spirit, from the throne of grace, will help us and teach us words, nay, write in our hearts the desires themselves. We have in Scripture instances where God puts words into sinners' mouths. "Take with you words," says he, "and say unto him, 'Receive us graciously and love us freely.'" (See Hosea 14:2-4.) He will put the desires, and put the expression of those desires into your spirit by His grace. He will direct your desires to the things which you ought to seek. He will teach you your wants, though as yet you know them not. He will suggest to you His promises, that you may be able to plead them. He will, in fact, be Alpha and Omega to your prayer, just as He is to your salvation; for as salvation is from first to last of grace, so the sinner's approach to the throne of grace is of grace from first to last. What comfort this is. Will we not, my dear friends, with the greater boldness draw near to this throne, as we suck out the sweet meaning of this precious word, "the throne of grace"?

If it be a throne of grace, then all the wants of those who come to it will be supplied. The King from such a throne will not say, "You must bring me gifts; you must offer me sacrifices." It is not a throne for receiving tribute; it is a throne for dispensing gifts. Come, then, you who are as poor as poverty itself; come you that have no merits and are destitute of virtues, come you that are reduced to a beggarly bankruptcy by Adam's fall and by your own transgressions; this is not the throne of majesty which supports itself by the taxation of its subjects, but a throne which glorifies itself by streaming forth like a fountain with floods of good things. Come you now and receive the wine and milk which are freely given; yea, come, buy wine and milk without money and without price. All the petitioner's wants shall be supplied, because it is a throne of grace.

And so, all the petitioner's miseries shall be compassionated. Suppose I come to the throne of grace with the burden of my sins; there is one on the throne who felt the burden of sin in ages long gone by, and has not forgotten its weight. Suppose I come loaded with sorrow; there is One there who knows all the sorrows to which humanity can be subjected. Am I depressed and distressed? Do I fear that God himself has forsaken me? There is One upon the throne who said, "My God, my God, why hast thou forsaken me?" (Mark 15:34). It is a throne from which grace delights to look upon the miseries of mankind with tender eye, to consider them and to relieve them.

Come, then; come, then; come, then, you that are not only poor, but wretched, whose miseries make you long for death, and yet dread it. You captive ones, come in your chains; you slaves, come with the irons upon your souls; you who sit in darkness, come forth all blindfolded as you are. The throne of grace will look on you if you cannot look on it, and will give to you, though you have nothing to give in return, and will deliver you, though you cannot raise a finger to deliver yourself.

"The throne of grace." The phrase grows as I turn it over in my mind, and to me it is a most delightful reflection that if I come to the throne of God in prayer, I may feel a thousand defects, but yet there is hope. I usually feel more dissatisfied with my prayers than with anything else I do. I do not believe that it is an easy thing to pray in public so as to conduct the devotions of a large congregation aright. We sometimes hear persons commended for preaching well, but if any shall be enabled to pray well, there will be an equal gift and a higher grace in it. But, brethren, suppose in our prayers there should be defects of knowledge. It is a throne of grace, and our Father knows that we have need of these things. Suppose there should be defects of faith; He sees our little faith and still does not reject it, small as it is. He does not in every case measure out His gifts by the degree of our faith, but by the sincerity and trueness of faith. And if there should be grave defects even in our spirit, and failures in the fervency or in the humility of the prayer, still, though these should not lie there and are much to be deplored; grace overlooks all this, forgives all this, and still its merciful hand is stretched out to enrich us according to our needs. Surely this ought to induce many to pray who have not prayed, and should make us who have been long accustomed to use the consecrated art of prayer, to draw near with greater boldness than ever to the throne of grace.

3. Now regarding our text as a whole, it conveys to us the idea of *grace enthroned*. It is a throne, and who sits on it? It is grace personified that is here installed in dignity. And, truly, today grace is on a throne. In the Gospel of Jesus Christ grace is the most predominant attribute of God. How does it come to be so exalted? Well, grace has a throne by conquest. Grace came down to Earth in the form of the well-beloved, and it met with sin. Long and sharp was the struggle, and grace appeared to be trampled underfoot by sin; but grace at last seized sin, threw it on its own shoulders, and, though all but crushed beneath the burden, grace carried sin up to the Cross and nailed it there, slew it there, put it to death forever, and triumphed gloriously. For this cause at this hour grace sits on a throne, because it has conquered human sin, has borne the penalty of human guilt, and overthrown all its enemies.

Grace, moreover, sits on the throne because it has established itself there by right. There is no injustice in the grace of God. God is as just when He forgives a believer as when He casts a sinner into hell. I believe in my own soul that there is as much and as pure a justice in the acceptance of a soul that believes in Christ as there will be in the rejection of those souls who die impenitent, and are banished from Jehovah's presence. The sacrifice of Christ has enabled God to be just, and yet the justifier of Him that believeth.

He who knows the word "substitution," and can spell out its meaning aright, will see that there is nothing due to punitive justice from any believer, seeing that Jesus Christ has paid all the believer's debts, and how God would be unjust if He did not save those for whom Christ vicariously suffered, for whom His righteousness was provided, and to whom it is imputed. Grace is on the throne by conquest, and sits there by right. Grace is enthroned this day, brethren, because Christ has finished His work and gone into the heavens. It is enthroned in power. When we speak of its throne, we mean that it has unlimited might. Grace sits not on the footstool of God; grace stands not in the courts of God, but it sits on the throne; it is the reigning attribute; it is the king today.

This is the dispensation of grace, the year of grace. Grace reigns through righteousness unto eternal life. We live in the era of reigning grace, for seeing He ever lives to make intercession for the sons of men. Jesus "is able also to save them to the uttermost that come unto God by him" (Hebrews 7:25). Sinner, if you were to meet grace in the byway, like a traveler on his journey, I would bid you make its acquaintance and ask its influence; if you should meet grace as a merchant on the exchange, with treasure in his hand, I would bid you court its friendship, it will enrich you in the hour of poverty; if you should see grace as one of the peers of Heaven, highly exalted, I would bid you seek to get its ear; but, oh, when grace sits on the throne, I beseech you close in with it at once. It can be no higher, it can be no greater, for it is written "God is love," which is an alias for grace. Oh, come and bow before it; come and adore the infinite mercy and grace of God.

Doubt not, halt not, hesitate not. Grace is reigning; grace is God; God is love. Oh that you, seeing grace is thus enthroned, would come and receive it. I say, then that grace is enthroned by conquest, by right, and by power, and, I will add, it is enthroned in glory, for God glorifies His grace. It is one of His objects now to make His grace illustrious. He delights to pardon penitents, and so to show His pardoning grace; He delights to look upon wanderers and restore them, to show His reclaiming grace; He delights to look upon the brokenhearted and comfort them, that He may show his consoling grace. There is grace to be had of various kinds, or rather the same grace acting in different ways, and God delights to make His grace glorious. There is a rainbow round about the throne that is like unto an emerald, the emerald of His compassion and His love. O happy souls that can believe this, and believing it can come at once and glorify grace by becoming instances of its power.

4. Lastly, our text, if rightly read, has in it *sovereignty resplendent in glory—the glory of grace*. The mercy seat is a throne; though grace is there, it is still a throne. Grace does not displace sovereignty. Now, the attribute of sovereignty is very high and terrible; its light is like unto a jasper stone, most precious, and like unto a sapphire stone, or, as Ezekiel calls it, "the terrible crystal" (Ezekiel 1:22). Thus saith the

King, the Lord of hosts,'I will have mercy on whom I will have mercy, and I will have compassion on whom I will have compassion.... Who art thou, O man, that repliest against God? Shall the thing formed say to him that formed it, Why hast thou made me thus? Hath not the potter power over the clay, to make of the same lump one vessel unto honour and another unto dishonour?" (Romans 9:15, 20-21). These are great and terrible words, and are not to be answered. He is a King, and He will do as He wills. None shall stay His hand, or say unto Him, "What doest thou?"

But, ah! lest any of you should be downcast by the thought of His sovereignty, I invite you to the text. It is a throne—there is sovereignty; but to every soul that knows how to pray, to every soul that by faith comes to Jesus, the true mercy seat, divine sovereignty wears no dark and terrible aspect, but is full of love. It is a throne of grace; from which I gather that the sovereignty of God to a believer, to a pleader, to one who comes to God in Christ, is always exercised in pure grace. To you, who come to God in prayer, the sovereignty always runs thus: "I will have mercy on that sinner; though he deserves it not, though in him there is no merit, yet because I can do as I will with my own, I will bless him, I will make him my child, I will accept him; he shall be mine in the day when I make up my jewels." On the mercy seat God never executed sovereignty otherwise than in a way of grace. He reigns, but in this case grace reigns through righteousness unto eternal life by Jesus Christ our Lord.

There are these two or three things to be thought of, and I will be done. On the throne of grace sovereignty has placed itself under bonds of love. I must speak with choice and picked words here, and I must hesitate and pause to get right sentences, lest I err while endeavoring to speak the truth in plainness. God will do as He wills; but, on the mercy seat, He is under bonds—bonds of His own making, for He has entered into covenant with Christ, and so into covenant with His chosen. Though God is and ever must be a sovereign, He never will break his covenant, nor alter the Word that is gone out of His mouth. He cannot be false to a covenant of His own making. When I come to God in Christ, to God on the mercy seat, I need not imagine that by any act of sovereignty God will set aside His covenant. That cannot be; it is impossible. Moreover, on the throne of grace, God is again bound to us by His promises. The covenant contains in it many gracious promises, exceeding great and precious. "Ask, and it shall be given you; seek, and ye shall find; knock, and it shall be opened unto you" (Matthew 7:7).

Until God had said that word or a word to that effect, it was at His own option to hear prayer or not, but it is not so now; for now, if it be true prayer offered through Jesus Christ, His truth binds Him to hear it. A man may be perfectly free, but the moment he makes a promise, he is not free to break it; and the everlasting God wants not to break His promise. He delights to fulfill it. He has declared that all His promises are yea and amen in Christ Jesus; but, for our consolation, when we survey God under the high and terrible aspect of a sovereign, we have this to reflect on, that He is under covenant bonds of promise to be faithful to the souls that seek Him. His throne must be a throne of grace to His people.

And, once more, and sweetest thought of all, every covenant promise has been endorsed and sealed with blood, and far be it from the everlasting God to pour scorn upon the blood of His dear Son. When a king has given a charter to a city, he may before have been absolute, and there may have been nothing to check his prerogatives, but when the city has its charter, then it pleads its rights before the king. Even thus God has given to His people a charter of untold blessing, bestowing upon them the sure mercies of David. Very much of the validity of a charter depends upon the signature and the seal, and, my brethren, how sure is the charter of covenant grace. The signature is the handwriting of God himself, and the seal is the blood of His only begotten Son. The covenant is ratified with blood, the blood of His own dear Son. It is not possible that we can plead in vain with God when we plead the blood-sealed covenant, ordered in all things and sure. Heaven and Earth shall pass away, but the power of the blood of Jesus with God can never fail. It speaks when we are silent, and it prevails when we are defeated. Better things than that of Abel does it ask for, and its cry is heard. (See Hebrews 12:24.) Let us come boldly, for we bear the promise in our hearts. When we feel alarmed because of the sovereignty of God, let us cheerfully sing:

The gospel cheers my spirit up,

A faithful and unchanging God

Lays the foundation for my hope

In oaths, and promises, and blood.

From this time forward may God the Holy Spirit help us to use aright "the throne of grace." Amen.

PRAYER IN THE DAY OF TROUBLE

"And call upon me in the day of trouble; I will deliver thee, and thou shalt glorify me." (Psalm 50:15)

The Lord God in this Psalm is described as having a controversy with His people. He summons Heaven and Earth to hear Him while He utters His reproof. This indictment will show us what it is that the Lord sets the greatest store by, for His complaint will evidently touch upon that point. We are informed most plainly that the Lord had no controversy with His people concerning the externals of His worship. He does not reprove them for their sacrifices and burnt offerings. He even speaks deprecatingly of these symbolical sacrifices, and says, "I will take no bullock out of thy house, nor he goats out of thy folds" (Psalm 50:9).

His complaint was not concerning visible ceremony and outward ritual; and this shows that He does not attach so much importance to outward things as most men suppose Him to do. His complaint was concerning inner worship, soul worship, spiritual worship. His reproof was that His people did not offer thanksgiving and prayer, and that their conduct was so inconsistent with their professions that clearly their hearts went not with their outward formalities. This was the essence of the charge against them. They were not faulty in visible religiousness, but in the internal and vital part of godliness. They had no true spiritual communion with God, though they kept up the appearance of it. We see, then, that heart worship is the most precious thing in the sight of the Lord. We learn what is that priceless jewel, which must be set in the gold ring of religion if the Lord is to accept it.

It is not hard to see why this is so, for it is plain that a man might keep the ritual of the old law to the very full, yet not be in sincerity a worshiper of God at all. He might drive whole flocks of his sheep to the Temple door for sacrifice, and yet he might feel no spiritual reverence for the Most High. It has, in fact, been proven times without number that the most careful and zealous attention to external ceremonies is quite consistent with the absolute absence of any true apprehension of God and hearty love for Him. Habit may keep a man outwardly religious long after his mind has forgotten the Lord. The conscious lack of inward and vital grace may drive a man to a more intense zeal in formalities in order to conceal his defect. It is written, "Israel hath forgotten his Maker, and buildeth temples" (Hosea 8:14).

You would think if he built temples, he must recognize his God, but it was not so. Within those buildings he hid himself from Him who dwells not in temples made with hands. (See Acts 17:24, 28.) Beneath the folds of vestments men smother their hearts, so that they come not to God. Much music drowns the cry of the contrite soul, and the smoke of incense becomes a cloud that conceals the face of the Most High. Great sacrifices might often be an offering made to a rich man's personal pride. No doubt certain kings that gave great contributions to the house of God did it to show their wealth, or to display their generosity, somewhat in the spirit of Jehu, who said to Jehonadab, the son of Rechab, "Come with me, and see my zeal for the LORD" (2 Kings 10:16). A great sacrifice might be nothing more than a bid for popularity, and so an offering to selfishness and vanity.

With such sacrifices God would not be well pleased. Alas! how easy it is to defile the worship of God and nullify its quality, until like milk that is soured, it may be utterly rejected. I am sure you know right well that it may be so in the simplest form of public worship, such as our own. Bare as is our mode of service, there is room for self. Singers may lift up sweet voices, that others may hear how charmingly they sing, ministers may preach with graceful eloquence, that they may be admired as men who are models of exquisite speech, and believers may even pray devoutly so that their fellow Christians may see how gracious they are. Alas! this blight of self may come into any and every part of outward service, and turn the worship of God into an occasion for self-glorification. Thus does Belshazzar drink out of the vessels of the sanctuary, while the buyers and sellers turn the Temple into a den of thieves. Wonder not, therefore, that God looks with but scant complacency—I was about to say with bare tolerance—upon the abundance of outward worship, because He sees how easy it is for it not to be His worship at all, but a mere exhibition of man's carnal glorying.

Many, too, have performed outward worship with a view to merit something from the Lord. They have supposed that God would be their debtor if they were zealous in furnishing His altars and frequenting His courts. If they have not put it in that coarse a form, it has certainly come to their hoping to be held worthy of particular regard if they are zealous above others. Some have superstitiously dreamed of obtaining prosperity in this world by observing holy days and seasons, and many more have hoped to have it set to their account at the last great day that they have heaped up the offertory, or given a painted window, or built an almshouse [a home for the poor that is maintained by private charity], or attended daily service year by year. Now, what is this but an offering to selfishness? The man performs pious and charitable deeds for his own good, and this motive flavors the whole of his life, so that the taint of self is in every particle of it. The Jew might offer bullocks or sheep for his own salvation, and what would this be but the manifest worship of self? It brought no glory to God, and did not mean to praise Him. Wonder not, therefore, if the Lord speaks slightingly of it all.

What the Lord missed in His people was not Temple rites and offerings, for in these they abounded, but He missed the fruit of the lips giving glory to His name. He missed first their thankfulness, for He says unto them, "Offer unto God thanksgiving; and pay thy vows unto the most High" (Psalm 50:14). He next missed in them that holy, trustful confidence that would lead them to resort to Him in the hour of their need; hence He says, "Call upon me in the day of trouble; I will deliver thee, and thou shalt glorify me."

Brethren and sisters, have you failed in these two precious things? Do you fail in thankfulness? The Lord multiplies His favors to many of us; do we multiply our thanks? The Earth gives back a floweret for every dewdrop; are we alike responsive to plenteous mercy? Do the bounties of His providence and the favors of His grace teach us how to sing psalms unto our ever merciful God? Do we not too often permit divine mercies to come and go in silence as if they were not worthy of a thankful word? Have we a time and season for God's praise? Is it not too often huddled into a corner? We have a closet for our prayers, but no chamber for our praises. Do we make it a point in life that no matter what else is neglected, the praises of God shall have full expression? Do you, my brethren, give thanks in everything? Do you carry out to the full this sentence: "From the rising of the sun to the going down of the same the LORD's name is to be praised" (Psalm 113:3)?

May I also venture to ask whether you pay your vows to Him? In times of sickness and sorrow you say, "Gracious Lord, if I am recovered, or if I am brought out of this condition, I will be more believing, I will be more consecrated. I will devote myself alone to you, O my Savior, if you will now restore me." Are you mindful of these vows? It is a delicate question, but I put it pointedly, because a vow unredeemed is a wound in the heart. If you have failed in your grateful acknowledgments, remember that these are the things God looks for more than for any ceremonial observance or religions service. He would have you bring your daily thankfulness and your faithful vows unto Him, for He is worthy to be praised, and it is meet that unto Him the vow should be performed.

It is not to thankfulness, however, that I am going to ask attention this morning, so much as to the other sacrifice—namely, prayer in the day of trouble. Let me say at the outset that I am struck with wonder that God should regard it as being one of the most acceptable forms of worship, that we should call upon Him in the day of trouble. Such prayers seem to be all for ourselves, and to be forced from us by our necessities, and yet such is His condescending love, that He puts them down as being choice sacrifices, and places them side by side with the thankful paying of our vows. He tells us that our call for His help in the hour of distress will be more acceptable to Him than the oblations that His own law ordained, more pleasing than all the bullocks and rams that liberal princes could present at His altars.

Be not backward then, beloved, to cry to Him in your hour of need. If it pleases Him and profits you, you ought not to want a single word from me to excite you to do what seems so natural, so comforting, so beneficial. Are our cries of anguish and our appeals of hope acceptable to God? Then let us cry mightily unto Him. Are any of you in the black waters? Call upon Him. Are you in the hungry desert? Call upon Him. Are you in the lions' dens, and among the mountains of the leopards? Call upon Him. Whether you are in peril as to your souls or your bodies, do not hesitate to pray at once, but say to yourself, "Why should I linger? Let me tell the Lord my grief right speedily, for if He counts my call a worthy sacrifice, assuredly I will present it with my whole heart." Let us look to this matter and see the value of this form of adoration. Our first head, therefore, is that calling upon God in the day of trouble brings honor to God in the very act. Our second is it brings honor to God in His answer, for there is coupled with such a prayer the blessed assurance, "I will deliver thee." And third, it brings honor to God in our after conduct, for it is written, "Thou shalt glorify me."

1. May the Holy Spirit, the Comforter, enable us to see that *calling upon God in the day of trouble brings glory to Him in itself.* I beg you to notice the time that is specially mentioned. Calling upon God at any time honors Him, but calling upon Him in the day of trouble has a special mark set against it as peculiarly pleasing to the Lord because it yields

peculiar glory to His name. Note then, first, that when a man calls upon God sincerely in the day of trouble, it is a truthful recognition of God. Outward devotions suppose a God, but prayer in the day of trouble proves that God is a fact to the suppliant. The tried pleader has no doubt that there is a God, for he is calling upon Him when mere form can yield no comfort. He wants practical matter-of-fact help, and he so realizes God that he treats Him as real, and appeals to Him to be his helper. God is not a mere name or a superstition to him. He is sure that there is a God, for he is calling upon Him in an hour when a farce would be a tragedy, and an imposture would be a bitter mockery. The afflicted suppliant perceives that God is near him, for he would not call upon one who was not within hearing. He has a perception of God's omnipotence by which He can help, and of God's goodness, which will lead Him to help. You can see that he believes in God's hearing prayer, for a man does not call upon one whom he judges to be a deaf deity, or upon one whose palsied hand is never outstretched to help.

The person who calls upon God in the day of trouble, evidently possesses a real and sincere belief in the existence of God, in His personality, His power, His condescension, and in His continual active interposition in the affairs of men; otherwise, he would not call upon Him. Many of your beliefs in God are a sort of religious parade, and not the actual walk of faith. Many have a holiday faith that enables them to repeat the creed, and say with the congregation, "I believe in God the Father Almighty," but in very deed they have no such belief.

Do you, my hearer, believe in God the Father Almighty when you are in trouble? Do you go to the great Father at such times and expect help from Him? This is real work and not hypocritical play. There is solid metal about the faith that follows the Lord in the dark, cries to Him when the rod is in His hand, and looks to Him not for sentimental comforts in prosperity, but for substantial help in bitter adversities. What we want is facts, and trial is the test of fact. Sharp furnace work does away with mere pretense, and this is one of its great uses, for that grace which, like the salamander, lives in the fire is grace, indeed.

I say again that very many publicly declared creed faiths are mere shams, which like the leaves of autumn's trees, would wither and fall if one sharp winter's frost should pass over them. It is not so when a man in the dire hour of his distress casts himself upon God, and believes that he is able to succor and to help him. Then there is evidence of true reliance and real confidence in a real God, whom the mind's eye sees and rejoices in. It is this actuality, this making God real to the soul, that makes our calling upon God in the day of trouble so acceptable to Him.

There is more here, however, than this first good thing. When a man calls upon God in the day of trouble it is because he seeks and in some measure enjoys a spiritual communion with God. "Call upon me in the day of trouble." That call is heart language addressed to God; it is the soul really speaking to the great Father beyond all question. How easy it is to say a prayer without coming into any contact with God! Year after year the tongue repeats pious language, just as a barrel-organ grinds out the old tunes, and there may be no more converse with the Lord than if the man had muttered to the ghosts of the slain. Many prayers might as well be said backwards as forwards, for there would be as much in them one way as the other. The abracadabra of the magician has quite as much virtue in it as any other set of mere words. The Lord's Prayer, if it be merely rehearsed as a form, may be a solemn mockery. But prayer in the day of trouble is honest speech with God, or at least a sincere desire in that direction. Many are the words that pass between the Lord and the afflicted saint. He cries, "Make haste to help me, O Lord, my salvation" (Psalm 38:22). "Be pleased, O LORD, to deliver me" (Psalm 40:13). "Hide not thy face from me, for I am in trouble" (Psalm 102:2). "Hear my cry, O God, attend unto my prayer!" (Psalm 61:1). With multiplied entreaties does the heart thus hold converse with the Lord, and the Lord takes pleasure in it. He loves to have His people draw near to Him in spirit and in truth, and because calling upon Him in the day of trouble is an undoubted form of fellowship, He, therefore, regards it with complacency.

Now, as I have already said, in the sacrifice of bullocks there was no spiritual conversation with God in the case of a great many, and in external devotion, whether it is performed in a cathedral or in a humble barn, there is frequently no coming near to God. But when we believingly call upon God in the day of trouble there is no mistake in the matter, for we are holding converse with God. "The righteous cry, and the LORD heareth" (Psalm 34:17). Spiritual conversation with the unseen, spiritual Father is genuine indeed when it is carried on against wind and tide, under pressure of sorrow and weight of distress—may the Lord give us the grace to carry it on, whatever may happen to us.

Yet is there more than this, for the soul not only comes into God's presence, but in calling upon God in the day of trouble it is filled with a manifest hope in God. It hopes in

God for His goodness, for it is a belief in that goodness that is the reason why it feels able to pray at all. It also hopes in His mercy, or it would dwell in silence and never lift up another cry to Heaven. Amid a sense of deserved wrath, the heart has a trust in infinite grace, and hence its call.

A soul calling upon God honors His condescension. The troubled one says within himself, "I am less than the least of all His mercies, yet He will regard me. When I consider the heavens, the work of His fingers, I wonder that He should visit man, but I believe that He will do so, and that He will condescend to look upon the contrite and humble, and will deliver them out of their distresses." (See Isaiah 57:15.) There is a hope, then, in such a prayer that honors God's goodness and condescension, and equally pays tribute to His faithfulness and His all-sufficiency. He has promised to help those that call upon Him, therefore do we call upon Him; and He has all power to keep His promise; therefore, do we come to Him and spread our case before Him.

Little as the act of calling upon God in the day of trouble seems to be, it puts crowns upon all the attributes of God in proportion to the spiritual knowledge of the suppliant. I venture to say that if the greatest king of Israel had presented before God, on some solemn day, ten thousand of the fat of fed beasts, and poured out rivers of oil, it might be highly possible that God would not be so well pleased with all that royal zeal as with the cry of a poor, humble woman whose husband was dead, and whose two sons were about to be taken for bondmen, who had nothing in the house save a little oil, and then in her extremity cried, "O God, the Father of the fatherless, and the judge of the widow, out of the depths deliver me." (See Psalm 68:5.) There may be more honoring of the Lord in a ploughboy's tear than in a princely endowment, more homage to the Lord in the humble hope of a dying pauper than in the pealing anthems of the cathedral, or in the great shout of our own mighty congregation. The publican's confession and his hope in the mercy of God had more worship in it than the blast of the silver trumpets, the ringing out of the golden harps, and the songs of the white-robed choristers, who stood in the courts of the Lord's house and led the far-sounding hallelujahs of Israel.

This calling upon God in the day of trouble, again, pleases the Lord because it exhibits a clinging affection to Him. When an ungodly man professes religion, as such men often do, he is all very well with God, as long as God pleases him. Sunshiny weather makes such a man bless the sun—if God smiles upon him, he says that God is good. Yes, but a true child of God loves a chastening God. He does not turn his back when the Lord seems angry with him, but falls prostrate in humble supplication and cries, "Show me why you contend with me. I will not believe you have any real spite against me. If you smite me, there must be some wise and good cause for it; therefore, show me, I beseech you." (See Job 10:2.)

It is very sweet, brethren, when God sends you a great deal of trouble, to love Him all the more for it. This is a sure way of proving that ours is not a hireling love, which abides while it gets its price, and goes when wages fail. God forbid that we should have Balaam's love of reward, and Judas's treacherous greed. Any dog will follow a man as long as he throws him a bone, but it is a man's own dog that will follow him when he strikes him with the whip, and will even fawn upon him when he speaks roughly to him. Such Christians ought we be who will keep close to God when He is robed in thunder. It is ours to will that God shall do what He wills and ours to call upon Him in the day of trouble, and not to call out against Him when times are hard.

I would trust my God as unreservedly as Alexander trusted his friend, who was also his physician. The physician had mixed a medicine for Alexander, who was sick, and the potion stood by Alexander's bed for him to drink. Just before he drank, a letter was delivered to him in which he was warned that his physician had been bribed to poison him, and had mingled poison with the medicine. Alexander read the letter, and summoned the physician into his presence, and when he came in Alexander at once drank up the cup of medicine, and then handed his friend the letter. What grand confidence was this! To risk his life upon his friend's fidelity! Such a man might well have friends. He would not let the accused know of the libel till he had proved beyond all disputes that he did not believe a word of it.

Is not our heavenly Father in Christ Jesus worthy of even a grander faith? Shall I ever mistrust him? *The Devil tells me, my Lord, that this affliction which I am suffering will work me ill. I do not believe it. Not for a moment do I believe it, and to prove that I have no suspicion, I accept it joyfully at your hands. I joy and rejoice in it, because you have ordained it, and I call upon you to make it work to my lasting good. I will take bitter at your hand as well as sweet, and the gall shall be honey to me.* If we act this way, we shall be imitating the patience of Job. When his wife bade him curse God and die, what said he? "Thou speakest as one of the foolish women speaketh. What? shall we receive good at the hand of God, and shall we not receive evil?" (Job 2:10).

It seems to me we cannot glorify God better than by calling upon Him in the day of trouble, and showing that we do not believe ill of Him, or suspect Him either of error or unkindness. We go further, and are assured that infallible wisdom and infinite love is at the bottom of every trial that afflicts our spirit: thus we glorify the Lord. There is in connection with this clinging affection a most steadfast confidence. They who call upon God in the day of trouble become quiet and unshaken, and abide in full assurance as to the Lord on whom they rely. O troubled one, do not be agitated, do not run away to others, but call upon God in calm faith. Do not sit down in silent despair and fretfulness, but call upon God. Do not be soured into a morose state of mind, nor go into the sulks, but call upon the Lord, as one who cannot be driven to curse or to be in a passion, but gives himself to prayer. It is a blessed thing when we can say, "Though he slay me, yet will I trust in him" (Job 13:15), and can feel that whatever happens to us we never will stray aside from our firm conviction that the Lord is good, and "his mercy endureth for ever" (1 Chronicles 16:34).

It was a brave speech of Zwingli [Ulrich Zwingli, a 16th century Protestant Reformer] when amid furious persecutions he said, "Had I not perceived that the Lord was preserving the vessel I should long ago have abandoned the helm. I behold Him through the tempest strengthening the cordage, adjusting the yards, spreading the sails, and commanding the very winds. Should I not, then, be a coward, and unworthy the name of a man, were I to abandon my post? I commit myself wholly to His sovereign goodness. Let Him govern; let Him hasten or delay; let Him plunge us into the bottom of the abyss; we will fear nothing." That is the word which I admire. "Let him plunge us into the bottom of the abyss: we will fear nothing." This is the bravery of a child who knows no dread because he is in his father's hand, and his trust in his father cannot admit a fear.

Calling upon God enables men to face trouble and play the man, since they doubt not of a blessed outcome from all things, however contrary they may seem to be. Our business is to be as confident in God at one time as at another, since He is the same evermore, and mere changes in circumstances are matters unworthy to be taken into the estimate. What are circumstances while Almighty God has the rule of them? In brief, this it is that God accepts as honoring Him, that in the day of trouble we should take all our troubles to Him, pour out our hearts before Him, and then leave the whole case in His hands. The childlike uncovering of the heart to God alone is very precious to Him. There are times when it is wise to advise a troubled heart to be quiet before men.

Bear and forbear and silent be,

Tell no man thy misery.

But it is always wise to bare the bosom to the Lord's eye. Is the slander too vile to be communicated even to a single friend? Then follow the example of Hezekiah and spread Rabshakeh's letter before the Lord. Is the trial too severe, inasmuch as others are obliged to suffer with you, and are therefore turned to speak bitterly against you? Then imitate David at Ziklag, and encourage yourself in the Lord your God. Hide nothing. Reserve nothing. Tell it all, and then trust about it all. When you have once put the burden before the Lord leave it with Him. Do all that lies in you, that prudence can dictate, or common sense suggest, or industry effect, but still make the Lord your mainstay, your buckler, your shield, your fortress, and your high tower. (See Psalm 18:2.) Say to yourself, "My soul, wait thou only upon God, for my expectation is from him" (Psalm 62:5).

If you can do this, not once and again, but throughout your whole life, you will glorify the Lord greatly, and in your holy confidence and childlike faith the Lord will take as much delight as in the golden harps that ring out His perfect praises before His eternal throne. If we could reproduce Job and Enoch in one person, the patient saint continually walking with God, we should indeed show forth the glory of our heavenly Father. And why not? Blessed Spirit of God, You can work us to this selfsame thing!

A critic may sneeringly say, "It is a very natural thing for a man to cry out to God in the day of trouble, and certainly a selfish thing to run to the Lord because you need His help."

"Besides," says another, "it must be a very distracted prayer that such a person offers, and faith under troublesome circumstances is a very elementary virtue."

But, my good sirs, listen. Surely the Lord knows best what pleases Him, and if He declares His delight in our calling upon Him in the day of trouble, why should we dispute with Him? It is so, for He has said it. As for us, who dare not raise such quibbles, let us not be moved by them, but continue to call upon Him in the day of trouble, and we shall certainly glorify His name.

2. When we call upon God in the day of trouble *it brings honor to God through the answer* the prayer obtains. "I will deliver thee." I ask you, troubled saints, to follow me while I repeat the text with variations, for that is about all I shall

attempt. "Call upon me in the day of trouble"—there is the prayer commanded. "I will deliver thee"—there is the answer promised. In these words we have a practical answer. It is not merely, "I will think about you, I will hear you, I will propose plans for you, and somewhat aid you in working them out," but, "I will deliver you." You shall have solid, substantial aid. Either I will keep you out of the trouble of which you are afraid, or you shall be delivered by never having to endure it. The Egyptians you see today you shall see no more forever. You dread the stone at the mouth of the sepulcher, but you shall find it rolled away.

Or else, if you must come into the trouble, I will deliver you while you are in it. Like Noah, you shall be surrounded by the deluge, but the floods shall not overflow you. Like the three holy children, you shall be in the furnace, but the fire shall not kindle upon you. You shall go through the trouble triumphantly, as Israel went through the Red Sea on foot. You shall have such sustaining grace that you shall glory in tribulation, and rejoice in affliction. I will also bring you out of it altogether, for these things have an appointed end. Like Joseph, you shall come forth out of prison to sit upon the throne. Like David, you shall leave the caves and the rocks of the wild goats, and I will set your feet in a large room. Like Daniel, you shall be taken from among lions and set among princes. The promise may be kept in several forms, but in one shape or another it must be carried out, for He who cannot lie has said, "I will deliver thee."

Dear friend, grip those words and never let them go. You troubled ones, the Lord says, "Call upon me." Have you been already much in supplication? Now, then, take to yourselves what the Lord himself gives you: "I will deliver thee." Somehow or other a way of escape must be made, for God's Word never fails, and He has said, "I will deliver thee." Notice, next, that it is a positive answer. It is not, "I may, perhaps, deliver thee"; but, "I will." It is not, "I will endeavor to do it," but, "I will deliver thee." Did unbelief say, "But how?" Friend, leave the "how" with God.

Ways and means are with Him. He says, "I will deliver thee." To turn round and ask, "How?" is to forget that He is God and all sufficient.

Remember that omnipotence has servants everywhere.

Unbelief is very ready with its questions, and too often it enquires, "When?" Friend, leave the "when" with God. He does not tell us when, but the deliverance must come at the right time, because if He were not to deliver us till after we had perished, it would be no deliverance at all. If deliverance came too late, it would be a mere mockery. The promise comprehends within itself the implied condition that it shall be a timely deliverance, for otherwise how should the delivered one live to glorify the name of the Lord? Again I would say to you, dear friend, get a grip on this promise, "I will deliver thee." Do not let my Master's promise be blown away like the dry leaves from the trees, but hold it fast for life. Wave this before you, and your foes will flee as from a two-edged sword. Quote the divine Word, "I will deliver thee," and legions of devils will flee before you. Remember how Paul put it: "Who delivered us from so great a death, and doth deliver: in whom we trust that he will yet deliver us" (2 Corinthians 1:10).

Notice next, that the promise is personal. "I will deliver thee." It is not said, "My angels shall do it," but "*I* will deliver thee." The Lord God himself undertakes to rescue

His people. "For I, saith the LORD, will be unto her a wall of fire round about" (Zechariah 2:5). "I the LORD do keep it; I will water it every moment: lest any hurt it, I will keep it night and day" (Isaiah 27:3).

Then, too, it is personal to its object: it is the same man who calls upon God in trouble who shall be a partaker of the blessing. "Call upon me in the day of trouble, I will deliver thee." It is personal—personal to you. Therefore, dear friend, personally believe in this personal promise of your God.

Remember, also, that it is permanent. Some of you pleaded this promise fifty years ago; it is as sure today as it was then. If you have a banknote, and take it to the bank and get the cash, it is done with: but my Master's banknotes are self-renewing. You can plead His promise hundreds of times over, for His Word abides forever; it is fulfilled only to be fulfilled again. Like a springing well, which is always full and flowing, so my Lord's words of grace abide and continue in all their wealth of blessing. God's promise made two thousand years ago is as valid as if it had been uttered this morning, and never yet expended upon a single soul. "Call upon me in the day of trouble, and I will deliver thee" is a word for this very hour.

Where are you at this moment, you troubled, downcast one? You said just now, "I shall never be happy anymore." Recall those words. Eat them with bitter herbs of repentance: "Trust ye in the LORD for ever, for in the LORD JEHOVAH is everlasting strength" (Isaiah 26:4). You said, "That blow has crushed me. I could have borne anything else, but this trial I cannot bear." Hush! Do you know what you can bear? What said the apostle? "I can do all things through Christ which strengtheneth me" (Philippians 4:13). Only have faith in God, and obey and believe the text: "Call upon me in the day of trouble; I will deliver thee." Can you not take God at His word? If you can, you shall find His promise true, and God will be glorified in delivering you. What praise will come to His name if He lifts you up out of the low dungeon, if He snaps your fetters, if He tears away your entanglements, if He makes plain your complicated path, if He brings you through difficulties that now seem to be impossibilities, and if he causes you to rejoice in Him through them all! Why, then, His name will be glorified far more than by the offering of ten thousand bullocks and rivers of oil.

3. Lastly, if you trust your God in your distress and are, therefore, delivered, *the Lord will be glorified in your conduct afterwards.* When a man prays to God in the hour of trouble, and gets deliverance, as he is sure to get it, then he honors his great Helper by admiring the way in which the promise has been kept, and by adoring and blessing the loving Lord for such a gracious intervention. I know some of you have seen enough of the hand of the Lord in your own cases to make you wonder and to admire Him forever and ever.

Next, you will honor Him by the gratitude of your heart, in which the memory of His goodness will forever be recorded. This devout gratitude of yours will lead you in due season to bear testimony to His faithfulness. You will be indignant at unbelief and will war against it by personal witnessing. You will be very tender towards those who are now in trouble, as you once were, and you will long to tell them of the blessed rescue, which God is prepared to perform for them, as He did for you. Your mouth will be open, your witness will be enlarged, and you will speak as a man who has tasted and handled these things for himself. Others will be impressed as you tell the story of what the Lord has done for your soul. At the same time, you will personally grow in faith by the experience of your heavenly Father's love and power, and in days to come you will glorify Him by increased patience and confidence. You will say, "He has been with me in six troubles, and He will be with me in the seventh. I have tried and proved my God, and I dare not doubt Him." Your serenity of mind will be more deep and lasting, and you will be able to defy the power of Satan to drive you out of your joy in God.

I know also that you will try to live more to His praise. As you see Him bring you out of one difficulty and then another you will feel bound to His service by fresh bonds. You will become a more consecrated man than you ever have been. You will jealously protect your remaining days from being wasted by idleness or desecrated by sin. And let me tell you that even when you die, and come up the banks of Jordan on the other side, you will long to glorify your God. When the angels meet you I should not wonder but what one of the first things you will do will be to say, "Bright spirits, I long to tell you what the Lord has done for me." Even as you are going up towards the celestial gates, as Bunyan pictures, I should not wonder if you began to say to your guide:

Help me to sing; I cannot be silent.

I feel I must sing with rapture and surprise

His loving kindness in the skies.

Should the bright spirit remind you that you are climbing to the choirs where all the singers meet, you may answer, "Yes, but I am a special case: I came through such deep waters; I was greatly afflicted. If one in Heaven can praise Him more than another, I am just that one." The angel will smile and say, "I have escorted many a score up to glory who said just the same." We each owe most to God's grace, and hope to praise Him best. Some of you may think you are love's deepest debtors, but I know better. I am not going to quarrel with you, but I know one who is so undeserving and yet receives such mercy that he claims to take the lowest place, and most humbly to reverence boundless grace. Yea, I myself, less than the least of all saints, claim to have received most at His hands. I would happily love Him most, for towards me He has shown the utmost love in treating me as He has done. Am I not saying for myself that which you would say for yourself? I know it is so, and that's why it is that God is glorified by the reverence and love of those whom He delivers in answer to prayer. I want you to notice with care the persons mentioned in the first clause of the text. You do not see yourself'; you only hear of yourself. It is "Call upon me." God is there. There is no direct mention of you; you are hidden; you are such a poor, broken down, dispirited creature, that all you can do is to utter a cry and lie in the dust. There stands the mighty God, and you call upon Him.

Now, look at the next clause, "I will deliver thee." Here are two persons: the Lord stands first, the ever-glorious and blessed "I," and far down there are you. "I will deliver thee," poor, humble, but grateful "thee." Thus we see the Lord unites with His poor servant, and the link is deliverance.

When you come to the third clause, do you see where you are? You are placed first, for the Lord now calls you into action: "Thou shalt glorify me." What a wonderful thing it is! For God to put glory upon us is easy enough, but for us to put glory upon Him, this is a miracle of condescension on the part of our God. "Thou shalt glorify me." "But," says one in this place, "I do love the Lord, but I cannot glorify Him. I wish I could preach, I wish I could write sweet hymns, I wish I had a clear voice with which to sing out the Redeemer's praises, but I have no gifts or talents, and, therefore, I shall never be able to glorify Him."

Listen. You will be cast into trouble one of these days, and when you are in trouble you will find out how to glorify Him. Your extremity will be your opportunity. Like a lamp that shines not by day you will blaze up in the dark. When the day of trouble is come you will cry, "Lord, I could not do anything for you, but you can do everything for me. I am nothing, but, Lord, in my nothingness, I, poor I, do trust you, and fling myself upon you." Then you shall find that you have glorified Him by your faith. I think you might almost be content to have the trouble, might you not? It seems as if you could not glorify Him any other way, and to glorify Him is the main object of your existence. Some Christians would scarcely have brought any glory to God it they had not been led by paths of sorrow, and made to wade through seas of grief. God gets very little glory out of many who profess belief in Him, and He would have still less if they had been allowed to rust their souls away in comfort. The brightest of the saints owe much of their clearness to the fire and the file. It is by the sharp needle of sorrow that we are embroidered with the praises of the Lord. We must be tried, so the Lord may be glorified. We cannot call upon Him in the day of trouble if we have no such day, and He cannot deliver us if we have no trouble to be delivered from. We cannot glorify Him if we are not made to see the danger and the need in which He displays His love.

I leave the blessed subject of the text with you, as a souvenir, till we meet again. The Lord be with you till the day break and the shadows flee away. Pray, also, that He may abide with me, and with all my brethren in the ministry; and may we all in yonder world of rest glorify Him who will then have delivered us completely from all evil, to whom be glory forever. Amen.

PRAYER—THE FORERUNNER OF MERCY

*"Thus saith the LORD GOD; I will yet for this be
enquired of by the house of Israel to do it for them; I will
increase them with men like a flock" (Ezekiel 36:37).*

In reading this chapter we have seen the great and exceeding
precious promises which God had made to the favored
nation of Israel. God in this verse declares, that though the
promise was made, and though He would fulfill it, yet He
would not fulfill it until His people asked Him to do so. He
would give them a spirit of prayer by which they should cry
earnestly for the blessing, and then when they have cried aloud
unto the living God, He will be pleased to answer them from
Heaven, His dwelling place.

The word used here to express the idea of prayer is a
suggestive one. "I will yet for this be enquired of by the house
of Israel." Prayer, then, is an enquiry. No man can pray aright,
unless he views prayer in that light. First, I enquire what the
promise is. I turn to my Bible and I seek to find the promise
whereby the thing which I desire to seek is certified to me as
being a thing which God is willing to give. Having enquired
so far as that, I take that promise, and on my bended knees
I enquire of God whether He will fulfill His own promise. I
take to Him His own word of covenant, and I say to Him, "O

Lord, will you not fulfill it, and will you not fulfill it now?" So that there, again, prayer is enquiry.

After prayer I look out for the answer; I expect to be heard, and if I am not answered, I pray again, and my repeated prayers are but fresh enquiries. I expect the blessing to arrive; I go and enquire whether there is any news of its coming. I ask, and thus I say, "Will you answer me, O Lord? Will you keep your promise? Or will you shut up your ear, because I misunderstand my own wants and mistake your promise?"

Brethren, we must use enquiry in prayer, and regard prayer as being, first, an enquiry for the promise, and on the strength of that promise an enquiry for the fulfillment. We expect something to come as a present from a friend; we first have the note, whereby we are informed it is upon the road. We enquire as to what the present is by the reading of the note, and then, if it arrive not, we call at the accustomed place where the parcel ought to have been left, and we ask or enquire for such and such a thing. We have enquired about the promise, and then we go and enquire again, until we get an answer that the promised gift has arrived and is ours.

So with prayer. We get the promise by enquiry, and we get the fulfillment of it by again enquiring at God's hands. Now, this morning I shall try, as God shall help me, first to speak of prayer as the prelude of blessing; next, I shall try to show why prayer is thus constituted by God as the forerunner of His mercies, and then I shall close by an exhortation, as earnest as I can make it, exhorting you to pray, if you would obtain blessings.

1. Prayer is the *forerunner of mercies*. Many despise prayer. They despise it, because they do not understand it. He who knows how to use that sacred art of prayer will obtain so much thereby, that from its very profitableness he will be led to speak of it with the highest reverence. Prayer, we assert, is the prelude of all mercies. We bid you turn back to sacred history, and you will find that never did a great mercy come to this world, unheralded by prayer. The promise comes alone, with no preventing merit to precede it, but the blessing promised always follows its herald, prayer. You shall note that all the wonders that God did in the old times were first of all sought at His hands by the earnest prayers of His believing people. But last Sunday we beheld Pharaoh cast into the depths of the Red Sea, and all his hosts "still as a stone" in the depths of the waters. Was there a prayer that preceded that magnificent overthrow of the Lord's enemies? Turn to the Book of Exodus, and you will read, "The children of Israel sighed by reason of the bondage, and they cried, and their cry came up unto God by reason of the bondage" (Exodus 2:23). And note that just before the sea parted and made a highway for the Lord's people through its bosom, Moses had prayed unto the Lord, and cried earnestly unto Him, so that Jehovah said, "Wherefore criest thou unto me?" (Exodus 14:15).

A few Sundays ago, when we preached on the subject of the rain that came down from Heaven in the days of Elijah, you will remember how we pictured the land of Judea as an arid wilderness, a mass of dust, destitute of all vegetation. Rain had not fallen for three years; the pastures were dried up; the brooks had ceased to flow; poverty and distress stared the nation in the face. At an appointed season a sound was heard of abundance of rain, and the torrents poured from the skies, until the Earth was deluged with the happy floods. Do you ask me, whether prayer was the prelude to that? I point you to the top of Carmel. Behold a man kneeling before his God, crying, "O my God! send the rain;" lo! the majesty of his faith—he sends his servant Gehazi to look seven times for the clouds, because he believes that they will come, in answer to his prayer. And mark the fact, the torrents of rain were the offspring of Elijah's faith and prayer. (See 1 Kings 18:40-45.)

Wherever in Holy Scripture you shall find the blessing, you shall find the prayer that went before it. Our Lord Jesus Christ was the greatest blessing that men ever had. He was God's best boon to a sorrowing world. And did prayer precede Christ's advent? Was there any prayer that went before the coming of the Lord, when He appeared in the Temple? Oh, yes, the prayers of saints for many ages had followed each other. Abraham saw his day, and when he died Isaac took up the note, and when Isaac slept with his fathers, Jacob and the patriarchs still continued to pray; yea, and in the very days of Christ, prayer was still made for Him continually. Anna the prophetess, and the venerable Simeon, still looked for the coming of Christ; and day by day they prayed and interceded with God, that He would suddenly come to His temple.

Yes, and remember this, as it has been in the Bible, so it shall be with regard to greater things that are yet to happen in the fulfillment of promise. I believe that the Lord Jesus Christ will one day come in the clouds of Heaven. It is my firm belief, in common with all who read the sacred Scriptures correctly, that the day is approaching when the Lord Jesus shall stand a second time upon the Earth, when He shall reign with illimitable sway over all the habitable parts of the globe, when kings shall bow before Him, and queens shall be nursing mothers of His Church, but when shall that time come? We shall know its coming by its prelude, when prayer shall become more loud and strong, when supplication shall become more universal and more incessant, then, even as when the tree puts forth her first green leaves, we expect that the spring approaches, even so when prayer shall become more hearty and earnest, we may open our eyes, for the day of our redemption draws near. Great prayer is the preface of great mercy, and in proportion to our prayer is the blessing we may expect.

It has been so in the history of the modern Church. Whenever she has been roused to pray, it is then that God has awaked to her help. Jerusalem, when you have shaken yourself from the dust, your Lord has taken His sword from the scabbard. When you have suffered your hands to hang down, and your knees to become feeble, He has left you to become scattered by your enemies; you have become barren and your children have been cut off, but when you have learned to cry, when you have begun to pray, God has restored unto you the joy of His salvation, He has gladdened your heart, and multiplied your children.

The history of the Church has been a series of waves, a succession of ebbs and flows. A strong wave of religious prosperity has washed over the sands of sin, again it has receded, and immorality has reigned. In English history it has been the same. Did the righteous prosper in the days of Edward VI? They shall again be tormented under a bloody Mary. Did Puritanism become omnipotent over the land; did the glorious Cromwell reign, and did the saints triumph? Charles the second's debaucheries and wickedness became the black receding wave. Again, Whitefield and Wesley poured throughout the nation a mighty wave of religion, which like a torrent drove everything before it. Again it receded, and there came the days of Payne, and of men full of infidelity and wickedness. Again there came a strong impulse, and again God glorified himself.

And up to this date, again, there has been a decline. Religion, though more fashionable than it once was, has lost much of its vitality and power. Much of the zeal and earnestness of the ancient preachers has departed, and the wave has receded again. But, blessed be God, the floodtide has again set in; once more God has aroused His Church. We have seen in these days what our fathers never hoped to see: we have seen the great men of a Church, not too noted for its activity, at last coming forth—and God being with them in their coming forth! They have come forth to preach unto the people the unsearchable riches of God. I do hope we may have another great wave of religion rolling in upon us. Shall I tell you what I conceive to be the moon that influences these waves? My brethren, even as the moon influences the tides of the sea, even so does prayer (which is the reflection of the sunlight of Heaven, and is God's moon in the sky) influence the tides of godliness; for when our prayers become like the crescent moon, and when we stand not in conjunction with the sun, then there is but a shallow tide of godliness, but when the full orb shines upon the Earth, and when God Almighty makes the prayers of His people full of joy and gladness, it is then that the sea of grace returns to its strength. In proportion to the prayerfulness of the Church shall be its present success, though its ultimate success is beyond the reach of hazard.

And now again, to come nearer home: this truth is true of each of you, my dearly beloved in the Lord, in your own personal experience. God has given you many an unsolicited favor, but still great prayer has always been the great prelude of great mercy with you. When you first found peace through the blood of the Cross you had been praying much beforehand and earnestly interceding with God, that He would remove your doubts and deliver you from your distresses. Your assurance was the result of prayer. And when at any time you have had high and rapturous joys, you have been obliged to look upon them as answers to your prayers, when you have had great deliverances out of sore troubles, and mighty helps in great dangers, you have been able to say, "I cried unto the Lord, and He heard me, and delivered me out of all my fears." Prayer, we say, in your case, as well as in the case of the Church at large, is always the preface to blessing. And now some will say to me, "In what way do you regard prayer, then, as affecting the blessing? God the Holy Ghost grants prayer before the blessing; but in what way is prayer connected with the blessing?" I reply, "Prayer goes before the blessing in several senses."

It goes before the blessing, as the blessing's shadow. When the sunlight of God's mercy rises upon our necessities, it casts the shadow of prayer far down upon the plain. Or, to use another illustration, when God piles up a hill of mercies, He himself shines behind them, and He casts on our spirits the shadow of prayer, so that we may rest certain; if we are in prayer, our prayers are the shadows of mercy. Prayer is the rustling of the wings of the angels that are on their way, bringing us the blessings of Heaven. Have you heard prayer in your heart? You shall see the angel in your house. When the chariots that bring us blessings do rumble, their wheels do sound with prayer. We hear the prayer in our own spirits, and that prayer becomes the token of the coming blessings.

Even as the cloud foreshadows rain, so prayer foreshadows the blessing; even as the green blade is the beginning of the harvest, so is prayer the prophecy of the blessing that is about to come.

Again, prayer goes before mercy, as the representative of it. Oftentimes the king, in his progress through his realms, sends one before him who blows a trumpet; and when the people see him they know that the king is coming, because the trumpeter is there. But, perhaps, there is before him a more-important personage, who says, "I am sent before the king to prepare for his reception, and I am this day to receive whatever you have to send the king, for I am his representative." So prayer is the representative of the blessing before the blessing comes. The prayer comes, and when I see the prayer, I say, "Prayer, you are the vice-regent [ruler or manager in place of another] of the blessing; if the blessing is the king, you are the regent. I know and look upon you as being the representative of the blessing I am about to receive."

But I do think also that sometimes, and generally, prayer goes before the blessing, even as the cause goes before the effect. Some people say, when they get anything, that they get it because they prayed for it, but if they are people who are not spiritually minded, and who have no faith, let them know, that whatever they may get it is not in answer to prayer, for we know that God hears not sinners, and "The sacrifice of the wicked is an abomination to the LORD" (Proverbs 15:8).

"Well," says one, "I asked God for such-and-such a thing the other day. I know I am no Christian, but I got it. Don't you consider that I got it through my prayers?"

No, sir. No more than I believe the reasoning of the old man who affirmed that the Goodwin Sands had been caused by the building of Tenterden Steeple, for the sands had not been there before, and the sea did not come up till it was built, and, therefore, said he, the steeple must have caused the flood. Now, your prayers have no more connection with your blessing than the sea with the steeple; in the Christian's case it is far different. Often the blessing is actually brought down from Heaven by the prayer. An objector may reply, "I believe that prayer may have much influence on yourself, sir, but I do not believe that it has any effect on God."

Well, sir, I shall not try to convince you; because it is as useless for me to try to convince you to believe the testimonies I bring as it would be to convince you of any historical fact by simply reasoning about it. I could bring out of this congregation not one, nor twenty, but many hundreds, who are rational, intelligent persons, and who would, each of them, most positively declare, that some hundreds of times in their lives they have been led to seek, most earnestly, deliverance out of trouble, or help in adversity, and they have received the answers to their prayers in so marvelous a manner that they themselves did no more doubt their being answers to their cries than they could doubt the existence of God. They felt sure that He heard them; they were certain of it. Oh, the testimonies to the power of prayer are so numberless, that the man who rejects them flies in the face of good testimonies. We are not all enthusiasts; some of us are cool-blooded enough; we are not all fanatics; we are not all quite wild in our piety, some of us in other things, we reckon, act in a tolerably common-sense way.

But yet we all agree in this, that our prayers have been heard; and we could tell many stories of our prayers, still fresh upon our memories, where we have cried unto God, and He has heard us. But the man, who says he does not believe God hears prayer, knows He does. I have no respect to his skepticism, any more than I have any respect to a man's doubt about the existence of God. The man does not doubt it; he has to choke his own conscience before he dares to say he does. It is complimenting him too much to argue with him. Will you argue with a liar? He affirms a lie, and knows it is so. Will you condescend to argue with him, to prove that he is wrong! The man is incapable of reasoning; he is beyond the pale of those who ought to be treated as respectable persons. If a man rejects the existence of God, he does it desperately against his own conscience, and if he is bad enough to stifle his own conscience so much as to believe that, or pretend that he believes it, we think we shall demean ourselves if we argue with so loose a character. He must be solemnly warned, for reason is thrown away upon deliberate liars.

But you know, sir, that God hears prayer; because if you do not, either way you must be a fool. You are a fool for not believing so, and a worse fool for praying yourself; when you do not believe He hears you. "But I do not pray, sir." Do not pray? Did I not hear a whisper from your nurse when you were sick? She said you were a wonderful saint when you had the fever. You do not pray! No, but when things do not go quite well in business you would to God that they would go better, and you do sometimes cry out to Him a kind of prayer that He cannot accept, but that is still enough to show that there is an instinct in man that teaches him to pray. I believe that even as birds build their nests without any teaching, so men use prayer in the form of it (I do not mean spiritual prayer);I say, men use prayer from the very instinct of nature.

There is something in man that makes him a praying animal. He cannot help it; he is obliged to do it. He laughs at himself when he is on the dry land, but he prays when he is on the sea and in a storm. He snickers at prayer when he is well, but when he is sick he prays as fast as anybody. He would not pray when he is rich, but when he is poor he prays then strongly enough. He knows God hears prayer, and he knows that men should pray. There is no disputing with him. If he dares to deny his own conscience, he is incapable of reasoning; he is beyond the pale of morality, and therefore we dare not try to influence him by reasoning. Other means we may and hope we shall use with him, but not that which compliments him by allowing him to answer.

O saints of God, whatever you can give up, you can never give up this truth, that God hears prayer; for if you did disbelieve it today, you would have to believe it again tomorrow, for you would have such another proof of it through some other trouble that would roll over your head that you would be obliged to feel, if you were not obliged to say, "Verily, God hears and answers prayer." Prayer, then, is the prelude of mercy, for very often it is the cause of the blessing; that is to say, it is a part cause; the mercy of God being the great first cause; prayer is often the secondary agency whereby the blessing is brought down.

2. And now I am going to try to show you, in the second place, *why it is that God is pleased to make prayer the trumpeter of mercy, or the forerunner of it.*

(1) I think it is, in the first place, because God wants that man should have some reason for having a connection with him. Says God, "My creatures will shun me, even my own people will too little seek me—they will flee from me, instead of coming to me. What shall I do? I intend to bless them; shall I lay the blessings at their doors so that when they open them in the morning they may find them there, unasked and unsought?"

"Yes," says God, "many mercies I will so do with; I will give them much that they need, without their seeking for it, but in order that they may not wholly forget me, there are some mercies that I will not put at their doors, but I will make them come to my house after them."

"I love my children to visit me," says the heavenly Father, "I love to see them in my courts, I delight to hear their voices and to see their faces; they will not come to see me if I give them all they want; I will keep them sometimes without, and then they will come to me and ask, and I shall have the pleasure of seeing them, and they will have the profit of entering into fellowship with me."

It is as if some father should say to his son who is entirely dependent upon him, "I might give you a fortune at once, so that you might never have to come upon me again; but, my son, it delights me, it affords me pleasure to supply your wants. I like to know what it is you require, that I may oftentimes have to give you, and so may frequently see your face. Now I shall give you only enough to serve you for such a time, and if you want to have anything, you must come to my house for it. O my son, I do this because I desire to see you often;

I desire often to have opportunities of showing how much I love you."

So does God say to His children, "I do not give you all at once; I give all to you in the promise, but if you want to have it in the detail, you must come to me to ask me for it: so shall you see my face, and so shall you have a reason for often coming to my feet."

(2) But there is another reason. God would make prayer the preface to mercy, because often prayer itself gives the mercy. You are full of fear and sorrow, you want comfort; God says, "Pray, and you shall get it. The reason is because prayer is of itself a comforting exercise. We are all aware that when we have any heavy news upon our minds, it often relieves us if we can tell a friend about it. Now there are some troubles we would not tell to others, for perhaps many minds could not sympathize with us. God has, therefore, provided prayer as a channel for the flow of grief. "Come," says He, "your troubles may find vent here; come, put them into my ear; pour out your heart before me, and so will you prevent its bursting. If you must weep, come and weep at my mercy seat; if you must cry, come and cry in the closet, and I will hear you." And how often have you and I tried that! We have been on our knees, overwhelmed with sorrow, and we have risen up, and said, "Ah! I can meet it all now!"

> *Now I can say my God is mine*
> *Now I can all my joys resign,*
> *Can tread the world beneath my feet,*
> *And all that Earth calls good or great.*

Prayer itself sometimes gives the mercy. Take another case. You are in difficulty, and you don't know which way to go nor how to act. God has said that He will direct His people. You go forth in prayer and pray that God will direct you. Are you aware that your very prayer will frequently of itself furnish you with the answer? For while the mind is absorbed in thinking over the matter, and in praying concerning the matter, it is just in the likeliest state to suggest to itself the course that is proper, for while in prayer I am spreading all the circumstances before God. I am like a warrior surveying the battlefield, and when I rise I know the state of affairs, and I know how to act. Often, thus, you see, prayer gives the very thing we ask for in itself. Often when I have had a passage of Scripture that I cannot understand, I am in the habit of spreading the Bible before me, and if I have looked at all the commentators, and they do not seem to agree, I have spread the Bible on my chair, kneeled down, put my finger upon the passage, and sought instruction of God. I have thought that when I have risen from my knees I understood it far better than before, I believe that the very exercise of prayer did of itself bring the answer, to a great degree, for the mind being occupied upon it, and the heart being exercised with it the whole man was in the most excellent position for truly understanding it.

John Bunyan says, "The truths that I know best I have learned on my knees." He also said, "I never know a thing well till it is burned into my heart by prayer." Now that is in a great measure through the agency of God's Holy Spirit; but I think that it may in some measure also be accounted for by the fact that prayer exercises the mind upon the thing, and then the mind is led by an insensible process to lay hold upon the right result. Prayer, then, is a suitable prelude to the blessing, because often it carries the blessing in itself.

(3) Again, it seems but right, just, and appropriate, that prayer should go before the blessing, because in prayer there is a sense of need. I cannot as a man distribute assistance to those who do not represent their case to me as being destitute and sick. I cannot suppose that the physician will trouble himself to leave his own house to go into the house of one that is ill, unless the need has been specified to him, and unless he has been informed that the case requires his assistance. Neither can we expect of God that He will wait upon His own people, unless His own people should first state their need to Him, shall feel their need, and come before Him crying for a blessing. A sense of need is a divine gift; prayer fosters it and is, therefore, highly beneficial.

(4) Yet again, prayer before the blessing serves to show us the value of it. If we had the blessings without asking for them, we should think them common things; but prayer makes the common pebbles of God's temporal bounties more precious then diamonds. Spiritual prayer cuts the diamond and makes it glisten more. The thing was precious, but I did not know its preciousness till I had sought for it, and sought it long. After a long chase, the hunter prizes the animal because he has set his heart upon it and is determined to have it; and yet more truly, after a long hunger he that eats finds more relish in his food. So prayer does sweeten the mercy.

Prayer teaches us its preciousness. It is the reading over of the bill, the schedule, the account, before the estate and the properties are themselves transferred. We know the value of the purchase by reading over the will of it in prayer, and

SPURGEON'S SERMONS ON PRAYER

when we have groaned out our own expression of its peerless price, then it is that God bestows the benediction upon us. Prayer, therefore, goes before the blessing, because it shows us the value of it. But doubtless even reason itself suggests that it is but natural that God, the All-good, should give His favors to those who ask. It seems but right that He should expect of us that we should first ask at His hands, and then He will bestow. It is goodness great enough that His hand is ready to open. Surely it is but little that He should say to His people, "For this thing will I be enquired of by the house of Israel to do it for them."

3. Let me close *by stirring you up to use the holy art of prayer as a means of obtaining the blessing.*

Do you ask, "And for what shall we pray?" The answer is upon my tongue. Pray for yourselves, pray for your families, pray for the Church, pray for the one great Kingdom of our Lord on Earth.

Pray for yourselves. Sure you will never lack some subject for intercession. So broad are your wants, so deep are your necessities, that until you are in Heaven you will always find room for prayer. Do you need nothing? Then I fear you do not know yourself. Have you no mercy to ask of God? Then I fear you have never had mercies of Him, and are yet "in the gall of bitterness and in the bond of iniquity" (Acts 8:23). If you are a child of God, your wants will be as numerous as your moments and you will need to have as many prayers as there are hours. Pray that you may be holy, humble, zealous, and patient; pray that you may have communion with Christ and enter into the banqueting house of His love. Pray for yourself, that you may be an example unto others, that you may honor God here, and inherit His Kingdom hereafter.

In the next place, pray for your families, for your children. If they are pious, you can still pray for them, that their piety may be real, that they may be upheld in their profession. And if they are ungodly, you have a whole fountain of arguments for prayer. So long as you have a child unpardoned, pray for him or her; so long as you have children alive that are saved, pray for them, that they may be kept. You have enough reason to pray for those who have proceeded from your own loins.

And then pray for the Church. Let the minister have a place in your heart. Mention his name at your family altar, and in your closet. You expect him to come before you day after day, to teach you the things of the Kingdom, and exhort and stir up your pure minds by way of remembrance. If he is a true minister, there will be work to be done in this matter. He cannot write his sermon and read it to you; he does not believe Christ said, "Go and read the gospel to every creature." Do you know the cares of a minister? Do you know the trouble he has with his own church—how the erring ones do grieve him, how even the right ones do vex his spirit by their infirmities—how, when the church is large, there will always be some great trouble in the hearts of some of his people? And he is the reservoir of all; they come to him with all their grief; he is to "weep with them that weep" (Romans 12:15). And in the pulpit what is his work? God is my witness, I scarcely ever prepare for my pulpit with pleasure. Study for the pulpit is to me the most irksome work in the world. I have never come into this house that I know of with a smile upon my heart; I may have sometimes gone out with one, but never have I had one when I entered.

Preach, preach twice a day I can and will do, but still there is a travailing in preparation for it, and even the utterance is not always accompanied with joy and gladness, and God knows that if it were not for the good that we trust is to be accomplished by the preaching of the Word, it is no happiness to a man's life to be well known. It robs him of all comfort to be from morning to night heated for labor, to have no rest for the sole of his foot or for his brain—to be a great religious hack—to bear every burden—to have people asking, as they do in the country, when they want to get into a cart, "Will it hold it?"—never thinking whether the horse can drag it. It is not a joy to have them asking, "Will you preach at such a place? You are preaching twice, couldn't you manage to get to such a place and preach again?" Every one else has a constitution; the minister has none, until he kills himself and is condemned as imprudent. If you are determined to do your duty in that place to which God has called you, you need the prayers of your people, that you may be able to do the work, and you will need their abundant prayers, that you may be sustained in it. I bless God that I have a valiant corps of men, who day and night besiege God's throne on my behalf. I would speak to you, my brothers and sisters, again, and beseech you, by our loving days that are past, by all the hard fighting that we have had side by side with each other, not to cease to pray now. The time was when in hours of trouble, you and I have bended our knees together in God's house and we have prayed to God, that He would give us a blessing. You remember how great and sore troubles did roll over our heads—how men did ride over us. We went through fire and through water, and now God has brought us into a large place, and so multiplied us; therefore, let us not cease to pray. Let us still cry out unto the living God, that He may give us a blessing. Oh, may God help me if you cease to pray for me! Let me know the day, and I must cease to preach. Let me know when you intend to cease your prayers, and I shall cry, "O my God, give me this day my tomb, and let me slumber in the dust."

Lastly, let me bid you pray for the Church at large. This is a happy time we live in. A certain race of croaking souls, who are never pleased with anything, are always crying out about the badness of the times. They cry, "Oh, for the good old times!" Why, these are the good old times; time never was so old as it is now. These are the best times. I do think that many an old Puritan would jump out of his grave if he knew what was doing now. If they could have been told of the great movement at Exeter Hall, there is many a man among them who once fought against the Church of England, who would lift his hand to Heaven and cry, "My God, I bless you that I see such a day as this!" In these times there is a breaking down of many of the barriers. The bigots are afraid; they are crying out most desperately, because they think God's people will soon love each other too well. They are afraid that the trade of persecution will soon be done with, if we begin to be more and more united. So they are making an outcry, and saying, "These are not good times." But true lovers of God will say they have not lived in better days than these; and they all hopefully look for greater things still.

Unless you professors of religion are eminently in earnest in prayer, you will disgrace yourselves by neglecting the finest opportunity men ever had. I do think that your fathers who lived in days when great men were upon Earth, who preached with much power—I do think, if they had not prayed, they would have been as unfaithful as you will be. For now the good ship floats upon a flood tide. Sleep now, and you will not cross the bar at the harbor's mouth. Never did the sun of prosperity seem to shine much more fully on the Church during the last hundred years than now. Now is your time; neglect now to sow your seed in this good time of seed sowing; neglect now to reap your harvest in these good days when it is ripe, and darker days may come, and those of peril, when God shall say, "Because they would not cry to me, when I stretched out my hands to bless them, therefore will I put away my hand, and will no more bless them, until again they shall seek me."

And now to close. I have a young man here who has been lately converted. His parents cannot bear him; they entertain the strongest opposition to him, and they threaten him, that if he does not leave off praying, they will turn him out of doors. Young man, I have a little story to tell you. There was once a young man in your position; he had begun to pray, and his father knew it. He said to him, "John, you know I am an enemy to religion, and prayer is a thing that never shall be offered in my house." Still, the young man continued in earnest supplication. "Well," said the father one day, in a hot passion, "you must give up either God or me. I solemnly swear that you shall never darken the threshold of my door again, unless you decide that you will give up praying. I give you till tomorrow morning to choose." The night was spent in prayer by the young disciple. He rose in the morning, sad to be cast away by his friends, but resolute in spirit, that come what might, he would serve his God. The father abruptly accosted him, "Well, what is the answer?"

"Father," he said, "I cannot violate my conscience; I cannot forsake my God."

"Leave immediately," his father said. And the mother stood there; the father's hard spirit had made hers hard, too, and though she might have wept, she concealed her tears. "Leave immediately," the father repeated.

Stepping outside the threshold, the young man said, "I wish you would grant me one request before I go; and if you grant me that, I will never trouble you again."

"Well," said the father, "you shall have anything you like, but hear me, you go after you have had that. And you shall never have anything again."

"It is," said the son, "that you and my mother would kneel down, and let me pray for you before I go."

Well, they could hardly object to it; the young man was on his knees in a moment, and began to pray with such unction and power, with such evident love for their souls, with such true and divine earnestness, that they both fell flat on the ground, and when the son rose, there they were, and the father said, "You need not go, John. Ccome and stop; come and stop." It was not long before not only he, but the whole of them began to pray, and they were united to a Christian church.

So do not give way. Persevere kindly but firmly. It may be that God shall enable you not only to have your own souls saved, but to be the means of bringing your persecuting parents to the foot of the Cross. That such may be the case is our earnest prayer.

THE GOLDEN KEY OF PRAYER

*"Call unto me, and I will answer thee, and shew thee
great and mighty things, which thou knowest not."
(Jeremiah 33:3)*

Some of the most learned works in the world smell of the
midnight oil; but the most spiritual and most comforting
books and sayings of men usually have a savor about them of
a damp prison. I might quote many instances: John Bunyan's
Pilgrim's Progress may suffice instead of a hundred others.
And this good text of ours (see above), all moldy and chill
with the prison in which Jeremiah lay, has nevertheless a
brightness and a beauty about it, which it might never have
had if it had not come as a cheering word to the prisoner of
the Lord, locked up in the court of the prison. God's people
have always in their worst condition found out the best of
their God. He is good at all times, but He seems to be at His
best when they are at their worst.

"How could you bear your long imprisonment so well?"
said one to the Landgrave of Hesse, who had been imprisoned
for his attachment to the principles of the Reformation.

He replied, "The divine consolations of martyrs were
with me."

Doubtless there is a consolation more deep, more strong than any other, which God keeps for those who, being His faithful witnesses, have to endure exceeding great tribulation from the enmity of man. There is a glorious aurora for the frigid zone, and stars glisten in northern skies with unusual splendor. Rutherford had a quaint saying, that when he was cast into the cellars of affliction he remembered that the great King always kept His wine there, and he began to seek at once for the wine bottles and to drink of the "wines on the lees well refined" (Isaiah 25:6).

They who dive in the sea of affliction bring up rare pearls. You know, my companions in affliction, that it is so. You whose bones have been ready to come through the skin through long lying upon the weary couch; you who have seen your earthly goods carried away from you and have been reduced well nigh to poverty; you who have gone to the grave yet seven times, till you have feared that your last earthly friend would be borne away by unpitying death; you have proved that He is a faithful God and that even as your tribulations abound, so your consolations also abound by Christ Jesus.

In taking this text this morning, my prayer is that some other prisoners of the Lord may have its joyous promise spoken home to them, that you who are strictly shut up and cannot come forth by reason of present heaviness of spirit may hear Him say, as with a soft whisper in your ears and in your hearts, "Call unto me, and I will answer thee, and show thee great and mighty things which thou knowest not."

The text naturally splits itself up into three distinct particles of truth. Upon these let us speak as we are enabled by God the Holy Spirit. First, prayer commanded, "Call unto me." Second, an answer promised, "And I will answer thee." Third, faith encouraged, "And shew thee great and mighty things which thou knowest not."

1. The first part is *prayer commanded*. We are not merely counseled and recommended to pray, but we are bidden to pray. This is great condescension. A hospital is built; it is considered sufficient that free admission shall be given to the sick when they seek it, but no order in council is made that a man must enter its gates. A soup kitchen is well provided for in the depth of winter. Notice is promulgated that those who are poor may receive food on application, but no one thinks of passing an Act of Parliament, compelling the poor to come and wait at the door to take the charity. It is thought to be enough to proffer it without issuing any sort of mandate that people shall accept it. Yet so strange is the infatuation of man, on the one hand, which makes him need a command to be merciful to his own soul, and so marvelous is the condescension of our gracious God on the other, that He issues a command of love without which not a man of Adam-born would partake of the gospel feast, but would rather starve than come. In the matter of prayer it is even so. God's own people need, or else they would not receive it, a command to pray.

How is this? Because, dear friends, we are very subject to fits of worldliness, if indeed that be not our usual state. We do not forget to eat, we do not forget to take the shop shutters down, we do not forget to be diligent in business, and we do not forget to go to our beds to rest. But we often do forget to strive with God in prayer, and to spend, as we ought to spend, long periods in consecrated fellowship with our Father and our God. With too many who profess being Christians, the ledger is so bulky that you cannot move it. And the Bible, representing their devotion, is so small that you might almost put it in your waistcoat pocket. Hours for the world! Moments for Christ! The world has the best, and our prayer closet the parings of our time. We give our strength and freshness to the ways of mammon, and our fatigue and indifference to the ways of God. Hence, we need to be commanded to attend to that very act which ought to be our greatest happiness, as it is our highest privilege to perform—namely, to meet with our God. "Call unto me," He says, for He knows that we are apt to forget to call upon God. "What meanest thou, O sleeper? arise, call upon thy God" (Jonah 1:6) is an exhortation that is needed by us as well as by Jonah in the storm.

God understands what heavy hearts we have sometimes, when we are under a sense of sin. Satan says to us, "Why should you pray? How can you hope to prevail? In vain you say, 'I will arise and go to my Father' (Luke 15:18), for you are not worthy to be one of His hired servants. How can you see the King's face after you have played the traitor against Him? How will you dare to approach the altar when you have defiled it, and when the sacrifice that you would bring there is a poor, polluted one?"

O brethren, it is well for us that we are commanded to pray, or else in times of heaviness we might give it up. If God commands me, unfit as I may be, I will creep to the footstool of grace; and since He says, "Pray without ceasing" (1 Thessalonians 5:17), though my words fail me and my heart itself will wander, yet I will stammer out the wishes of my hungering soul and say, "O God, at least teach me to pray and help me to prevail with you." Are we not commanded to pray also because of our frequent unbelief? Unbelief whispers,

"What profit is there if you should seek the Lord upon such and such a matter?" This is a case quite out of the list of those things wherein God has interposed. Therefore (says the devil), if you were in any other position you might rest upon the mighty arm of God; but here your prayer will not avail you. Either it is too trivial a matter, or it is too connected with temporal matters, or it is a matter in which you have sinned too much, or it is too high, too hard, too complicated a piece of business—you have no right to take that before God! So suggests the foul fiend of hell.

Therefore, an everyday precept that is suitable to every case into which a Christian can be cast stand written, "Call unto me—call unto me." Are you sick? Would you be healed? Cry unto me, for I am the Great Physician. Does providence trouble you? Are you fearful that you shall not provide things honest in the sight of man? Call unto me! Do your children vex you? Do you feel that which is sharper than an adder's tooth—a thankless child? Call unto me. Are your grief's little, yet painful, like small points and pricks of thorns? Call unto me! Is your burden heavy as though it would make your back break beneath its load? Call unto me! "Cast thy burden upon the LORD, and he shall sustain thee: he shall never suffer the righteous to be moved" (Psalm 55:22). In the valley, on the mountain, on the barren rock, in the briny sea, submerged beneath the billows, and lifted up by-and-by upon the crest of the waves, in the furnace when the coals are glowing, in the gates of death when the jaws of hell would shut themselves upon you, cease not, for the commandment addresses you evermore with "Call unto me." Still prayer is mighty and must prevail with God to bring you deliverance. These are some of the reasons why the privilege of supplication is also in holy

Scripture spoken of as duty. There are many more, but these will suffice this morning.

We must not leave our first part till we have made another remark. We ought to be very glad that God has given us this command in His Word that it may be sure and abiding. You may turn to fifty passages where the same precept is uttered. I do not often read in Scripture, "Thou shalt not kill," or "Thou shalt not covet" (Romans 13:9). Twice the Law is given, but I often read gospel precepts, for if the Law be given twice, the gospel is given seventy times seven. For every precept that I cannot keep, by reason of my being weak through the flesh, I find a thousand precepts, which are sweet and pleasant for me to keep, by reason of the power of the Holy Spirit that dwells in the children of God. This command to pray is insisted upon again and again.

It may be a seasonable exercise for some of you to find out how often in Scripture you are told to pray. You will be surprised to find how many times such words as these are given: "Call upon me in the day of trouble: I will deliver thee" (Psalm 50:15). "Ye people, pour out your heart before him" (Psalm 62:8). "Seek ye the LORD while he may be found; call ye upon him while he is near" (Isaiah 55:6). "Ask, and it shall be given you; seek, and ye shall find; knock, and it shall be opened, unto you" (Matthew 7:7). "Watch ye and pray, lest ye enter into temptation" (Mark 14:38). "Pray without ceasing" (1 Thessalonians 5:17). "Come boldly unto the throne of grace" (Hebrews 4:16). "Draw nigh to God, and he will draw nigh to you" (James 4:8). "Continue in prayer" (Colossians 4:2). I need not multiply where I could not possibly exhaust. I pick two or three out of this great bag of pearls.

Come, Christian, you ought never to question whether you have a right to pray. You should never ask, "May I be permitted to come into His presence?" When you have so many commands (and God's commands are all promises, and all His enabling), you may come boldly unto the throne of heavenly grace, by the new and living way through the rent veil. (See Hebrews 10:20.) But there are times in the Bible when God not only commands His people to pray, but He also commands them to pray directly by the admonitions of His Holy Spirit. You who know the inner life, comprehend me at once. You feel on a sudden, possibly in the midst of business, the pressing thought that you must retire to pray. It may be that you do not at first take particular notice of the inclination, but it comes again and again and again: "Retire and pray!"

I find that in the matter of prayer, I am very much like a waterwheel that runs well when there is plenty of water, but that turns with very little force when the brook is growing shallow. Or, like the ship that flies over the waves, putting out all her canvas when the wind is favorable, but which has to tack about most laboriously when there is but little of the favoring breeze. Now, it strikes me that whenever our Lord gives you the special inclination to pray, that you should double your diligence. You "ought always to pray, and not to faint" (Luke 18:1); yet when He gives you the special longing after prayer, and you feel a peculiar aptness and enjoyment in it, you have, over and above the command that is constantly binding, another command that should compel you to cheerful obedience. At such times I think we may stand in the position of David, to whom the Lord said, "When thou hearest the sound of a going in the tops of the mulberry trees, that then thou shalt bestir thyself"

(2 Samuel 5:24). That "going in the tops of the mulberry trees" may have been the footsteps of angels hastening to the help of David, and then David was to smite the Philistines, and when God's mercies are coming, their footsteps are our desires to pray, and our desires to pray should be at once an indication that the set time to favor Zion has come.

Sow plentifully now, for you can sow in hope. Plow joyously now, for your harvest is sure. Wrestle now, Jacob, for you are about to be made a prevailing prince, and your name shall be called Israel. Now is your time, spiritual merchantmen; the market is high, so trade much, and your profit shall be large. See to it that you use right well the golden hour, and reap your harvest while the sun shines. When we enjoy visitations from on high, we should be peculiarly constant in prayer, and if some other duty less pressing should be laid aside for a season, it will not be done so amiss and we shall not be losers. When God bids us specially pray by the admonitions of His Spirit, then should we stir ourselves up in prayer.

2. Let us now take the second part—*an answer promised*. We ought not to tolerate for a minute the ghastly and grievous thought that God will not answer prayer. His nature, as manifested in Christ Jesus, demands it. He has revealed himself in the gospel as a God of love, full of grace and truth; and how can He refuse to help those of His creatures who humbly, in His own appointed way, seek His face and favor? Upon one occasion the Athenian senate found it most convenient to meet together in the open air. As they were sitting in their deliberations, a sparrow, pursued by a hawk, flew in the direction of the senate. Being hard pressed by the bird of prey, it sought shelter in the bosom of one of the senators. He,

being a man of rough and vulgar mold, took the bird from his bosom, dashed it on the ground and killed it. Whereupon the whole senate rose in uproar, and without one single dissenting voice, condemned him to die as being unworthy of a seat in the senate with them, or to be called an Athenian, if he did not render succor to a creature that confided in him.

Can we suppose that the God of Heaven, whose nature is love, could tear out of His bosom the poor, fluttering dove that flies from the eagle of justice into the bosom of His mercy? Will He give the invitation to us to seek His face, and when we, as He knows, with so much trepidation of fear, yet summon courage enough to fly into His bosom, will He then be unjust and ungracious enough to forget to hear our cry and to answer us? Let us not think that way about the God of Heaven. Let us remember, His past character as well as His nature. I mean the character that He has won for himself by His past deeds of grace. Consider, my brethren, that one stupendous display of bounty; if I were to mention a thousand, I could not give a better illustration of the character of God than that one deed: "He that spared not his own Son, but delivered him up for us all." This is not my inference only, but the inspired conclusion of an apostle, "How shall he not with him also freely give us all things?" (Romans 8:32).

If the Lord did not refuse to listen to my voice when I was a guilty sinner and an enemy, how can He disregard my cry now that I am justified and saved? How is it that He heard the voice of my misery when my heart did not know it and would not seek relief, if after all He will not hear me now that I am His child, His friend? The streaming wounds of Jesus are the sure guarantees for answered prayer. George Herbert tells about this in that quaint poem of his, "The Bag."

If ye have anything to send or write

(I have no bag, but here is room)

Unto my Father's hands and sight,

(Believe me) it shall safely come.

That I shall mind what you impart

Look, you may put it very near my heart,

Or if hereafter any of friends

Will use me in this kind, the door

Shall still be open; what he sends

I will present and somewhat more

Not to his hurt.

Surely, George Herbert's thought was that the atonement was in itself a guarantee that prayer must be heard, that the great gash made near the Savior's heart, which let the light into the very depths of the heart of deity was a proof that He who sits in Heaven would hear the cry of His people. You misread Calvary, if you think prayer is useless. But, beloved, we have the Lord's own promise for it, and He is a God who cannot lie. "Call upon me in the day of trouble: I will deliver thee" (Psalm 50:15). Has He not said, "Whatsoever ye shall ask in prayer, believing, ye shall receive" (Matthew 21:22)? We cannot pray, indeed, unless we believe this doctrine, "For he that cometh to God must believe that he is, and that he is the rewarder of them that diligently seek him" (Hebrews 11:6). If we have any question at all about whether our prayer will be heard, we are comparable to him who wavers, "For he who wavereth is like a wave of the sea driven with the wind and tossed; For let not that man think that he shall receive any thing of the Lord" (James 1:6-7).

Furthermore, it is not necessary, still it may strengthen the point, if we add that our own experience leads us to believe that God will answer prayer. I must not speak for you, but I may speak for myself. If there be anything I know, anything that I am quite assured of beyond all question, it is that praying breath is never spent in vain. If no other man here can say it, I dare to say it, and I know I can prove it. My own conversion is the result of prayer—long, affectionate, earnest, importunate prayer. Parents prayed for me, and God heard their cries, and here I am to preach the gospel. Since then I have ventured upon some things that were far beyond my capacity as I thought, but I have never failed, because I have cast myself upon the Lord. You know as a church that I have not scrupled to indulge large ideas of what we might do for God, and we have accomplished all that we purposed. I have sought God's aid, assistance, and help, in all my manifold undertakings, and though I cannot tell here the story of my private life in God's work, yet if it were written, it would be a standing proof that there is a God who answers prayer.

He has heard my prayers, not now and then, nor once nor twice, but so many times that it has grown into a habit with me to spread my case before God with the absolute certainty that whatsoever I ask of God, He will give to me. It is not now just a perhaps or a possibility. I know that my Lord answers me, and I dare not doubt. It would indeed be folly if I did. As I am sure that a certain amount of leverage will lift a weight, so I know that a certain amount of prayer will get anything from God. As the rain cloud brings the shower, so prayer brings the blessing. As spring scatters flowers, so supplication ensures mercies. In all labor there is profit, but most of all in the work of intercession; I am sure of this, for I have reaped it. As I put trust in the queen's money, and have never failed yet to buy what I want when I produce the cash, so I put trust in God's promises and mean to do so till I find that He shall once tell me that they are base coin, and will not do to trade with in Heaven's market. But why should I speak?

O brothers and sisters, you all know in your own selves that God hears prayer; if you do not, then where is your Christianity? Where is your religion? You will need to learn what are the first elements of the truth, for all saints, young or old, set it down as certain that He does hear prayer. Still remember that prayer is always to be offered in submission to God's will; that when we say that God hears prayer, we do not intend that He always gives us literally what we ask for. We do mean, however, that He gives us what is best for us. If He does not give us the mercy we ask for in silver, He bestows it upon us in gold. If He does not take away the thorn in the flesh, He says, "My grace is sufficient for thee" (2 Corinthians 12:9), and that comes to the same in the end.

Lord Bolingbroke said to the Countess of Huntingdon, "I cannot understand, your ladyship, how you can make out earnest prayer to be consistent with submission to the divine will."

"My lord," she said, "that is a matter of no difficulty. If I were a courtier of some generous king, and he gave me permission to ask any favor I pleased of him, I should be sure to put it thus, 'Will your majesty be graciously pleased to grant me such-and-such a favor; but at the same time, though I very much desire it, if it would in any way detract from your majesty's honor, or if in your majesty's judgment it should seem better that I did not have this favor, I shall be quite as content to go without it as to receive it.' So you see I might earnestly offer a petition, and yet I might submissively leave it in the king's hands."

So with God. We never offer up prayer without inserting that clause, either in spirit or in words, "Nevertheless, not as I will, but as thou wilt" (Matthew 26:39)—not my will, but yours be done. We can only pray without an "if" when we are quite sure that our will must be God's will, because God's will is fully our will. A much-slandered poet has well said:

Man, regard thy prayers as a purpose of love to your soul,

Esteem the providence that led to them as an index of God's good will;

So shall you pray aright, and your words shall meet with acceptance.

Also, in pleading for others, be thankful for the fullness of your prayer;

For if you are ready to ask, the Lord is more ready to bestow

The salt preserves the sea, and the saints uphold the Earth;

Their prayers are the thousand pillars that prop the canopy of nature.

Verily, an hour without prayer, from some terrestrial mind,

*Were a curse in the calendar of time, a spot of the blackness
of darkness.*

*Perchance the terrible day, when the world must rock
into ruins,*

*Will be one unwhitened by prayer—shall He find faith
on the Earth?*

*For there is an economy of mercy, as of wisdom and
power, and means;*

*Neither is one blessing granted, unbesought from the
treasury of good:*

*And the charitable heart of the Being, to depend upon
whom is happiness,*

*Never withholdeth a bounty, so long as His subject
prays.*

Yea, ask what you will, to the second throne in Heaven,

*It is yours for whom it was appointed; there is no limit
unto prayer:*

*But and if you cease to ask, tremble, you self-suspended
creature,*

*For your strength is cut off as was Samson's: and the hour
of your doom is come.*

3. Our third part is *encouragement to faith*. I think this is
full of encouragement to all those who exercise the hallowed
art of prayer, "I will shew thee great and mighty things which
thou knowest not."

Let us just remark that this was originally spoken to a prophet in prison; therefore, it applies in the first place to every teacher. Indeed, as every teacher must be a learner, it has a bearing upon every learner in divine truth. The best way by which a prophet, teacher and learner, can know the reserved truths, the higher and more mysterious truths of God, is by waiting upon God in prayer. I noticed very specially yesterday in reading the Book of Daniel, how Daniel understood Nebuchadnezzar's dream. The soothsayers, the magicians, the astrologers of the Chaldees, brought out their curious books and their strange-looking instruments, and began to mutter their abracadabra and all sorts of mysterious incantations, but they all failed.

What did Daniel do? He set himself to prayer, and knowing that the prayer of a united body of men has more prevalence than the prayer of one, we find that Daniel called together his brethren, and bade them unite with him in earnest prayer that God would be pleased of His infinite mercy to open up the vision. "Then Daniel went to his house and made the thing known to Hananiah, Mishael, and Azariah, his companions, that they would desire mercies of the God of heaven concerning this secret; that Daniel and his fellows should not perish with the rest of the wise men of Babylon" (Daniel 2:17-18).

And in the case of John, who was the Daniel of the New Testament, you remember how he saw a book in the right hand of Him who sat on the throne—a book sealed with seven seals that none was found worthy to open or to look thereon. What did John do? The book was by-and-by opened by the Lion of the tribe of Judah, who had prevailed to open the book; but it is written first before the book was opened, "I wept much"

307

(Revelation 5:4). Yes, and the tears of John, which were his liquid prayers, were, as far as he was concerned, the sacred keys by which the folded book was opened.

Brethren in the ministry, you who are teachers in the Sabbath school, and all of you who are learners in the college of Christ Jesus, I pray you remember that prayer is your best means of study. Like Daniel, you shall understand the dream, and the interpretation thereof, when you have sought God; and like John, you shall see the seven seals of precious truth unloosed, after you have wept much. "Yea, if thou criest after knowledge, and liftest up thy voice for understanding; if thou seekest her as silver, and searchest for her as for hid treasures; then shalt thou understand the fear of the LORD, and find the knowledge of God" (Proverbs 2:3-5).

Stones are not broken, except by an earnest use of the hammer; and the stone breaker usually goes down on his knees. Use the hammer of diligence, and let the knee of prayer be exercised, too, and there is not a stony doctrine in Revelation that is useful for you to understand that will not fly into shivers under the exercise of prayer and faith. "*Bene orasse est bene studuisse*" was a wise sentence of Luther, which has been so often quoted, that we hardly venture but to hint at it. "To have prayed well is to have studied well." You may force your way through anything with the leverage of prayers. Thoughts and reasonings may be like the steel wedges that may open a way into truth; but prayer is the lever, the price that forces open the iron chest of sacred mystery, that we may get the treasure that is hidden therein for those who can force their way to reach it. The Kingdom of Heaven still "suffereth violence, and the violent take it by force" (Matthew 11:12).

Take care that you work away with the mighty implement of prayer, and nothing can stand against you.

We must not, however, stop there. We have applied the text to only one case; it is applicable to a hundred. We single out another. The saint may expect to discover deeper experience and to know more of the higher life and scriptural life by being much in prayer. There are different translations of my text. One version renders it, "I will shew thee great and fortified things which thou knowest not." Another reads it, "Great and reserved things which thou knowest not." Now, all the developments of spiritual life are not easy of attainment. There are the common frames and feelings of repentance, faith, joy, and hope, which are enjoyed by the entire family; but there is an upper realm of rapture, communion, and conscious union with Christ, which is far from being the common dwelling place of believers. All believers see Christ; but all believers do not put their fingers into the prints of the nails, nor thrust their hand into His side. We have not all the high privilege of John to lean upon Jesus' bosom, nor of Paul, to be caught up into the third heaven.

In the ark of salvation we find a lower, second, and third story; all are in the ark, but all are not in the same story. Most Christians, as to the river of experience, are only up to the ankles; others have waded till the stream is up to their knees; a few find it breast high; and but a few—oh! how few!—find it a river to swim in, the bottom of which they cannot touch. My brethren, there are heights in experimental knowledge of the things of God that the eagle's eye of acumen and philosophic thought has never seen; and there are secret paths that the lion's whelp of reason and judgment has not as yet learned to travel. God alone can bear us there; but the chariot in which He takes us up, and the fiery steeds with which that chariot is pulled are prevailing prayers. Prevailing prayer is victorious. "By his strength he had power with God: yea, he had power over the angel, and prevailed: he wept, and made supplication unto him: he found him in Bethel, and there he spake with us" (Hosea 12:3-4). Prevailing prayer takes the Christian to Carmel, and enables him to cover Heaven with clouds of blessing, and Earth with floods of mercy. Prevailing prayer bears the Christian aloft to Pisgah and shows him the reserved inheritance; yes, and it elevates him to Tabor and transfigures him, till in the likeness of his Lord, as He is, so are we in this world. If you would reach to something higher than ordinary groveling experience, look to the rock that is higher than you. (See Psalm 61:2.) Look with the eye of faith through the windows of importunate prayer.

To grow in experience, then, there must be much prayer. You must have patience with me while I apply this text to two or three more cases. It is certainly true of the sufferer under trial: if he waits much upon God in prayer, he shall receive greater deliverances than he has ever dreamed of— "great and mighty things which thou knowest not." Here is Jeremiah's testimony: "Thou drewest near in the day that I called upon thee: thou saidst, Fear not. O LORD, thou hast pleaded the causes of my soul; thou hast redeemed my life" (Lamentations 3:57-58). And David's is the same: "I called upon the LORD in distress: the LORD answered me, and set me in a large place ... I will praise thee: for thou hast heard me, and art become my salvation" (Psalm 118:21). And yet again: "Then they cried unto the LORD in their trouble, and He delivered them out of their distresses. And He led them forth by the right way, that they might go to a city of habitation" (Psalm 107:6-7). "My husband is dead," said the poor woman, "and my creditor is come to take my two sons as bondsmen." She hoped that Elijah would possibly say, "What are your debts? I will pay them." Instead of that, he multiplies her oil till it is written, "Go thou and pay thy debt, and"—what was the "and"?—"live thou and thy children of the rest" (2 Kings 4:7).

So often it will happen that God will not only help His people through the miry places along the way, so that they may just stand on the other side of the slough, but He will bring them far on the journey safely. That was a remarkable miracle, when in the midst of the storm, Jesus Christ came walking upon the sea, the disciples received Him into the ship, and not only was the sea calm, but it is recorded, "Immediately the ship was at the land whither they went" (John 6:21). That was a mercy over and above what they asked. I sometimes hear you pray and make use of a quotation which is not in the Bible—"He is able to do exceeding abundantly above what we can ask or even think." It is not so written in the Bible. I do not know what we *can* ask or what we *can* think. But it is said, "Now unto him that is able to do exceeding abundantly above all that we ask or think" (Ephesians 3:20). Let us, then, dear friends, when we are in great trial say only, "Now I am in prison; I will pray as Jeremiah did, for I have God's command to do it, and I will look out as he did, expecting that He will show me reserved mercies, which I know nothing of at present." He will not merely bring His people through the battle, covering their heads in it, but He will bring them forth with banners waving, to divide the spoil with the mighty, and to claim their portion with the strong. Expect great things of God, who gives such great promises as these.

311

Again, here is encouragement for the worker. Most of you are doing something for Christ; I am happy to be able to say this, knowing that I do not flatter you. My dear friends, wait upon God much in prayer, and you have the promise that He will do greater things for you than you know of. We know not how much capacity for usefulness there may be in us. That ass's jawbone lying there upon the ground, what can it do? Nobody knows what it can do. Then it gets into Samson's hands; what can it not do now? No one knows what it cannot do now that a Samson wields it. And you, friend, have often thought yourself to be as contemptible as that bone, and you have said, "What can I do?" Yes, but when Christ by His Spirit grips you, what can you not do? Truly, you may adopt Paul's language and say, "I can do all things through Christ which strengtheneth me" (Philippians 4:13). However, do not depend upon prayer without effort.

In a certain school there was one girl who knew the Lord; she was a very gracious, simple-hearted, trustful child. As usual, grace developed itself in the child according to the child's position. Her lessons were always best said of any in the class. Another girl said to her, "How is it that your lessons are always so well said?"

"I ask God to help me," she said, "to learn my lesson."

Well, thought the other, *then I will do the same*. The next morning when she stood up in the class she knew nothing, and when she was in disgrace she complained to the other, "I prayed for God to help me learn my lesson, and I do not know anything of it. What is the use of prayer?"

"But did you sit down and try to learn it?"

"Oh, no," she said. "I never looked at the book."

"Ah," then said the other, "I asked God to help me to learn my lesson; but I then sat down to it studiously, and I kept at it till I knew it well, and I learned it easily, because my earnest desire, which I had expressed to God was, 'Help me to be diligent in endeavoring to do my duty.'"

So is it with some who come to prayer meetings and pray, and then they fold their arms and go away, hoping that God's work will go on. Like the woman who sings, "Fly abroad, thou mighty gospel," but does not put a penny in the plate. Her friend touched her and said, "But how can it fly if you don't give it wings to fly with?" There are many who appear to be very mighty in prayer and wondrous in supplications, but, then, they require God to do what they can do themselves, and, therefore, God does nothing at all for them.

"I shall leave my camel untied," said an Arab once to Mahomet [Muhammad], "and trust to providence."

"Tie it up tight," said Mahomet, "and then trust to providence."

So you that say, "I shall pray and trust my church or my class or my work to God's goodness," may rather hear the voice of experience and wisdom which says, "Do your best; work as if all rested upon your toil; as if your own arm would bring your salvation; and when you have done all, cast yourself on Him without whom it is in vain to rise up early and to sit up late, and to eat the bread of carefulness: and if He speed you, give Him the praise."

I shall not detain you many minutes longer, but I want to notice that this promise ought to prove useful for the comforting of those who are intercessors for others. You who are calling upon God to save your children, to bless your neighbors, to remember your husbands or your wives in mercy, may take comfort from this, "Call unto me, and I will answer thee, and show thee great and mighty things, which thou knowest not" (Jeremiah 33:3). A celebrated minister in the last century, a Mr. Bailey, was the child of a godly mother. This mother had almost ceased to pray for her husband, who was a man of a most ungodly stamp and a bitter persecutor. The mother prayed for her boy, and while he was yet eleven or twelve years of age, eternal mercy met with him. So sweetly instructed was the child in the things of the Kingdom of God, that the mother requested him—and for some time he always did so—to conduct family prayer in the house. Morning and evening this little one laid the Bible open; and, though the father would not deign to stop for the family prayer, yet on one occasion he was rather curious to know, "What sort of an out the boy would make of it." Therefore, he stopped on the other side of the door, and God blessed the prayer of his own child, who was under thirteen years of age, by granting his conversion. The mother might well have read my text with streaming eyes, and said, "Yes, Lord, you have shown me great and mighty things, which I knew not. You have not only saved my boy, but through my boy you have brought my husband to the truth."

You cannot guess how greatly God will bless you. Only go and stand at His door. You cannot tell what is in reserve for you. If you do not beg at all, you will get nothing; but if you beg, He may not only give you, as it were, the bones and broken meat, but He may say to the servant at His table,

"Take that dainty meat, and set that before the poor man." Ruth went to glean; she expected to get a few good ears, but Boaz said, "Let her glean even among the sheaves, and reproach her not." He said, moreover, to her, "At mealtime come thou hither, and eat of the bread, and dip thy morsel in the vinegar" (Ruth 2:14-15). She found a husband when she only expected to find a handful of barley.

So in prayer for others, God may give us such mercies that we shall be astounded at them, since we expected but little. Hear what is said of Job, and learn this lesson: "And the Lord said, My servant Job shall pray for you: for him will I accept: lest I deal with you after your folly, in that ye have not spoken of me the thing which is right, like my servant Job.... And the LORD turned the captivity of Job, when he prayed for his friends: also the LORD gave Job twice as much as he had before" (Job 42:8-10).

Now, this word to close with. Some of you are seekers for your own conversion. God has quickened you to solemn prayer about your own souls. You are not content to go to hell, you want Heaven; you want washing in the precious blood; you want eternal life. Dear friends, I pray you take this text—God himself speaks it to you—"Call unto me, and I will answer thee, and shew thee great and mighty things, which thou knowest not." At once take God at His Word. Get home, go into your chamber and shut the door, and try Him. Young man, I say, try the Lord. Young woman, prove Him, see whether He is true or not. If God is true, you cannot seek mercy at His hands through Jesus Christ and get a negative reply. He must, for His own promise and character bind Him to it, open mercy's gate to you who knock with all your heart. God help you, believing in Christ Jesus, to cry aloud unto

God, and His answer of peace is already on the way to meet you. You shall hear Him say, "Your sins which are many are all forgiven." (See Luke 7:47.)

The Lord bless you for His love's sake. Amen.

PART 3

SPURGEON'S SUNDAY MORNING PRAYERS

ORIGINAL PREFACE TO

SPURGEON'S SUNDAY MORNING PRAYERS

A man of faith and prayer is an apt description of the late pastor of the Tabernacle. His faith was responsive to the divine call and obedient to the divine command; it grasped the promises of God and proved the secret of his strength for service and endurance.

Familiar with the mercy seat, he sought for heavenly guidance and found in the exercise of prayer a wellspring of joy and the inspiration for his ministry. Things not seen and eternal ever lay within the range of his soul's vision, and he lived as one who had business with eternity.

Mr. D. L. Moody in commencing his first address in the Tabernacle, October 9, 1892, especially recalled the time when he first entered the building twenty-five years ago. He had come four thousand miles to hear Mr. Spurgeon. What impressed him most was not the praise, though he thought he had never heard such grand congregational singing; it was not Mr. Spurgeon's exposition, fine though it was, nor even his sermon; it was his prayer. He seemed to have such access to God that he could bring down power from Heaven; that was the great secret of his influence and his success.

The following selection of Mr. Spurgeon's Sunday morning prayers, reported verbatim, will be welcomed as a precious memorial of a life and ministry by which God was honored, souls were saved, believers were edified, and "workers together with God" were encouraged in all holy service. They will furnish stimulus for the preacher in the pulpit and aids to devotion to saints in solitude.

The sermons to which the prayers were preludes are published in the *Metropolitan Tabernacle Pulpit,* and the hymns are contained in *Our Own Hymn Book.*

GOD'S THOUGHTS AND WAYS FAR ABOVE OURS

"For my thoughts are not your thoughts, neither are your ways my ways, saith the LORD. For as the heavens are higher than the earth, so are my ways higher than your ways, and my thoughts than your thoughts."
(Isaiah 55:8-9)

O God, most high and glorious, the thought of your infinite serenity has often cheered us, for we are toiling and churning about, troubled and distressed here below beneath the moon, but you sit forever in perfect happiness. Your designs cause you no care or fear, for you will surely carry them out. Your purposes stand fast as the eternal hills; your power knows no bound, your goodness no limit. You bring order out of confusion, and our defeats are but your victories. We sow in tears, but you allow us to reap in joy. Our everlasting felicity is present to you, even while groans and mourning are our present lot. Glory be to the Lord most high, who sits on the clouds, who sits as King forever and ever.

Our hearts rejoice to hear the gladsome tidings that the Lord reigns. Let His Kingdom be established over the sons of men, for His Kingdom must come, and of it there will be no end. Behold, we come to your throne this morning, bearing about with us a body of sin and death, and consequently much of sin, and much of care, and it may be much of sorrow; but we would be unburdened at your mercy seat now. As for our cares, we are ashamed that we have them, seeing that you care for us. We have trusted you now for many years, and your faithfulness has never been under suspicion, nor your love a matter of question. We, therefore, leave every concern about our families, ourselves, our business, or about our souls entirely with our God. And as for our sin, we bless you for a sight of the precious blood of Jesus, for when you see it you pass over us. No angel of justice smites where once the blood is sprinkled. Oh, let us have a sight of the blood of Jesus, too, and rest because you have forever put away our sin, because we believe in Jesus. Thus, Lord, help us to stand before you, entering into your rest, as we enter into your presence; and may this be a time of peace, wherein the peace of God which passes all understanding, shall keep the hearts and minds of His people through Christ Jesus.

Still, Lord, we have a burden which we must now lay before you, and ask you to help us in it. We mourn over the condition of your Church, for on every side, as we look around, we see men endeavoring to undermine the doctrines of the everlasting gospel. There was a time when a man was famous for lifting up his axe upon the trees of the forest, but now they with axes break down the carved work of your sanctuary, and they despoil your truth. There is scarce a single doctrine of your Word which the wise men among us do not deny. Yea, and those who pretend to be the ministers of the gospel are among the first to speak against it, denounce it, and sanction license to sin because you will no more punish it, and to declare that Jesus Christ is not your Son.

O Lord God, our hearts often sink within us; we are apt to wish to lay our hand upon the ark to steady it, for the oxen shake it; but we know it is in your hand, and having spread the case before you, we leave it there. Many a Rabshakeh's letter [The Bible mentions Rabshakeh as one of Sennacherib's messengers to Hezekiah—2 Kings 18:17] have we read of late; behold, we bring it into the sanctuary and spread it before the Lord. O Lord our God, rebuke the unbelief, rebuke the skepticism of those who assail both you and your Christ and the gospel of your truth.

And we would ask you to do it thus if it pleases you; revive deep spirituality in the hearts of your own children. Oh, that we might live so near to the great Shepherd as to be familiar with His voice, to know its tones, that a stranger we may not follow, for we know not the voice of strangers. If it were possible, they would deceive even the very elect, and how shall your elect be kept from their deceptions but by abiding in the truth and walking in the power of the Holy Spirit? Oh, revive your Church, we pray you! Give to those who know you intense faith in the eternal verities, burning into us by experience the things that we do know; may they be beyond all question to us. And may we never be ashamed to glory in the good old way, the way the fathers trod, the way that leads to Heaven and to God. May we not be ashamed to vindicate it and to bear reproach; for your gospel has of old been to the Jews a stumbling block, and to the Greeks foolishness, and so we expect it ever to be a stumbling block to those who go after the way of superstition, and also to be foolishness to the wise men of the world. O God, again confuse the knowledge of men by what they think to be the foolishness of the gospel. Let it again be seen that the foolishness of God is wiser than men, and the weakness of God is stronger than men.

O Jesus, Son of the Highest (see Luke 1:32), we know that the truth is powerful, because you are the soul of it—the very essence of it. Put your life into it, we pray you. May the eternal Spirit go with every word that God-sent ministers shall proclaim, and may the Lord grant, that as the mists fly before the sun and the clouds before the wind, so error and superstition may be driven away by the rising of the Sun of Righteousness in all the glory of His brightness.

We have also to bring before you another burden, and that is the godlessness of this present age. It is not alone the wise men but, behold, even the men who know not do not seek after God. O Lord, the multitudes delight in sin. Drunkenness defiles our city, and filthy words are heard on every side. Be not wrathful with this nation, we beseech you, for it has been entrusted with wondrous privileges. Forgive it and have mercy upon its aggravated sin. Lay not its heavy responsibilities to its charge, but let this nation be saved. We pray for it, as we are in duty bound to do and as our love constrains us to do. Oh, let the masses of the people yet come to seek after Christ, or by some means, by all means, by every means, may the ears of men be reached and their hearts be touched. May they hear, that their souls may live; and may the Lord who in everlasting covenant sets forth His Son, glorify Him in the midst of the nations. Let all the nations know the Christ of God.

Our Father, we ask you to help the few, the valiant few, who press forward into the dense area of the enemy. Help them to fight valiantly! May these pioneers of the Christian host in mission lands be increased in number, may they be kept in good heart, may they have confidence in God, and may the Lord send the day of victory much sooner than our feeble faith has dared to hope. But, Lord, we have yet another burden—it is that we ourselves do not love you as we should, that oftentimes we grow lukewarm and chill, and doubt creeps over us; unbelief mars our confidence, and we sin and forget our God. O Lord, help us! Pardon is not enough; we want sanctification. We beseech you, let the weeds that grow in the seed plot of our soul be cut up by the roots. We do want to serve you. We long that every thought we think and every word we say or write, should be all for you. We want to lead consecrated lives, for we are persuaded that we only live as we live unto God, that anything else is but trifling. Oh, to be taken up as offerings wholly to be consumed upon the altar of the Lord, joyfully ascending to Him in every outgoing of our life.

Now this morning be pleased to refresh us. Draw nigh unto us, most gracious God; it is only your presence that can make us happy, holy, devout, or strong. Shadow us now with your wings, cover us with your feathers, and under your wings may we trust. May we follow very near to you, and so feel the quickening warmth, the joy which only your nearness can bring. If any in your presence this morning are unsaved, oh, save them now. Do grant that the service of this morning may bring such glad tidings to their ears, that their hearts shall leap at the sound of it, and they shall return unto God, who will abundantly pardon. Bless every preacher of the Word today and all Sabbath schools, classes of young men and women, all tract distributing and street preaching, and preaching in the theaters, and every form of holy service. Accept the prayers and praises of your people. Receive them even from the sick beds of those detained at home. Let not one of your mourners, the weary watchers of the night, be kept without a smile from you.

The Lord bless us now, and all His chosen people. Our soul cries out for it. Break, O everlasting morning, break over the dark hills! Let our eyes behold you, and till the day break and the shadows flee away, abide with us. O our Beloved, abide with us now. Amen.

JESUS INTERCEDING FOR TRANSGRESSORS

"He bare the sin of many, and made intercession for the transgressors." (Isaiah 53:12)

Gracious God, we praise you with our whole hearts for the wondrous revelation of your love in Christ Jesus our Lord. We think every day of His passion, for all our hope lies in His death, but as often as we think upon it, we are still filled with astonishment that you should so love the world as to give your only begotten Son, that whosoever believes in Him should not perish but have everlasting life; that Heaven's eternal Darling should come to Earth to be made a man, and in manhood's form to be despised and rejected of the very men whom He came to bless; and then should be made to bear the sin of many and to be numbered with the transgressors, and being found in that number, to die a transgressor's death—a felon's death upon the gibbet of the Cross.

Oh, this surpasses all belief, if it had not indeed been actually so and if the sure word of prophecy had not of old declared it, we could not have imagined it. It would have seemed blasphemy to have suggested such a thought; yet you have done it. Your grace has almost out-graced itself, your love has reached its height of love to rebels—such love that even your Son could not be spared. O God, we are afflicted in our hearts to think we do not love you more after such love as this. Oh, were there not a stone in our hearts, we would melt in love to you; we would account that there was no thought fit to occupy the mind but this one stupendous thought of God's love to us, and, henceforth, this would be the master key to our hearts, the key that should unlock or lock them at your will, and give access to the great love wherewith you have loved us. We lie in the very dust before you in utter shame, to think that we have sometimes heard this story without emotion and even told it without tenderness. The theme truly has never become stale to us. We can say in your presence that the story of Christ's death still brings joy and makes our hearts leap. But yet, Lord, it never has affected us as we could have expected it would. Give us more tenderness of heart; give us the ability to feel the wounds of Jesus till they wound our sins to death. Give us a heart pierced even as His was pierced, with deep sympathy for His griefs and an all-consuming love for His blessed person.

We adore you, O Father, for your great love in the gift of Jesus. We equally adore you, most blessed Jesus, for resigning your life for our sakes, and then we adore the blessed Spirit who has led us to know this mystery and to put our trust in Jesus. Unto the one God of Abraham, Isaac, and Jacob do we pay our reverent homage this morning; only we see Him yet more clearly than the patriarchs of old did, for God in the time of Jesus Christ is seen in the clearest light that mortal eye can bear.

And now we have a prayer to present to you, great God, and it is this, that in us your dear Son may see some portion of the travail of His soul. Lord, let Him see a reward for His sufferings in all of us being repentant for sin, trusting in God and confessing His name. We fear there are among us this morning some who still indulge in the sins that brought Christ to death; some are still trusting in their own righteousness and so are despising His, because if their wills suffice then His was superfluous. O God, we beseech you to bring men away from all their false trusts to rest in the great sacrifice of your dear Son. Let not one person here be so callous to the merit of Christ as not to love Him, or so indifferent to the efficacy of His blood as not to desire to be cleansed in it.

Oh, bring every one of us now to believe in Jesus Christ with our whole heart unto eternal life, so that the thousands in this tabernacle may belong to Jesus, that He may have a portion with the great. But even those who have believed in Christ have a need to give the same prayer. Our Lord and Master, Redeemer and Savior, come and take entire possession of us. We own your right, but you must take by force what you have purchased, or you will never have it. By force of arms, the arms must be those of love, will you capture our willful, wayward spirit. Come and divide the spoil with the strong in us, we pray you. Take every faculty and use it, overpower and sanctify it. Help us to use every moment of our time for you, and may we breathe every breath to your honor. We feel that there is unconquered territory in our nature yet. Subdue, Lord, we beseech you, our corruptions; cast them out and rule and conquer within. Set up your eternal throne our spirits. "Wean our hearts from every creature, thee to love and thee alone."

We do pray this with our whole hearts. Assist us, we ask, most blessed Redeemer, to show forth your praises in our lives.

Sanctify us in our households. May we go in and out before you showing the name and nature of Christ. Help us in our business, that in all we do among our fellow men we may act as Christ would have us act. Strengthen us in secret, that there we may be mighty in prayer. Guard us in public, that neither in act nor word we may slip away from you. Above all, cast cords of love around our hearts. Oh, hold us, Savior; never let us go. Suffer no professed Christian here ever to violate the loyalty of his obedience to his King. May those dear wounds of His have more sway over us than a silver scepter even had over the subjects of earthly princes. May we feel that if He drank for us the vinegar and gall, whatever cup He sets before us we will cheerfully drink. Rule us, Savior; rule us, we beseech you. And let no believer here violate the chastity of his heart to the Beloved of his soul.

O Jesus, let us love you so intensely, that whatever else there may be of loving relationship, still this may cover all and swallow up all. Oh, to be wholly Christ's! We do mourn that we cannot attain to this—that in the secret of our hearts every devil should be cast out, every demon driven to its deep, every sin made hateful, every thought of sin made loathsome to us, until only pure desires and inward longings after perfect holiness shall predominate our natures. O God, let the scourge still be used to drive out the buyers and sellers; we would not ask to have them spared, but let the temple be the Lord's, seeing He has built it and has cleansed it with His blood.

Bless at this time very graciously the church to which we belong. Let us in this place know the power of prayer today and tomorrow. Especially pour out upon the members of this church an intense spirit of supplication. May we agonize tomorrow for the glory of God, and today also, and let it not depart from us so long as we live. Send us, Lord, a mighty groundswell of intense desire for the glory of God, and may these your servants banded together in church fellowship recognize their sweet obligations to their dying Lord and determine that the prayers of the church shall go up before Him like sweet perfume.

Lord, convert our friends who remain unsaved. Oh, mighty power of God, let none come into this house even accidentally and casually without receiving some devout impression. May the Spirit of God work mightily by our ministry and the ministration of all His servants now present, whether in the Sabbath school, in the streets, in the lodging houses, from door to door, or when they privately speak to individuals. Oh, glorify yourself in us. Dear Savior, we pray you, come and mark us all distinctly with the blood mark as being wholly yours, and henceforth may we say with Paul, "Let no man trouble me, for I bear in my body the marks of the Lord Jesus." As we have been buried with you by baptism into death, so would we be dead to all the world and only live for Christ. God grant that it may be so, and we will glorify you in life and death forever.

As you have bidden us to pray for all men, so do we now especially pray for our beloved country. May every blessing rest upon this favored isle. Upon the Queen let your mercies always descend. Keep this land in peace, we beseech you, and as for all other lands may peace yet reign. May oppression in every place be broken to shivers, and may truth and righteousness win the day. Break in pieces the power of antichrist, we pray you, and of the false prophet, and let the idols fall from their thrones, and may the Lord God omnipotent yet reign, even Jesus, King of kings and Lord of lords. We ask it all in His name. Amen.

THE DAY OF SALVATION

Behold, now is the accepted time;
behold, now is the day of salvation." (2 Corinthians 6:2)

O God, you are our exceeding joy. The very singing of your praises lifts our hearts; when we can join in the solemn psalm or the sacred hymn, our hearts leaps\ within us. And when your name is glorified, when we see sinners glorifying the name of Jesus, when we look forward to the brighter days when myriads shall flock to the crucified, when we contemplate His final triumph, then is our heart very restful and our spirit rejoices in God our Savior.

What a fountain of delight you are, and how richly have you promised to bless the men who delight themselves in you. You have said, "Delight thyself also in the LORD, and he shall give thee the desires of thine heart" (Psalm 37:4). Do you reward us for being delighted? Oh, pleasant duty, which has appended to it so divine a promise. Shall we have the desires of our heart when our heart finds all its desire in you?

Oh, blessed Lord, you do indeed meet them that work righteousness and that rejoice in your ways; and you fill your people with good things, so that their youth is renewed like the eagle's. We pray you to help us who know you to glorify you. We have known you from our youth, some of us, and hitherto have we declared your wondrous works. Oh, may there never be in our hearts, and above all may there never come from our lips, or in our lives, anything that might dishonor you. Oh, let us die a thousand deaths sooner than ever dishonor your hallowed name. This is dearer to us than the apple of our eye. We have loved the habitation of your house and the place where your honor dwells. Gather not our soul with sinners, nor our lives with cruel men; but let us be helped, even to the end, to follow the Lamb whithersoever He goes, even if it be to Gethsemane and Calvary. Oh, to be perfect in heart towards the Lord! Our lives are faulty, and we see much to grieve over, but we would have our whole heart towards your statutes; and we bless you that so it is, for our heart is in your ways, and we are willing to spend and to be spent for you.

Reservation would we not make to the very slightest, but we lay ourselves out for your honor only, for by us and in us, Father, glorify your name. Look down upon the great assemblies of this morning all over the world, and let your eye of tenderness rest here. You see here many that love you—may we love you more! You see many that live by the life of God—oh, life of God, live in us to the full! You see, also, we fear, some who are declining from your ways, in whom grace is but a flickering light. Lord, trim the lamps and bring back the wanderers, for there is no joy but in God. And, perhaps, nay we fear it must be so, that you see in this throng, ungodly ones who are careless and indifferent. Oh, sword of the Lord, pierce them through, that carelessness may be slain, and their souls may live. Oh, you who are as a polished shaft hidden in the quiver of the eternal, go forth today to smite to the heart the proud, the self-righteous, and those who will not stoop to ask mercy at your hands, but as for the humble and the contrite, look upon them; the broken-hearted and the heavy-laden do you relieve, and such as have no helper, do you succor.

Bring up the sinner from the prison house, and let the lawful captive be delivered. Let the mighty God of Jacob lead forth His elect, as once He led them out of Pharaoh's bondage. The Red Sea is already divided, that they may march through it. The Lord saves multitudes—He knows them that are His. Accomplish their number and let Jesus so be rewarded, though Israel be not gathered. Oh, Lord, we ask for ourselves strength to bear and to do. Some of us would ask, if it were your will, for restoration to health; but your will be done. Others would ask deliverance out of trouble—again, your will be done. Some would come before you with conscious guilt, and ask for a new application of the precious blood. We had better all ask for this; let us all have it.

O God, bless this church and these people more and more. How richly you have blessed them! When we look back upon past years, what has God wrought? Shall you be without our song? Even when we are not as we would be, shall our voice, if it be cracked and broken, still be silent? No, if every harp string shall be broken but one, that one shall still resound with the love of Jesus and the glory of God. As long as we live, we will bless your name, our King, our God of love, for there is none like you. "Whom have we in Heaven but you, and there is none upon Earth that we desire beside you." Our soul is clean divorced from all Earth's good, and married to the Christ of God forever. By bonds that never can be snapped we are one with Him, and who shall separate us from His Love?

The Lord be pleased to reveal himself to His servants. Oh, for the uplifting of the veil, for the drawing near of the people who are made glad by the blood, for the speaking of God unto the soul, and the speaking of our soul unto God. Oh, for converse with the eternal, for such fellowship as they may have who are raised up together with Christ, and made to sit in the heavenlies with Him. Oh, Savior, grant us a glimpse of your great love. One flash of your eye is brighter than the noonday. One word from your lips will be sweeter to us and more full of music than the harps of angels. Grant it to every one of your children all over the world, both to the sick and to the dying. Oh, how gloriously will they die!

And now, Lord, we ask you to bless our country at this time, and by your great and infinite mercy preserve us, we beseech you, from war. Oh, that peace may reign yet all over the world, but let not this nation intermeddle and be as one that takes a dog by the ear, but may there be wisdom given where we fear folly and strength given where wisdom reigns. The Lord grant that wars may utterly cease unto the ends of the Earth. Oh, make a way, we pray you, for the progress of Christianity, civilization, liberty, and everything that is honest and of good repute. May your Kingdom come, and your will be done on Earth, as it is in Heaven, for yours is the Kingdom, the power and the glory, forever and ever. Amen.

CHRIST IS ALL

Oh, the bitter shame and sorrow,
That a time could ever be
When I let the Savior's pity

Plead in vain, and proudly answered,

"All of self, and none of you."

Yet He found me. I beheld Him

Bleeding on the accursed tree,

Heard Him pray, "Forgive them, Father!"

And my wistful heart said faintly,

"Some of self, and some of you."

Day by day His tender mercy,

Healing, helping, full and free,

Sweet and strong, and ah! so patient,

Brought me lower, while I whispered,

"Less of self, and more of you!"

Higher than the highest heavens,

Deeper than the deepest sea,

Lord, thine love at last hath conquered;

Grant me now my soul's desire, —

"None of self, and all of you!

THE PERSONAL TOUCH

"If I may touch but his clothes, I shall be whole."
(Mark 5:28)

O Lord God, the great I Am, we do confess and cheerfully acknowledge that all of us were made by you. You have made us and not we ourselves, and the breath in our nostrils is kept there by your continued power. We owe our sustenance, our happiness, our advancement, our ripening, and our very existence entirely to you. We would bless you for all the mercies with which you surround us, for all things which our eyes see that are pleasant, which our ears hear that are agreeable, and for everything that makes existence to be life. Especially do we own this dependence when we deal with spiritual things. O God, we are less than nothing in the spiritual world. We do feel this increasingly, and yet even to feel this is beyond our power. Your grace must give us even to know our need of grace. We are not willing to confess our own sinfulness until you show it to us. Though it stares us in the face, our pride denies it, and our own inability is unperceived by us. We steal your power and call it our own till you compel us to say that we have no strength in ourselves.

Now, Lord, would we acknowledge that all good must come of you through Jesus Christ by your Spirit, if ever we are to receive it. And we come humbly, first of all acknowledging our many sins. We cannot calculate how many they are, how black they are, how deep their ill effects; yet, we do confess that we have sinned ourselves into hopeless misery, unless your free, undeserved grace rescues us from it. Lord, we thank you for any signs of penitence—give us more of it. Lay us low before you under a consciousness of our undeserving state. Let us feel and mourn the atrocity of our guilt. O God, we know a tender heart must come from you. By nature our hearts are stony, and we are proud and self-righteous.

Help everyone here to make an acceptable confession of sin, with much mourning, deep regret, self-loathing, and the absence of anything like a pretense to merit or to excuse. Here we stand, Lord, a company of publicans and sinners, with whom Jesus deigns to sit down. Heal us, Emmanuel! Here we are, needing that healing. Good Physician, come and manifest your healing power!

There are many of us who have looked unto Jesus and are lightened, but we do confess that our faith was the gift of God. We had never looked with these bleary eyes of ours to that dear Cross unless first the heavenly light had shone, and the heavenly finger had taken the thick scales away. We trace, therefore, our faith to that same God who gave us life, and we ask now that we may have more of it. Lord, maintain the faith you have created, strengthen it, let it be more and more simple. Deliver us from any sort of reliance upon ourselves, whatever shape that reliance might take, and let our faith in you become more childlike every day that we live; for, O dear

Savior, there is room for the greatest faith to be exercised upon your blessed person and work.

O God, the most high and all-sufficient, there is room for the greatest confidence in you. O Divine Paraclete, the Holy Ghost, there is now sufficient room for the fullest faith in your operations. Grant us this faith. Oh, work it in us now while at the same time we do confess that if we have it not—it is our shame and sin. We make no excuse for unbelief, but confess it with detestation of it that we should ever have doubted the truthful, the mighty, the faithful God. Yet, Lord, we shall fall into the like sin again, unless the grace that makes us know it to be sin shall help us to avoid it.

And now, Lord, we ask you to accept of us this morning whatever offerings we can bring. We bring our hearts to you, full of love for what you have done, full of gratitude, faith, hope, and joy. We feel glad in the Lord. But we do confess that if there be anything acceptable in these our offerings, they are all first given to us by you. No praise comes from us till first it is wrought in us, for:

Every virtue we possess,

And every victory won;

And every thought of holiness,

Are yours, great God, alone.

May we lay those fruits at your feet that were grown in your garden, and that gold, silver, and frankincense that you did bestow, only first give us more! Oh, to love the Savior with a passion that can never cool! Oh, to believe in God with a confidence that can never stagger! Oh, to hope in God with an expectation that can never be dim! Oh to delight in God with a holy, overflowing rejoicing that can never be stopped, so that we might live to glorify God at the highest level of our powers, living with enthusiasm, burning, blazing, being consumed with the indwelling God who works all things in us according to His will!

Thus, Lord, would we praise and pray at the same time. We would confess and acknowledge our responsibilities, but also bless the free and sovereign grace that makes us what we are. O God of the eternal choice, O God of the ransom purchased on the tree, O God of the effectual call—Father, Son, and Spirit—our adoration rises to Heaven like the smoke from the altar of incense. Glory, honor, majesty, power, dominion, and might be unto the only God, forever and ever. And all the redeemed by blood will say, "Amen."

Look at this time, we beseech you, upon us as a church and give us greater prosperity. Add to us daily. Knit and unite us together in love. Pardon church sins. Have mercy upon us, that we do not more for you. Accept what we are enabled to do. Qualify each one of us to be vessels fit for the Master's use, then use each one of us according to the measure of our capacity. Be pleased to bless the various works carried on by the church. May they all prosper. Let our Sabbath school especially be visited with the dew of Heaven, and may the schools that belong to us and are situated a little distance from here also have an abundant shower from the Lord. May the Sabbath schools throughout the world be richly refreshed and bring forth a great harvest for God.

Bless our college, O God; let every brother sent out be clothed with power, and may the many sons of this church that have been brought up at her side, preach with power today. It is sweet for us to think of hundreds of voices this day declaring the name of Christ. Blessed is the church that has her quiver full of them; she shall speak with her adversaries in the gate. The Lord bless us in this thing also, for except you build the house, they labor in vain who build it. Bless our dear boys at the orphanage. We thank you for the conversion of many. May they all be the children of God, and as you have taken yet another away to yourself, prepare any whom you intend to take. We pray you spare their lives, but if at any time any must depart, may they go out of the world unto the Father. May the Lord bless all the many works that are carried on by us, or rather which you carry on through our feeble instrumentality.

May our colporteurs [distributors of books and tracts], in going from house to house, be graciously guided to speak a good word for Jesus. And, Lord, bless us. We live unto you; our one aim in life is to glorify you. For you we hope we would gladly die; yes, for you we will cheerfully labor while strength is given; but, oh, send prosperity, and not to us only, but to all workers for Jesus, to all missions in foreign lands and missions in the heathendom at home.

Bless all your churches far and near, especially the many churches speaking our own language across the Atlantic, as well as in this land. The Lord send plenteous prosperity to all the hosts of His Israel. May your Kingdom come! And, Lord, gather in the unconverted. Our prayers can never conclude without pleading for the dead in sin. Oh, quicken them, Savior, and if anyone here has a little daughter who lies dead in sin, like Jairus may they plead with Jesus to come and lay His hand upon her, please, that she may live. If we have any unsaved relatives, Lord, save them. Save our servants, save our neighbors, save this great city; yea, let your Kingdom come over the whole Earth. Let the nations melt into one glorious empire beneath the sole sway of Jesus, the Son of David and the Son of God.

Come quickly, O Lord Jesus, even so, come quickly. Amen.

TRUE PRAYER—HEART PRAYER

*For thou, O LORD of hosts, God of Israel, hast revealed
to thy servant, saying, I will build thee an house:
therefore hath thy servant found in his heart to pray
this prayer unto thee. (2 Samuel 7:27)*

O Lord, our song reminds us of what we were, and we begin our praise by the acknowledgment of our natural condition; we remember the miry clay and the rock from which we were hewn, for we were "by nature the children of wrath, even as others" (Ephesians 2:3). Well do we remember when we felt this, and when the bitterness and gall were in our mouths, of which we had to drink both day and night. How heavy was the load of sin! All our thoughts were engrossed with that sense of pressure and of dread. We looked on the right hand and there was no helper, and on the left and we found none; but then you did yourself deliver us by leading us to cast a faith look to the divine, only begotten and crucified Son. At this moment, is it vividly upon our recollection how you did bring us up out of the "horrible pit." We remember now the new song which you put into our mouths, as we found our feet fast on the rock and our goings established. It has been long since then with some of us, but all the way has been strewn with mercies, and we desire this morning to record, "Bless the LORD, O my soul, and forget not all His benefits" (Psalm 103:2). We thank you now, in retrospect, for the trials we have endured. Some of us have been brought very low with physical pain and mental weariness, and others have been sorely smitten with bereavement, losses, crosses, and persecutions, but there is not one out of all our trials that we could have afforded to have been without. No, Lord, all has been ordered well; there was a need for every twig of the rod, and we desire now to thank you that we can see in looking back, how all things have even now worked together for good, though we know we cannot see the end as yet.

O our good God, our blessed God, like David, we would happily sit down before you in silence and wait awhile, for our words when we do use them are totally inadequate to the expression of what we feel, much more of what we ought to feel concerning your goodness and your loving-kindness; yet we will bless your name with such language as we have. Jehovah, our God, let others worship whom they will and seek after what object of love they please, this God is our God forever and ever, He shall be our Guide even unto death. Father, Son, and Holy Spirit, the triune God of Israel, we express most solemnly the reverence we feel for you; and we render to you our humble adoration, as we acknowledge you to be the One and only God, by whom the heavens and the Earth were made, by whom all things consist, the Redeemer of your people, their Father and their Friend, forever and ever! All our hearts worship you, O glorious Lord!

And truly since we have received so many mercies from your hand, we do feel that you will never forsake us; and in any darkness that may be in our path in the future, you will not desert your own. You have done too much for us to desert us now. We have cost you so much—oh, wondrous price that you have paid for us—and you have spent so much wise thought and so many gracious acts upon us, that we are persuaded you will go through with the work your wisdom has undertaken. But give us faith to believe this when the stormy times come; let us not doubt, but what our helmsman will bring us to the desired haven. Though winds and waves assault our keel, may we still find perfect peace and rest in the thought that He who is in the hinder part of the ship is Master of the winds and waves. Comfort your children this morning, great Father, if any of them are in doubt just now; and bring them all into an assured confidence and perfect restfulness in the Lord their God.

Next, we would humbly ask that we may be permitted to do some great service for you before we leave this world. We do not mean great service in the wisdom of our fellows, but let it be all that we can do. If we cannot build a house for you, yet have we set our hearts upon doing something; and if it be your will, direct our minds to what it shall be, lest our minds should not be your mind, but let not one of us be barren or unfruitful. If we have, indeed, been redeemed by the blood of Christ, may we reckon that we must live to Him; may the love of Christ constrain us, and may something come of our lives that shall be a blessing to the sons of men before we go.

And, our Father, while we offer this prayer, we will also pray with a deep gratitude for all your mercies; may they take possession of our heartsso that, as when David sat in his house of cedar he "magnified the Lord," so may we also do the same whenever things go smoothly with us. Lord, may the gratitude we feel prompt us to say again, "What shall I render to the Lord for all His benefits towards me?" Make every child of yours here serve you every day; in serving you, may Heaven's work begin below and something of Heaven's pleasure be enjoyed even now. But, Lord, while we work for you, always keep us sitting at the feet of Jesus. Let our faith never wander away from the simplicity of its confidence in Him. Let our motive never be anything but His glory; may our hearts be taken up with His love, and our thoughts perpetually engaged about His person. Let us choose the good part that shall not be taken away, that if we serve with Martha, we may also sit with Mary.

Let this church, Lord, receive a fresh anointing of the Holy Ghost, that all its members may be spending themselves for the Master. Quicken, we pray you, every agency. In all our Sabbath schools, may there be no lack of teachers; may our young friends find it a delight to be teaching the little ones; may there be even a superabundance of workers in this department. Let not anything lack completion to which the church has set her hand. Prosper us in the education of our young men for the ministry! Bless us, we pray you, with our dear orphan boys; may they, all of them, be saved in the Lord with an everlasting salvation. Remember our colporteurs [peddlers of devout literature] scattered about this country, and prosper them in their going from house to house with the Word of God, and may they be great soul-winners, all of them, that the Lord's name may be glorified.

And all the thousand and one things that constitute the activities of the churches at large, do bless and prosper them so far as they are according to your will; and may it please you to give to the churches prayer in proportion to activity and faith in proportion to zeal. O Lord, visit your Church at this time, which is a time of peril, and in your mercy revive among us the love of the pure Gospel of Jesus Christ. Rebuke, we pray you, those who with their philosophy and vain deceit would mar and spoil the Gospel of Jesus Christ. Grant that in all deliberations of any part of your Church, which concern this great and grievous and crying evil, there may be decision and wisdom and help given, that all may be done and ordered to your glory.

Bless our nation, Lord, we pray you, and let the spirit of Christianity permeate it, enter into the high places, and flow down even to its darkest dens. And, we beseech you, let us have peace; may nothing happen to break it, may it be established on a firm and judicious footing, and for many a year may no sound of trumpet, or noise of cannon be heard throughout the whole Earth. Let the people praise you, O God, and learn war no more! Let all the nations be blessed! May the Gospel of Christ Jesus penetrate into the remotest regions, and where it is known, may the power of it be felt far more.

Bless our brethren across the sea of another land, but who with the same tongue worship our Lord in spirit and in truth, and our brethren on the southern side of the globe, and all the scattered saints in every nation; visit them with the dew of the Holy Ghost, and make the gardens of the Lord amidst the desert to be green, and blossom as the rose. Now help us this morning, give to every one a sense of pardoned sin, and forgive us, O Father, for Christ's sake! Give to each one of us also sanctifying power, that we may be cleansed from the influence of guilt. Give us power in the delivery of the gospel. May the truth sink into the soul, and may this be a good and happy, devout and beneficial occasion to all of us here. We ask it for Jesus' sake. Amen.

PRELUDE TO SERMON

TRUST AND PRAY

"For the people shall dwell in Zion at Jerusalem: thou shalt weep no more: he will be very gracious unto thee at the voice of thy cry; when he shall hear it, he will answer thee."
(Isaiah 30:19)

O Lord God, the strength and the hope of your people, we would approach you through Jesus Christ your Son with notes of thanksgiving, for we are not ashamed of our hope; neither has our confidence led us into confusion. We have proven it to be true, that they that trust in the Lord shall be as mount Zion, which can never be moved and abides forever.

We trusted in you with regard to our innumerable sins, and you have cast them behind your back. We trusted in you; yes, we trusted in you when many evils compassed us about, and we were sorely tried with temptation. You brought us out into a wealthy place. You did set our feet upon a rock and establish our goings. We trusted in you, though too feebly, in the hour of our distress when we were troubled exceedingly with earthly things. Still, you did not fail us, though our faith trembled, and, though we believed not, you did abide faithful. The Lord has helped His people, yea the Lord has been the strength and the help of His chosen. "Many are the afflictions of the righteous, but the LORD delivereth him out of them all" (Psalm 34:19), and at this moment, in looking back upon the past, we have nothing to do but to admire and to adore the constancy of lov and the faithfulness of grace.

We thank you, O God, on behalf of many of your people, our brethren, that you have dealt so well with them. We knew them many years ago when their young hearts first believed in you, and here they are still living in Zion, to praise you as they do this day. Their feet have sometimes almost gone, their steps have well nigh slipped, but you have held them up, and they are walking in their integrity, preserved as only grace could preserve them, living still to praise your name. We bless you on behalf of the much tried among your children. They went through fire and through water; men did go over their heads, yet have you preserved them. Their hope seemed to wither like the fading leaf, and the summer of their joy turned into a bleak winter of adversity, yet has the springtime come to them and the time of the singing of birds, yea, they begin to pluck their first ripe fruits, and they joy and exult in the Lord.

O Lord, we praise you for keeping alive a testimony for the truth in the land. There have been dark and evil days, and some that professed to be your servants have turned traitors to the gospel; still, you have heard the cry of the faithful, and the candle is not put out; neither has the sun gone down, but even unto this day the Lord, the God of Israel reigns in the midst of His people and His saints exult in His name. And now with this thankfulness upon our hearts, we would humbly ask you to strengthen us as to our future confidence in you. Are there any of your servants here at this time, or anywhere all over the world, whose confidence begins to fail them by reason of present affliction or deep depression of spirit? We beseech you, strengthen the things that remain that are ready to die, and let their faith no longer waver, but may they become strong in the Lord, in full assurance of faith. O God, you know the burden of every heart before you, the secret sighing of the prisoner comes up into your ears. Some of us are in perplexity, while others are in actual suffering of body. Some are sorely cast down in themselves, and others are deeply afflicted with the trials of those they love, but as for all these burdens, our soul would cast them on the Lord—in quietness and confidence shall be our strength, and we would this morning, all without exception who are tried and troubled, take up the place of sitting still, leaving with quiet acquiescence everything in the hands of God. Great Helmsman, you shall steer the ship and we will not be troubled. By your grace we will leave everything most sweetly in your hands. Where else should these things be left? And we will take up the note of joyous song in anticipation of the deliverance that will surely come.

Save your people from unbelief, and save them from confidence in the creature. Bring us one and all to be as to the world even as a weaned child. May we have done with these things, and as to you, O Lord, may we with strong desire seek after yet more of you, and cling to you as our sure confidence for evermore. As for the future, we desire to bless your name that you have covered it from our eyes; nor would we wish to lift even a corner of the veil that hides from us the things that are to be, but we delight to feel that He who has ruled all things for our good changes not. It may be that you have appointed for us great torrents of tribulation, but you will be with us if we pass through the river. Perhaps you will permit us to go through blazing fires of persecution or temptation, but we shall not be burned, for you have assured us it shall be so, that we shall go through the fires unhurt since you will be with us.

Peradventure it is written in the tablets of your eternal purpose that we shall soon end this mortal life and die. Well, be it so, we shall the sooner see your face, and the sooner drink eternal draughts of bliss. But if you have appointed for us gray hairs and a long and weary time of the taking down of the tabernacle, only grant us grace that by infirmity our faith may never fail us. But when the windows are darkened may we still look out to see the hope that is to be revealed, and when the grasshopper becomes a burden, still let our strength be as our days, even to the last day.

We now commit ourselves again to your keeping, O faithful Creator; to your keeping, O Savior of the pierced hand; to your keeping, O eternal Spirit, you who are able to keep us from falling, and sanctify us fully, that we may be made to stand among the saints in light. O God, we can trust you, and we do so. Our faith has gathered strength by the lapse of years. Each following birthday, we trust, confirms us in the fact that to rely upon God is our happiness and our strength, and we will do so, though the Earth be removed and the mountains be carried into the midst of the sea. We will not fear since God abides fast forever, and His covenant cannot fail.

And now today will you lead others to trust you? Oh, be so revealed wherever the congregations meet together, that men may come to you and live. Oh, that the people in this house this morning, might none of them go away as unbelievers. If they have been indifferent to these things and have never studied the ground of the believer's confidence, may they see it clearly this morning, and accept it as the rock on which they shall build. Oh, if there be in this audience, as we fear there must be, many that are living to trust in their wealth, their talents, their position in life, or who are trusting in nothing but raising their building without a foundation at all, oh, bring them this day to see that there is nothing worthy of an immortal soul's confidence except the immortal and ever-living God, and this day come by Christ Jesus unto the Father. May many a heart end all its weary wanderings and sit still at Christ's feet and see the salvation of God.

God bless our country! May faith be multiplied in the land! Preserve our nation at this juncture. Guide, we pray you, the deliberations of leaders and princes. May peace be preserved, and at the same time may the great purposes of God with regard to the spread of liberty and of the gospel be subserved by every decree of the council. O God, we beseech you, ease the world of the sway of every evil principle. Let the day come when all classes of men shall study the interests of others as well as their own, when the various nations shall yield to the one scepter of Christ, and like kindred tribe shall melt into one. Yes, hasten His coming and His reign when the shout shall go up to Heaven that the "Lord God omnipotent reigneth" (Revelation 19:6).

As you bid us to do, we pray for all who are in authority over us, especially asking that every blessing may rest upon the queen. We pray for other nations also, and especially for countries and colonies where our language is spoken and our God is worshiped—may the Lord's choicest blessings rest there. We also put up special prayer for any of our dear friends who are in trouble, asking you to help some who have been suffering bitter bereavement, others who are vexed with sickness in their own persons. The Lord be pleased to be gracious unto all who trust Him, and to make them trust Him in the darkest hour. And now, unto the Father, the Son, and the Holy Ghost, Israel's one God, be glory throughout all the world. Amen and Amen.

PART 4

SPURGEON'S
PULPIT
PRAYERS

ORIGINAL INTRODUCTION TO

SPURGEON'S PULPIT PRAYERS

The day on which a volume of C. H. Spurgeon's pulpit prayers appears is a day to be desired. Many will now rejoice to see that day. Decidedly this selection of the great preacher's prayers supplies a want. Many of us have long hoped for such a volume, and now we welcome it with warm gratitude.

Lovers of C. H. Spurgeon will delight in this treasury of devotion. They will not open the book without keen anticipation, and assuredly they will not close it with disappointment. It was memorable to hear this incomparable divine when he preached. It was often even more memorable to hear him pray. Dr. John Cairns, the golden-voiced preacher and scholar, much as he rejoiced in C. H. Spurgeon's sermons, rejoiced yet more in his prayers. Many can bear a similar witness. Who talked with God as Spurgeon did? His congregational prayers—and I heard many—are always echoing in my grateful heart. They are sweet and luminous, in the memory, as angel presences.

Never did I hear him pray without adoringly saying, "Lord, it is good for us to be here." How naturally prayer fell from the lips of that great apostle! We felt that he was only doing before the multitude what he was habituated to do in private. Prayer was the instinct of his soul, and the atmosphere of his life. It was his "vital breath" and "native air." How naturally he inhaled and exhaled it! The greatness of his prayers more and more impresses and delights me. He touched every note. He sped as on eagle's wings, into the Heaven of God.

The things that were given him to utter in prayer were often more profound and beautiful than the sayings that left his lips in preaching. This has often been a feature of the greatest ministries. A noble intellect shines with the glory that excels when it is turned towards God. A man of God is frequently at his intellectual best in prayer. Assuredly it was not seldom so with this beloved pastor. I once heard him speak thus with God: "O Lord, if some of us began to doubt you, we should begin to doubt our senses, for you have done such wonderful things for us. You have done more for us than you did for Thomas. You did allow Thomas to thrust his finger into your wounds, but you have often thrust your finger into our wounds and healed them." Did he not speak by the Spirit when he uttered those pathetic and lovely words?

His wonderful knowledge of Scripture made his prayers so fresh and edifying. No man can pray with high effect unless he is steeped in Scripture. Mr. Spurgeon lived and moved and had his being in the Word of God. He knew its remotest reaches, its nooks and crannies. Its spirit had entered into his spirit; and when he prayed, the Spirit of God brought all manner of precious oracles to his mind.

Then he lived so entirely in the spiritual world that he was ever ready to pray. He had not to school himself in those moments. His pulpit prayers were not art, but nature. Every prayer was the effluence of a consecrated personality. No liturgy could have restrained him. One could not imagine him making literary preparation for public prayer. The flower gave out its perfume without effort. The urn was ever being filled where the pure waters rise and so afforded at any moment abundant refreshment.

The quivering sympathy of Mr. Spurgeon's prayers thrilled all who heard them. You felt the throbbing of his mighty heart. He was royal in his tenderness. Whom did he forget in those powerful pleadings? The faith of this great saint indeed worked by love. His prayers grandly evinced this. How ardent were those incomparable prayers! No hint was there of the dull, slumberous, tedious quality which too often has vitiated pulpit prayer.

C. H. Spurgeon was a glowing-hearted "remembrancer" of God. The warmth of the baptism of fire diffused itself throughout his supplications. The prayers at the tabernacle kindled countless cold hearts. And the English was so delectable. We hesitate to call attention to the intellectual or literary aspect of prayer. Yet why should we? God's honored servant thought and studied so incessantly for God's glory that we reaped an intellectual harvest as well as a spiritual harvest from his devotions. Mr. Spurgeon loved God with his "mind," and our minds were stimulated when we heard him pray.

Let the holy urgency of his prayers be noted. He never lost his importunity. He pleaded for the immediate moment. "Now" was his plea; and verily then and there were we all blessed of God. As a perusal of this volume will reveal, Mr. Spurgeon's prayers were eminently "theological." It is a warning, well worthy to be heeded, that a devotional master gave, "Beware of an un-theological devotion." The theological quality of C. H. Spurgeon's prayers was very notable. How

he knew God—the Holy Trinity; Jesus, the Son of God and
Savior of men; the blessed Spirit. These noble prayers will be
seen to be full of theology. They were the utterances of one
who studied God, delighted in God, and walked with God,
especially with the God-man. Precious to him beyond compare
was the divine Redeemer. The blood of our redemption was
his glory. The atoning Cross was all in all to him. I would
specially commend the theological contents of these prayers,
for they are rich with enduring wealth.

The sweet and holy memories of the prayers we heard no
man takes from us. Many such memories will be aroused in
many of the readers of this book. To those who never heard
C. H. Spurgeon's glorious voice, these printed prayers will
be valuable as suggesting his prophetic power at the mercy
seat. We covet for this volume a great constituency. Of a
truth these prayers are ideals of how men ought to pray. They
are calculated to be great inspirations to ministers, as they
contemplate their congregational prayers. To all Christian
workers they will afford real enrichment. For quiet home
reading they will be invaluable. I am glad that the publishers
have associated with these prayers one of C. H. Spurgeon's
delightful and pungent sermons on prayer—an art, of all arts
the greatest, in which he was a master, indeed. Few could use
"The Golden Key of Prayer" as he so deftly could. May many
be enabled, through grace, by the study of these prayers, to
pray more abundantly and more effectually!

Dinsdale T. Young

[Dinsdale T. Young occupied two of the most renowned pulpits in
Methodism—Wesley's Chapel, London, for eight years, and then the Central
Hall, Westminster, from 1914 until his death in 1938.]

A PRAYER FOR HOLINESS

Our Father, we worship and love you. One major point of our worship is the truth that you are holy. There was a time when we loved you solely for your mercy beccause we knew no more than that. Now you have changed our hearts and made us in love with goodness, purity, justice, and true holiness. We understand now why "the cherubim and seraphim continually do cry, 'Holy, Holy, Holy is the LORD of hosts.'" (See Isaiah 6:3 and Revelation 4:8.) We adore you because you are holy, and we love you for your infinite perfection. We sigh and cry after holiness ourselves. Sanctify us wholly, spirit, soul, and body.

Lord, we mourn over the sins of our past life and our present shortcomings. We bless you, for you have forgiven us; we are reconciled to you by the death of your Son. There are many who know they have been washed from these sins, and that He who bears away sin has borne their sin away. These are they who now cry to you to be delivered from the power of sin, to be delivered from the power of temptation without, but especially from indwelling sin within.

Lord, purify us in head, heart, and hand; and if it be needful that we should be put into the fire to be refined as silver is refined, we would even welcome the fire if we may be rid of the dross. Lord, save us from constitutional sin, from sins of temperament, and from sins of our surroundings. Save us from ourselves in every way, and grant us especially to have the light of love strong within us. May we love God; may we love you, O Savior; may we love the people of God as being members of one body in connection with you. May we love the guilty world with that love which desires its salvation and conversion; and may we love not in word only, but in deed and in truth. May we help the helpless, comfort the mourner, sympathize with the widow and fatherless, and may we be always ready to put up with wrong, to be long suffering, to be very patient, full of forgiveness, counting it a small thing that we should forgive our fellowman since we have been forgiven of God. Lord, tune our hearts to love, and then give us an inward peace and a restfulness about everything.

May we have no burden to carry, because, though we have a burden, we have rolled it upon the Lord. May we take up our cross, and because Christ has once died on the Cross, may our cross become a comfort to us. May we count it all joy when we fall into diverse trials, knowing that in all this God will be glorified, His image will be stamped upon us, and the eternal purpose will be fulfilled, wherein He has predestinated us to be conformed unto the image of His Son.

Lord, look upon your people. We might pray about our troubles. We will not; we will only pray against our sins. We might come to you about our weariness, our sickness, our disappointment, and our poverty, but we will leave all that; we will only come about sin. Lord, make us holy and then do what you will with us. We ask you to help us to keep the doctrine of God our Savior in all things. As we fight against "the sin which doth so easily beset us" (Hebrews 12:1), Lord, lend us heavenly weapons and heavenly strength that we may cut the giants down, these men of Anak that come against us. We feel very feeble. Oh, make us strong in the Lord and in the power of His might. (See Ephesians 6:10.) May we never let sin have any rest in us, may we chase it, drive it out, slay it, hang it on a tree, abhor it, and may we "cleave to that which is good" (Romans 12:9).

Some of us are striving after some excellent virtue. Lord, help stragglers; enable those who contend against great difficulties to obtain greater grace, more faith, and so to bring them nearer to God. Lord, we will be holy; by your grace we will never rest until we are. You have begun a good work in us and you will carry it on. You will work in us to will and to do of your own good pleasure. (See Philippians 1:6, 2:13.)

Lord, help the converted child to be correct in his relation to his parents; help the Christian father or mother to be right in dealing with their children. "May they not provoke their children to anger lest they be discouraged" (Colossians 3:21). Take away willfulness from the young; take away impatience from the old. Lord, help Christian men of business. May they act uprightly; may Christian masters never be hard with their servants or their workpeople. May Christian workpeople give to their masters that which is just and equal in the way of work in return for wage. May we as Christians be always standing upon our rights, but always be willing to minister to the needs of others.

And, oh, that as Christians we might be humble! Lord, take away that stiff-necked attitude, that proud look; take away from us the spirit of "stand by, for I am holier than thou"; make us condescend to men of low estate; yes, even to men of low morals and low character. May we seek them out and seek their good. Oh, give to the Church of Jesus Christ an intense love for the souls of men. May it make our hearts break to think that they will perish in their sin. May we grieve every day because of the sin of this city. Set a mark upon our foreheads and let us be known to you as men that sigh and cry for all the abominations that are done in the midst of the city. O God, save us from a hard heart and an unkind spirit that is insensitive to the woes of others.

Lord, preserve your people also from worldliness, rioting, drunkenness, chambering, and wantonness. Keep us from strife and envy, from everything that would dishonor the name of Christ that we bear. Lord, make us holy. Our prayer comes back to this: make us holy; cleanse the inside and let the outside be clean, too. Make us holy, O God; do this for Christ's sake. Then we are saved from sin. Lord, help your poor children to be holy. Oh, keep us so if we are so; keep us even from stumbling and present us faultless before your presence at last.

We pray for friends who are ill, for many that are troubled because of the illnesses of others. We bring before you every case of trouble and trial that is known to us, and we ask for your gracious intervention. We pray for your ministers everywhere, and for your missionary servants. Remember brethren who are making great sacrifice out in the hot sun or in the cold and in the frozen north. Everywhere preserve those who for Christ's sake carry their lives in their hands. And our brethren at home, in poverty many of them, working for Christ, Lord, accept them and help us to help them. Sunday school teachers, do remember them; and the tract visitors from door to door and the city missionaries and the Bible women—all who in any way endeavor to bring Christ under the notice of others. O Lord, help them all.

We will offer but one more prayer, and it is this: Lord, look in pity upon any who are not in Christ. May they be converted. May they pass from death to life, and may they never forget it; may they see the eternal light for the first time, and they will remember it even in eternity.

Father, help us; bless us now for Jesus' sake. Amen.

HELP FROM ON HIGH

O thou who are King of kings and Lord of lords, we worship you. Before Jehovah's majestic throne we bow with sacred joy.

We can truly say that we delight in God. There was a time when we feared you, O God, with the fear of bondage. Now we reverence you, but we love you as much as we reverence you. The thought of your omnipresence was once horrible to us. We said: "Whither shall we flee from His presence?" and it seemed to make hell itself more dreadful, because we heard a voice saying, "If I make my bed in hell, behold, thou art there" (Psalm 139:8). But now, O Lord, we desire to find you. Our longing is to feel your presence, and it is the Heaven of heavens that you are there. The sick bed is soft when you are there. The furnace of affliction grows cool when you are there, and the house of prayer, when you are present, is none other than the house of God, and it is the very gate of Heaven.

Come near, our Father, come very near to your children. Some of us are very weak in body and faint in heart. Soon, O God, lay your right hand upon us and say unto us, "Fear not." Perhaps some of us are weak, and the world is attracting us. Come near to kill the influence of the world with your superior power. Even to worship may not seem easy to some. The dragon seems to pursue them, and floods from his mouth wash away their devotion. Give to them great wings as of an eagle, that each one may fly away into the place prepared for him and rest in the presence of God today.

Our Father, come and give rest to your children now. Take the helmet from our brow, remove from us the weight of our heavy armor for a while, and may we just have peace, perfect peace, and be at rest. Oh, help us, we pray you, now. As you have already washed your people in the fountain filled with blood and they are clean, now this morning wash us from defilement in the water. With the basin and with the pitcher, O Master, wash our feet again. It will greatly refresh; it will prepare us for innermost fellowship with you. So did the priests wash before they went into the Holy Place.

Lord Jesus, take from us now everything that would hinder the closest communion with God. Any wish or desire that might hamper us in prayer remove, we pray you. Any memory of either sorrow or care that might hinder the fixing of our affection wholly on our God, take it away now. What have we to do with idols any more? You have seen and observed us. You know where the difficulty lies. Help us against it, and may we now come boldly, not into the Holy Place alone, but into the Holiest of All, where we should not dare to come if our great Lord had not rent the veil, sprinkled the mercy seat with His own blood, and bidden us to enter. Now we have come close to you, to the light that shines between the wings of the cherubim, and we speak with you now as a man speaks with his friends.

Our God, we are yours. You are ours. We are now concerned with one business; we are joined together for one battle. Your battle is our battle, and our fight is your fight.

Help us, we pray you. You who did strengthen Michael and his angels to cast out the dragon and his angels, help poor flesh and blood, that to us also the word may be fulfilled: "The God of peace shall bruise Satan under your feet shortly" (Romans 16:20).

Our Father, we are very weak. Worst of all, we are very wicked if left to ourselves, and we soon fall prey to the enemy. Therefore, help us. We confess that sometimes in prayer when we are nearest to you, at that very time some evil thought comes in and some wicked desires appear. Oh, what poor simpletons we are. Lord, help us. We feel as if we would now come closer to you still and hide under the shadow of your wings. We wish to be lost in God. We pray that you may live in us; may Christ live in us and show himself in us and through us. Lord, sanctify us. Oh, that your Spirit might come and saturate every faculty, subdue every passion, and use every power of our nature for obedience to God.

Come, Holy Spirit, we do know you. You have often overshadowed us. Come more fully and take possession of us. Standing now as we feel we are right up at the mercy seat, our very highest prayer is for perfect holiness, complete consecration, and entire cleansing from every evil. Take our heart, our head, our hands, our feet, and use us all for you. Lord, take our substance; let us not hoard it for ourselves, nor spend it for ourselves. Take our talent; let us not try to educate ourselves, that we may have the repute of being wise, but let every gain of mental attainment be still that we may serve you better. May every breath be for you; may every minute be spent for you. Help us to truly live while we live and while we are busy in the world, as we must be, for we are called to it, may we sanctify the world for your service. May we be lumps of salt in the midst of society. May our spirit and temper, as well as our conversation, be heavenly; may there be an influence about us that shall make the world the better before we leave it. Lord, hear us in this thing.

And now that we have your ear, we would pray for this poor world in which we live. We are often horrified by it. O Lord, we wish that we did not know anything about it for our own comfort. We have said, "Oh, for a lodge in some vast wilderness." We hear of oppression and robbery and murder, and men seem to be against each other. Lord, have mercy upon this great and wicked city. What is to be done with these millions? What can we do? At least help every child of yours to do his utmost. May none of us contribute to the evil in the world directly or indirectly, but may we contribute to the good that is in it. We feel we may speak with you now about this, for when your servant Abraham stood before you and spoke with such wonderful familiarity to you, he pleaded for Sodom; and we plead for London. We would follow the example of the Father of the faithful and pray for all great cities, and, indeed, for all the nations.

Lord, let your Kingdom come. Send forth your light and your truth. Chase the old dragon from his throne, with all his hellish crew. Oh, that the day might come when even upon Earth the Son of the woman, the man-child, should rule the nations, not with a broken staff of wood, but with an enduring scepter of iron, full of mercy, full of power, full of grace, but yet irresistible. Oh, that that might soon come, the personal advent of our Lord! We long for the millennial triumph of His Word. Until then, O Lord, gird us for the fight, and make us to be among those who overcome through the blood of the

Lamb and through the word of our testimony, because we "love not our lives unto the death" (Revelation 12:11).

We lift our voices to you in prayer; also, for all our dear ones. Lord, bless the sick and make them well, as soon as it is right that they should be. Sanctify to them all they have to bear. There are also dear friends who are very weak and some who are trembling very much. God, bless them. While the tent is being taken down may the inhabitant within look on with calm joy, for we shall by and by "… be clothed upon with our house which is from Heaven" (2 Corinthians 5:2). Lord, may we live here like strangers and make the world not a house but an inn, in which we sup and lodge, expecting to be on our journey tomorrow.

Lord, save the unconverted and bring out, we pray you, from among them those who are converted, but who have not confessed Christ. May the Church be built up by many who, having believed, are baptized unto your sacred name. We pray you would go on and multiply the faithful in the land. Oh, that you would turn the hearts of men to the gospel once more. Your servant is often very heavy in heart because he witnesses so many departures from the faith. Oh, bring them back; let not Satan take away any more of the stars with his tail, but may the lamps of God shine brightly. Oh, you who walks among the seven golden candlesticks, trim the flame, pour forth the oil, and let the light shine brightly and steadily.

Now, Lord, we cannot pray any longer, though we have a thousand things to ask for. Your servant cannot do so. Therefore, I beg to leave a broken prayer at the Mercy Seat with this at the foot of it: we ask in the name of Jesus Christ your Son. Amen.

PRAYER ANSWERED AND UNANSWERED

God of Israel, God of Jesus Christ, our God forever and ever! Help us now by the sacred Spirit to approach you properly with deepest reverence, but not with servile fear; with holiest boldness, but not with presumption. Teach us, as children, to speak to the Father, and yet, as creatures, to bow before our Maker.

Our Father, we would first ask you whether you have ought against us as your children? Have we been asking of you amiss, and have you given us that which we have sought? We are not conscious of it, but it may be so, and now we are brought as an answer to our presumptuous prayers into a more difficult position than the one we occupied before. Now it may be that some creature comfort is nearer to us than our God; we would have better been without it and have dwelt in our God and have found our joy in Him.

But now, Lord, in these perilous circumstances give us grace that we may not turn away from you. If our position now be not such as you would have allotted to us had we been wiser, yet, nevertheless, grant that we may be taught to behave ourselves aright even now, lest the mercies you have given should become a cause of stumbling and the obtaining of our heart's desire should become a temptation to us. Rather, do we feel inclined to bless you for the many occasions in which you have not answered our prayer, for you have said that we did ask amiss and, therefore, we could not have, and we desire to register this prayer with you, that whenever we do ask amiss, you would in great wisdom and love be pleased to refuse us.

O Lord, if we at any time press our petition without a sufficiency of resignation do not regard us, we pray you. Though we cry unto you day and night concerning anything, yet if you see that we are in error, regard not the voice of our cry, we pray you. It is our heart's desire now, in our coolest moments, that this prayer of ours might stand on record as long as we live, "Not as I will, but as you will." But, O Lord, in looking back we are obliged to remember with the greatest gratitude the many occasions in which you have heard our cry. We have been brought into deep distress, and our heart has sunk within us, and then have we cried to you and you have never refused to hear us. The prayers of our lusts you have rejected, but the prayers of our necessities you have granted. Not one good thing has failed of all that you have promised.

You have given to us exceeding abundantly above what we asked or even thought, for there was a day when our present condition would have been regarded as much too high for us ever to reach, and in looking back, we are surprised that those who did lie among the pots of Egypt should now sit every man under his vine and fig tree, that those who wandered in the wilderness in a solitary way should now find a city to dwell in, that we who were prodigals in rags should now be children in the Father's bosom, and that we who were companions of swine, should now be made heirs of God and joint heirs with Christ. Oh, what encouragement we have to pray to such a prayer-hearing God, who far exceeds the requests of His children.

Blessed be the name of the Lord forever. Amen, blessed be His name! If it were only for answered prayer or even for some unanswered prayers, we would continue to praise and bless you as long as we have any being. And now, Lord, listen to the voice of your children's cry. Wherever there is a sincere heart seeking for greater holiness, answer that request; or wherever there is a broken spirit seeking for reconciliation with you, be pleased to answer it now. You know where there is prayer, though it be unuttered, and even the lips do not move. Oh, hear the publican who dares not lift his eyes to Heaven. Hear him while he cries, "God be merciful to me a sinner" (Luke 18:13). Hear such as seem to themselves to be appointed unto death. Let the sighing of the prisoner come before you! Oh, that you would grant peace and rest to every troubled spirit all over the world who now desires to turn his face to the Cross and to see God in Christ Jesus. O Lord, if there are any of your servants who are concerned and praying about the cases of others, we would thank you for them. Raise up in the Church many intercessors who shall plead for the prosperity of Zion, and give you no rest till you establish her and make her a joy in the land.

Oh, there are some of us who cried to you about our country. You know how in secret we groaned and sighed over evil times, and you have begun to hear us already, for which we desire to praise and bless your name. But we would not cease to pray for this land, that you would roll away from it all its sin, that you would deliver it from the curse of drunkenness, rescue it from infidelity, popery, ritualism, rationalism, and every form of evil, that this land might become a holy land. O Lord, bring the multitudes of working men to listen to the gospel. Break in, we pray you, upon their stolid indifference. Lord, give them a love of your house, a desire to hear your gospel, and then will you look upon the poor rich, for so many of them know nothing about you and are worshiping their own wealth. Lord, grant that the many for whom there are no special gospel services, but who are wrapped up in self-righteousness, may be brought to hear the Gospel of Jesus that they also, as well as the poor, may be brought to Christ.

God, bless this land with more of gospel light and with more of gospel life and love. You will hear us, O Lord. Then would we pray for our children, that they might be saved. Some of us can no longer pray for our children's conversion, because our prayers are heard already. But there are others who have children who vex them and grieve their hearts. O God, save sons and daughters of godly people. Let them not have to sigh over their children as Eli did and as Samuel did, and may they see their sons and daughters become the children of the living God. We would pray for our servants, our neighbors, our kinsfolk of near or far degree, that all might be brought to Jesus. Do this, O God, through your infinite mercy.

And, as we are now making intercession, we would, according to your Word, pray for all kings and all who are in authority, that we may lead quiet and peaceable lives. We pray for all nations also. O Lord, bless and remember the lands that sit in darkness, and let them see a great light, and may missionary enterprise be abundantly successful. Let the favored nations where our God is known, especially this land and the land across the mighty ocean that love the same Savior and speak the same tongue, be always favored with the divine presence and with abundant prosperity and blessing.

O Lord, you have chosen our race and favored it and multiplied it on the face of the Earth, and whereas with this staff it crossed this Jordan, it has now become two great nations. Lord, be pleased to bless the whole of the race and those absorbed into it, and then all other races that in us may be fulfilled the blessing of Abraham, "I will bless thee,... and thou shalt be a blessing" (Genesis 12:2).

And now, Father, glorify your Son! In scattering pardons through His precious blood, glorify your Son! In sending forth the eternal Spirit to convince men and women and bring them to His feet, Father, glorify your Son! In enriching your saints with gifts and graces and building them up into His image, Father glorify your Son! In the gathering together of the whole company of His elect and in the hastening of His kingdom and His coming, Father, glorify your Son! Beyond this prayer we cannot go: "Glorify thy Son, that thy Son also may glorify thee" (John 17:1). Unto Father, Son, and Holy Spirit be glory forever and ever. Amen.

THE ALL-PREVAILING PLEA

O Lord God, the fountain of all fullness, we, who are nothing but emptiness, come unto you for all supplies. We know we shall not come in vain, since we bear with us a plea that is all prevalent. Since we come as commanded by your Word, encouraged by your promise, and preceded by Christ Jesus, our great High Priest, we know that whatsoever we shall ask in prayer, believing, we shall receive. Do help us now to ask right things, and may the utterances of our mouth be acceptable in your sight, O God, our strength and our Redeemer.

We would first adore your blessed and ever-to-be-beloved name. "All the earth doth worship you, the Father everlasting." Heaven is full of your glory. Oh, that men's hearts were filled therewith, that the noblest creatures you have made, whom you did set in the Paradise of God, for whom the Savior shed His blood, loved you with all their hearts. The faithful, chosen, called, and separated join in the everlasting song. All your redeemed praise you, O God! As the God of our election, we extol you for your everlasting and immutable love. As the God and Father of our Lord Jesus Christ, we bless you for that unspeakable gift, the offering of your only begotten Son. Words are but air and tongues are but clay, and your compassion is divine; therefore, it is not possible that any words of ours should "reach the height of this great argument," or sound forth your worthy praise for this superlative deed of grace.

We bless you, also, divine Son of God, co-equal and co-eternal with the Father, that you did not disdain to be born of the virgin, and that, being found in fashion like a man, you did not refuse to be obedient unto death, even the death of the Cross. (See Philippians 2:8.) Let your brows be girt with something better than thorns; let the eternal diadem forever glitter there. You were slain, and have redeemed us to God by your blood; unto you be glory, honor, power, majesty, dominion, and might forever and ever! (See Revelation 5:9-13.)

And equally, most blessed Spirit, you who did brood over chaos and bring it into order, you who did beget the Son of God's body of flesh, you who did quicken us to spiritual life, by whose divine energy we are sanctified and hope to be made meet to be partakers of the inheritance of the saints in light (see Colossians 1:12), unto you, also, be hallelujahs, world without end!

O Lord, our soul longs for words of fire, but we cannot reach them! Oh, when shall we drop this clay that now is so uncongenial to our song? When shall we be able with wings to mount upward to your throne, and, having learned some flaming sonnets that have once been sung by cherubim above, we shall praise you forever? Yet even these are not rich enough for your glory. We would sing unto you a new song. We will, when we reach the heavenly shore, become leaders of the eternal music. "Day without night" will we "circle God's throne rejoicing," and count it the fullness of our glory, our bliss, our Heaven, to wave the palm and cast our crowns with our songs at your feet forever and ever!

Our Father, who is in Heaven, next to this we would offer prayer for those who never think of you; who, though created by you, are strangers to you; who are fed by your bounty, and yet never lift their voices to you, but live for self, for the world, for Satan, and for sin. Father, these cannot pray for themselves, for they are dead; your quickened children pray for them. These will not come to you, for, like sheep, they are lost; but do seek them, Father, and bring them back.

Oh, our glorious Lord, you have taught us to pray for others, for the grace that could have met with such undeserving sinners as we are must be able to meet with the vilest of the vile. Oh, we cannot boast of what we are; we cannot boast of what we have been by nature. Had we our doom we had now been in hell. Had we this day our proper, natural, and deserved position, we should still have been "… in the gall of bitterness, and in the bond of iniquity" (Acts 8:23). It is your rich, free, sovereign, distinguishing grace that has brought us up out of the miry clay, and set our feet upon a rock. (See Psalm 40:2.)

And shall we even refuse to pray for others? Shall we leave a stone unturned for their conversion? Shall we not weep for those who have no tears and cry for those who have no prayers? Father, we must and we will. "Fain our pity would reclaim, And snatch the fire-brands from the flame." There are those who are utterly careless about divine things. Will you impress them? May some stray shot reach their conscience! Oh, that they may be led solemnly to consider their position and their latter end! May thoughts of death and of eternity dash irresistibly like some mighty waves, against their souls! Oh, may Heaven's light shine into their consciences! May they begin to ask themselves where they are and what they are, and may they be turned unto the Lord with full purpose of heart.

There are others who are concerned, but they are halting between two opinions. There are some we love in the flesh who have not yet decided for God. Behold, it trembles in the balance! Cast in your Cross, O Jesus, and turn the scale! Oh, love irresistible, come forth, and carry by blessed storm the hearts that have not yet yielded to all the attacks of the Law! Oh, that some who never could be melted, even by the furnace of Sinai, may be dissolved by the beams of love from the tearful eyes of Jesus! Lord, if there be a heart that is saying, "Now, behold, I yield; lo, at your feet rebellion's weapons I lay down and cease to be your foe, you King of kings. If there be one who is saying, "I am willing to be espoused unto Christ, to be washed in His blood, to be called in His righteousness," bring that willing sinner in now! May there be no longer delay, but may this be the time when, once for all, the great transaction shall be done, and they shall be their Lord's, and He shall be theirs.

Oh, that we could pour out our soul in prayer for the unconverted! You know where they will all be in a few years! Oh, by your wrath, we pray you, let them not endure it! By the flames of hell, be pleased to ransom them from going down into the pit! By everything that is dreadful in the wrath to come, we do argue with you to have mercy upon these sons of men, even upon those who have no mercy upon themselves.

Father, have you not promised your Son to see of His soul's travail? We point you to the ransom paid; we point you once again to the groans of your Son, to His agony, and His bloody sweat! Turn your glorious eyes thither, and then look on sinners; speak the word and bid them live. Righteous Father, refresh every corner of the vineyard, and on every branch of the vine let the dew of Heaven rest. Oh that you would bless your Church throughout the world! Let visible union be established, or if not that, let the invisible union that has always existed be better recognized by believers. Will you repair our schisms? Will you repair the breaches that have been made in the walls of Zion? Oh! that you would purge us of everything unscriptural, till all Christians shall come to the Law and to the testimony, and still keep the ordinances and the doctrines, as they were committed to the apostles by Christ!

Remember our land in this time of need. Do be pleased by some means to relieve the prevalent distress. Quicken the wheels of commerce, that the many who are out of employment in this city may no longer be crying for work and bread. Oh, that you would make wars to cease to the ends of the Earth, or, when they break out, break the slave's fetters thereby, and though desperate be the evil, yet grant that Satan may cast out Satan, and may his kingdom be divided, and so fall. (See Matthew 12:26.)

Above all, you long-expected Messiah, do now come! Your ancient people who despised you once are waiting for you in your Second Coming, and we, the Gentiles, who knew you not, neither regarded you; we, too, are watching for your advent. Make no tarrying, O Jesus! May your feet soon stand again on Olivet! You shall not have this time there to sweat great drops of blood, but you shall come to proclaim the year of vengeance for your foes, and the year of acceptance for your people. "When wilt thou the heavens rend, in majesty come down?" (See Isaiah 64:1.) Earth travails for your coming. The whole creation groans in pain together until now. Your own expect you; we are longing till we are weary for your coming. Come quickly, Lord Jesus; come quickly. Amen and Amen.

THE WINGS OF PRAYER

O ur Father, your children who know you delight themselves in your presence. We are never happier than when we are near you. We have found a little Heaven in prayer. It has eased our load to tell you of its weight; it has relieved our wound to tell you of its sting; it has restored our spirit to confess to you its wanderings. No other place is like the mercy seat for us.

We thank you, Lord, that we have not only found benefit in prayer, but in the answers to it we have been greatly enriched. You have opened your hidden treasures to the voice of prayer; you have supplied our necessities as soon as we have cried unto you; yea, we have found this to be true: "Before they call I will answer; and while they are yet speaking, I will hear" (Isaiah 65:24).

We do bless you, Lord, for instituting the blessed ordinance of prayer. What could we do without it? We take great shame to ourselves that we should use it so little. We pray that we may be men and women of prayer, taken up with it, that it may take us up and bear us, as on its wings towards Heaven. And now at this hour will you hear the voice of our supplication?

First, we ask at your hands, great Father, for complete forgiveness for all our trespasses and shortcomings. We hope we can say with truthfulness that we do from our heart forgive all those who have in any way trespassed against us. There lies not in our heart, we hope, a thought of enmity towards any person. However we have been slandered or wronged, we would, with our inmost heart, forgive and forget it all.

We come to you and pray that, for Jesus' sake, and through the virtue of the blood once shed for many for the remission of sins, you would give us perfect pardon of every transgression of the past. Blot out, O God, all our sins like a cloud, and let them never be seen again. Grant us also the peace-speaking word of promise applied by the Holy Spirit, that being justified by faith we may have peace with God through Jesus Christ our Lord. (See Romans 5:1.) Let us be forgiven and know it, and may there remain no lingering question in our hearts about our reconciliation with God, but by a firm and full assurance, based upon faith in the finished work of Christ, may we stand as forgiven men and women against whom transgression shall be mentioned never again forever.

And then, Lord, we have another mercy to ask for that shall be the burden of our prayer. It is that you would help us to live such lives as pardoned men and women should live. We have but a little time to tarry here, for our life is but a vapor; soon it vanishes away, but we are most eager to spend the time of our sojourning here in holy fear, that grace may be upon us from the commencement of our Christian life even to the earthly close of it.

Lord, you know there are some who have not yet begun to live for you, and the prayer is now offered that they may today be born again. Others have been long in your ways, and are not weary of them. We sometimes wonder that you are not weary of us, but assuredly we delight ourselves in the ways of holiness more than we ever did. Oh, that our ways were directed to keep your statutes without slip or flaw. We wish we were perfectly obedient in thought, word, and deed, entirely sanctified. We shall never be satisfied till we wake up in Christ's likeness, the likeness of perfection itself. Oh, work us to this selfsame thing, we beseech you.

May experience teach us more and more how to avoid occasions of sin. May we grow more watchful; may we have a greater supremacy over our own spirit; may we be able to control ourselves under all circumstances, and so act that if the Master were to come at any moment, we should not be ashamed to give our account into His hands. Lord, we are not what we want to be. This is our sorrow. Oh, that you would by your Spirit help us in the walks of life to adorn the doctrine of God our Savior in all things. As men of business, as work people, as parents, as children, as servants, as masters, whatever we may be, may we be such that Christ may look upon us with pleasure. May His joy be in us, for then only can our joy be full.

Dear Savior, we are your disciples, and you are teaching us the art of living; but we are very dull and very slow, and, beside, there is such a bias in our corrupt nature, there are such examples in the world, and the influence of an ungodly generation affects even those who know you. O dear Savior, be not impatient with us, but still school us at your feet, till at last we shall have learned some of the sublime lessons of self-sacrifice, meekness, humility, fervor, boldness, and love that your life is fit to teach us. O Lord, we beseech you, mold us into your own image. Let us live in you and live like you. Let us gaze upon your glory till we are transformed by the sight and become Christlike among the children of men.

Lord, hear the confessions of any who have backslidden, who are marring your image rather than perfecting it. Hear the prayers of any who are conscious of great defects during the past. Give them peace of mind by pardon, but give them strength of mind, also, to keep clear of such mischief in the future. O Lord, we are sighing and crying more and more after you. The more we have of you, the more we want you; the more we grow like you, the more we perceive our defects, and the more we pine after a higher standard, to reach even unto perfection.

Oh, help us. Spirit of the living God, continue still to travail in us. Let the groanings that cannot be uttered still be within our spirit, for these are growing pains, and we shall grow while we can sigh and cry, while we can confess and mourn; yet this is not without a blessed hopefulness "... that he which hath begun a good work in you will perform it until the day of Jesus Christ" (Philippians 1:6).

Bless, we pray you, at this time, the entire Church of God in every part of the Earth. Prosper the work and service of Christian people, however they endeavor to spread the Kingdom of Christ. Convert the heathen; enlighten those who are in any form of error. Bring the entire Church back to the original form of Christianity. Make her first pure, and then she shall be united. O Savior, let your Kingdom come. Oh, that you would reign, and your will would be done in Earth, as it is in Heaven.

We pray that you would use every one of us according as we have ability to be used. Take us, and let no talent lie to corrode in the treasure house, but may every pound of yours be put out in trading for you in the blessed market of soul winning. Oh, give us success. Increase the gifts and graces of those who are saved. Bind us in closer unity than ever to one another. Let peace reign; let holiness adorn us. Hear us as we pray for all countries, and then for all sorts of men, from the Sovereign on the throne to the peasant in the cottage. Let the benediction of Heaven descend on men and women through Jesus Christ our Lord. Amen.

UNDER THE BLOOD

Jehovah, our God, we thank you for leaving on record the story of your ancient people. It is full of instructions for us. Help us to take its warning to avoid the faults into which they fell! You are a covenant-God, you keep your promises, and your Word never fails. We have proved this, so hitherto:

Thus far we find that promise good,

Which Jesus ratified with blood.

But, as for ourselves, we are like Israel of old, a fickle people, and, we confess it with great shame that there are days when we take the timbrel and we sing with Miriam, "… to the LORD, for he hath triumphed gloriously" (Exodus 15:21); and yet, we grieve to say it, not many hours after we are thirsty, and we are crying for water, and we are murmuring in our tents, the bitter Marah turns our hearts, and we are grieved with our God. (See Exodus 15:22-24.)

Sometimes we bow before you with reverence and awe when we behold your Sinai smoking; but there have been times when we have set up the golden calf and we have said of some earthly things, "These be your gods, O Israel." We believe with intensity of faith, and then we doubt with a horribleness of doubt. Lord, you have been very patient with us. Many have been our provocations, and many have been your chastisements, but:

Your strokes are fewer than our crimes,

And lighter than our guilt.

"He hath not dealt with us after our sins, nor rewarded us according to our iniquities" (Psalm 103:10). Blessed be your name!

And now fulfill that part of the covenant wherein you have said, "A new heart also will I give you, and a new spirit will I put within you;… I will put My fear in their hearts, that they shall not depart from me" (Ezekiel 36:26, Jeremiah 32:40). Hold us fast and then we shall hold fast to you. Turn us, and we shall be turned; keep us, and we shall keep your statutes. We cry to you, that we may no longer provoke you. We beg you, rather, to send the serpents among us than to let sin come among us. Oh, that we might have our eyes always on the brazen serpent that heals all the bites of evil, but may we not look to sin nor love it. Let not the devices of Balaam and of Balak prevail against us to lead your people away from their purity. Let us not be defiled with false doctrine or with unholy living, but may we walk as the separated people of God and keep ourselves unspotted from the world.

Lord, we would not grieve your Spirit. Oh, may we never vex you so as to lead you in your wrath to say, "They shall not enter into my rest" (Hebrews 3:11). Bear with us still for His dear sake whose blood is upon us. Bear with us still and send not the destroying angel, as you did to Egypt, but again fulfill that promise of yours, "When I see the blood I will pass over you" (Exodus 12:13). Just now may we be consciously passed over by the spirit of condemnation; may we know in our hearts that "There is therefore now no condemnation to them which are in Christ Jesus" (Romans 8:1). May we feel the peace-giving power of the divine absolution. May we come into your holy presence with our feet washed in the brazen laver, hearing our great High Priest say to us, "Ye are clean every whit." (See John 13:10.) Thus made clean, may we draw near to God through Jesus Christ our Lord.

Further, our heavenly Father, we come before you now washed in the blood, wearing the snow-white robe of Christ's righteousness, and we ask you to remember your people. Some are sore burdened; lighten the burden or strengthen the shoulder. Some are bowed down with fear; perhaps they mistrust; forgive the mistrust and give a great increase of faith, that they may trust you where they cannot trace you. Lord, remember any who bear the burden of others. Some cry to you day and night about the sins of the times, about the wanderings of your Church. Lord, hear our prayers! We would bear this yoke for you, but help us to bear it without fearing, so as to distrust you. May we know that you will take care of your own case and preserve your own truth, and may we, therefore, be restful about it all.

Some are crying to you for the conversion of relatives and friends; this burden they have taken up to follow after Jesus in the cross-bearing. Grant them to see the desires of their hearts fulfilled. God, save our children and our children's children, and if we have unconverted relatives of any kind, have mercy upon them for Christ's sake. Give us joy in them—as much joy in them as Christians as we have had sorrow about them as unbelievers.

Further, be pleased to visit your Church with the Holy Spirit. Renew the Day of Pentecost in our midst, and in the midst of all gatherings of your people may there come the downfall of the holy fire, the uprising of the heavenly wind. May matters that are now slow and dead become quick and full of life, and may the Lord Jesus Christ be exalted in the midst of His Church, which is His fullness, "... the fulness of Him that filleth all in all" (Ephesians 1:23). May multitudes be converted; may they come flocking to Christ with holy eagerness to find in Him a refuge, as the doves fly to their dovecotes. Oh, for salvation, work throughout these islands and across the sea and in every part of the world, especially in heathen lands. Bring many to Christ's feet, we pray you, everywhere where men are ready to lay down their lives, that they may impart the heavenly life of Christ. Work, Lord, work mightily! Your Church cries to you. Oh, leave us not! We can do nothing without you! Our strength is wholly yours! Come to us with great power, and let your Word have free course and be glorified.

Remember every one who calls you Father. May a Father's love look on all the children. May the special need of each one be supplied and the special sorrow of each one be assuaged. May we be growing Christians, may we be working Christians, may we be perfected Christians, may we come to the fullness of the stature of men in Christ Jesus. Lord Jesus, you are a great pillar; in you does all fullness dwell. You began your life by filling the water pots to the full; you filled Simon Peter's boat until it began to sink; you filled the house where your people met together with the presence of the Holy Ghost; you fill Heaven; you will surely fill all things; fill us today with all the fullness of God, and make your people thus joyful, strong, gracious, and heavenly!

But we cannot leave off our prayer when we have prayed for your people, though we have asked large things; we want you to look among the thousands and millions round about us who do not know you. Lord, look on the masses who go nowhere to worship. Have pity upon them; Father, forgive them, for they know not what they do. Give them a desire to hear your Word. Send upon the people a strong desire after their God. O Lord, take sinners in hand yourself. Oh, come and reach obstinate, obdurate minds; let the careless and the frivolous begin to think upon eternal things. May there be an uneasiness of heart, a sticking of the arrows of God in their loins, and may they seek, too, the Great Physician and find healing this very day. Lord, you say, "To day if ye will hear his voice" (Hebrews 3:7), and we take up the echo. Save men today, this very day. Bring them your Spirit in power, that they may be willing to rest in Christ. Lord, hear, forgive, accept, and bless for Jesus' sake. Amen.

STUDY GUIDE

BIOGRAPHY: THE BOY PREACHER

1. How old was Spurgeon when he was converted?

2. What was the Scripture verse that resulted in his conversion?

3. How old was he when he preached his first public sermon?

4. How old was he when the first person was converted under his ministry in Waterbeach?

5. How old was he when he became pastor of New Park Street church?

6. How many sermons had Spurgeon preached by the time he was called to New Park Street?

7. On what date did Spurgeon preach his first sermon at New Park Street?

8. How many people attended his first service?

9. Spurgeon preached once in a field to a crowd of how many?

10. When did he preach his first sermon in the Metropolitan Tabernacle?

11. Thousands attended his meetings in the Tabernacle; how did he get such a large congregation?

12. Spurgeon suffered from three diseases: what were they?

13. On what date did he die?

14. Where did he die?

15. On Spurgeon's coffin there was a Bible opened to a text; what was that text?

DEVOTIONALS

1. In one of his devotionals, Spurgeon said, "A prayerless soul is a _____ soul." (Fill in the blank.)

2. In his devotional "David Enquired of the Lord," what did Spurgeon say you could learn from David?

3. Who was the woman who said to God, "For this child I prayed"?

4. What are some of the reasons God sometimes makes us wait for an answer to our prayers? ("God Often Delays His Answer")

5. What are some of the things Spurgeon suggests we could pray about? ("Keep the Altar Burning")

6. What was Moses' mighty prayer?

7. How many times did Jesus pray the same thing?

8. What should follow answered prayer?

9. How long should you continue to pray for the same thing?

10. What is intercessory prayer?

11. Prayer is the forerunner of _____. (Fill in the blank.)

12. Spurgeon says that praying in the Holy Ghost is what?

13. What happened when Saul began to pray?

14. Complete this: "Sinking times are _____ times."

15. When you wait in faith for God to answer your prayers, what are you expressing toward Him? ("Wait On the Lord.")

SERMONS

A Golden Prayer

1. What should we daily say to ourselves?

2. Complete this: "Sin lies not in the conflict but in the _____."

3. What was the chief end and object of our Savior's life and death?

4. Our prayer should not be, "Father, help me to glorify thy name," but rather, "Father, _____ _____ ____." (Fill in the blanks.)

5. As Christians what is the greatest thing we could do in this life?

How to Converse With God

1. What are the two methods of sacred converse between God and the soul?

2. What is the purpose of Scripture?

3. What is needed if there is to be a conversation between God and you?

4. How should we constantly speak to the Most High?

5. Whatever God asks of you, what should you bring Him?

Intercessory Prayer

1. When did God turn the captivity of Job?

2. What is the first example of Abraham praying an intercessory prayer?

3. What was the last intercessory prayer of Jesus Christ?

4. What are some of the kinds of intercessory prayers mentioned in the New Testament?

5. In the Bible, find as many examples of intercessory prayers as you can.

6. Make a list of the people and other things you should be praying for.

Let Us Pray

1. What is the first and foremost way of drawing near to God?

2. Does the goodness, the effectiveness, of the prayer lie in the merit of the prayer itself?

3. The best commentator on the Word of God is ____ ____ _____. (Fill in the blanks.)

4. According to the Book of Hebrews, what is the one singular thing that faith did, which is as great a miracle as any of those listed—and that also can be said of prayer?

5. What does it mean to "steep your seed" in relation to prayer?

6. To what should you devote the best hours of your day?

Paul's First Prayer

1. What was the one thing Saul was doing that seemed to cause the Lord to send Ananias to him?

2. What made Martin Luther more fearful than facing his enemies?

3. What is it a sign of when a person prays?

4. Spurgeon says, "Secret prayer is one of the best tests of
_____ _____." (Fill in the blanks.)

5. According to Spurgeon, what are the marks of election?

6. Spurgeon said, "If you pray, you have a proof that you
are _____ _____" (Fill in the blanks.)

Prayer at the Throne of Grace

1. Spurgeon said, "True prayer is not a mere mental
exercise, nor a vocal performance, but it is deeper far
than that—it is _____ _____ ____ ___ _____
_____ _____ ____ _____." (Fill in the blanks.)

2. "Prayer is not truly prayer without the ____ _____" (Fill
in the blanks.)

3. What is the right spirit in which to approach God's
throne of grace?

4. What gives us the confidence to go boldly before God's
throne of grace?

5. If God's throne is a throne of grace, how many of your
wants can you expect to be supplied when you go before
it?

Prayer in the Day of Trouble

1. Should you pray more or less on the days you have
trouble?

2. Spurgeon asks, "have you failed in these two precious things." What things are they?

3. Calling upon God in the day of trouble brings *what* to God?

4. Spurgeon says that when you call upon God in the day of trouble you evidently possess five things in relation to God—what are they?

5. What does God promise to do if you call upon Him in the day of trouble?

6. What are some of the ways you can glorify God in the day of trouble, and after you have been delivered?

Prayer—the Forerunner of Mercy

1. What does Spurgeon say we should use in prayer?

2. How many instances in the Bible can you find of prayer preceding God's mercy and blessings?

3. Spurgeon says, "Great prayer is the preface of great ____." (Fill in the blank.)

4. Why has God made prayer the forerunner of mercy?

5. What does prayer itself sometimes give?

6. List some of the things that you should pray for.

The Golden Key of Prayer

1. Spurgeon said that in this sermon his text divided into three particles of truth; what are they?

2. Look through the Scriptures and find out how often you are told pray.

3. What does it indicate when you feel a sudden desire to pray?

4. "As the rain cloud brings the shower, so prayer brings
___ _____." (Fill in the blanks.)

5. When we pray, what clause does Spurgeon say we should always insert, whether in spirit or in words?

6. Martin Luther said, "To have prayed well is to have
_____ _____." (Fill in the blanks.)

7. Martin Luther also said, "I am so busy working for the Lord that I cannot afford to pray ... less than three hours a day." How often and how much do you pray?

TOPICAL INDEX

SCRIPTURE INDEX

Pure Gold Classics

AN EXPANDING COLLECTION OF THE
BEST-LOVED CHRISTIAN CLASSICS OF ALL TIME.

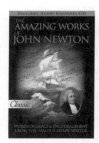

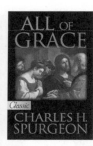

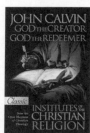

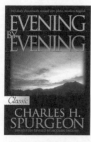
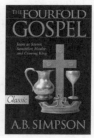

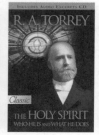
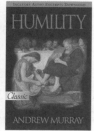

AVAILABLE AT FINE BOOKSTORES.

FOR MORE INFORMATION, VISIT WWW.BRIDGELOGOS.COM

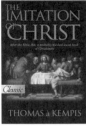

THE
IMITATION
of
CHRIST

After the Bible, this is probably the best-loved book of Christianity

Classic

THOMAS à KEMPIS

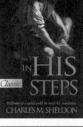

IN HIS STEPS

Millions of copies sold in over 41 countries

Classic

CHARLES M. SHELDON

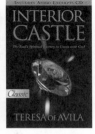

INTERIOR CASTLE

The Soul's Spiritual Journey to Union with God

Classic

TERESA OF AVILA

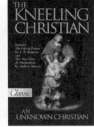

THE KNEELING CHRISTIAN

Classic

AN UNKNOWN CHRISTIAN

MADAME JEANNE GUYON

Classic

EXPERIENCING UNION WITH GOD THROUGH INNER PRAYER & THE WAY AND RESULTS OF UNION WITH GOD

MORNING BY MORNING

Classic

CHARLES H. SPURGEON

THE OVERCOMING LIFE

Classic

D.L. MOODY

THE PILGRIM'S PROGRESS
IN MODERN ENGLISH

Classic

JOHN BUNYAN

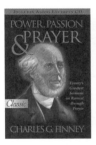

POWER, PASSION & PRAYER

Finney's Greatest Sermons on Revival through Prayer

Classic

CHARLES G. FINNEY

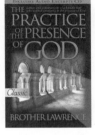

THE PRACTICE OF THE PRESENCE OF GOD

Classic

BROTHER LAWRENCE

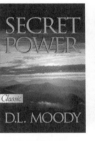

SECRET POWER

Classic

D.L. MOODY

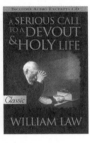

A SERIOUS CALL TO A DEVOUT & HOLY LIFE

Classic

WILLIAM LAW

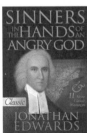

SINNERS IN THE HANDS OF AN ANGRY GOD

Classic

JONATHAN EDWARDS

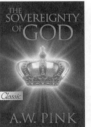

THE SOVEREIGNTY OF GOD

Classic

A.W. PINK

TORREY ON PRAYER

Classic

THE POWER OF PRAYER & THE PRAYER OF POWER

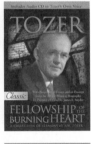

TOZER

Classic

FELLOWSHIP of the BURNING HEART
A COLLECTION OF SERMONS BY A.W. TOZER

TOZER ON THE HOLY SPIRIT

Classic

A.W. TOZER

WALKING WITH GOD

Classic

THE ANDREW MURRAY TRILOGY ON SANCTIFICATION

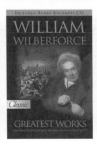

WILLIAM WILBERFORCE

Classic

GREATEST WORKS

WITH CHRIST IN THE SCHOOL OF PRAYER

Classic

ANDREW MURRAY